Historical Trajectories of Catholicism in Africa

Historical Trajectories of Catholicism in Africa

From *Catholicae ecclesiae* to *Ecclesia in Africa*

VALENTINE UGOCHUKWU IHEANACHO
Foreword by Paul Steffen

RESOURCE *Publications* · Eugene, Oregon

HISTORICAL TRAJECTORIES OF CATHOLICISM IN AFRICA
From *Catholicae ecclesiae* to *Ecclesia in Africa*

Copyright © 2021 Valentine Ugochukwu Iheanacho. All rights reserved. Except for brief quotations in critical publications or reviews, no part of this book may be reproduced in any manner without prior written permission from the publisher. Write: Permissions, Wipf and Stock Publishers, 199 W. 8th Ave., Suite 3, Eugene, OR 97401.

Resource Publications
An Imprint of Wipf and Stock Publishers
199 W. 8th Ave., Suite 3
Eugene, OR 97401

www.wipfandstock.com

PAPERBACK ISBN: 978-1-6667-3130-9
HARDCOVER ISBN: 978-1-6667-2366-3
EBOOK ISBN: 978-1-6667-2367-0

09/21/21

For Professor Rian Venter
Father, Friend and Mentor

Contents

Foreword by Paul Steffen		ix
Acknowledgments		xiii
Introduction		xvii
1	Brief perspective on missions in Africa	1
	A cursory overview	3
	"Pax Coloniae"	8
	Mission in rebound and its context	14
2	Missions in Africa in the twilight of the nineteenth century	27
	Great attention on Africa by Pius IX	28
	Missions within the general Leonine optics	32
	The anti-slavery campaign	37
	Territorial adjustments and mission jurisdictions	49
3	The broad ambient of plantatio ecclesiae	58
	Historical preview of plantatio ecclesiae	61
	Components and models of plantatio ecclesiae	64
	Plantatio ecclesiae as a missionary policy	67
	Flowering of the concept under Pope Pius XII	77
4	From missionary tutelage to indigenization	84
	Laying the foundation for indigenization	88
	A checkered path towards an indigenous Church	96
	The Vatican's policy of indigenization and contestation	103
5	A populous church—Quo vadis?	123
	Progress and pitfalls post-missionary era	124
	In search of an identity pre- and post-1994	128
	Avant-garde for human promotion and development	140

> Confronting the "ecclesiastical cake" mentality 147
> Ecclesial commitment for inclusion and harmony 151
> A continental church concerned about ecology 155

Conclusion 163

Bibliography 169

Index 183

Foreword

Valentine Ugochukwu Iheanacho, author of the study *Historical trajectories of Catholicism in Africa: From Catholicae Ecclesiae to Ecclesia in Africa*, is a member of the Missionary Society of St Paul of Nigeria. This fact already points to the central theme of his research, the Catholic Church in sub-Saharan Africa.

During his ecclesiastical studies at the Roman Pontifical Gregorian University (2005–2008; 2011–2015), Valentine Iheanacho was intensively engaged with the work of two popes in both his licentiate thesis and doctoral dissertation.

His licentiate thesis dealt with the theme: *Catholic missionary expansion in Africa under the Pontificate of Pope Leo XIII (1878–1903)* and his doctoral dissertation explored the topic: *Maximum illud: The missionary thinking of Benedict XV (1914–1922) and prospects of a local church in mission territories*. At the University of the Free State, Bloemfontein, Iheanacho (post-doctoral research fellow 2019–2020) recently completed his post-doctoral research on *Historical trajectories of Catholicism in Africa: From Catholicae Ecclesiae to Ecclesia in Africa*. In 2015, Iheanacho published his doctoral dissertation under the title *Maximum Illud and Benedict XV's missionary thinking: Prospects of a local church in mission territories* (Scholars' Press, Germany).

His book, *Historical trajectories of Catholicism in Africa: From Catholicae Ecclesiae to Ecclesia in Africa*, is the result of profound research for over a decade. This study, with its five chapters tracing the historical trajectories of contemporary Catholicism in Africa, will be of great benefit to a worldwide readership. The author highlights the turns and courses that the Church took to reach its current status. This was only possible through the activity of countless missionaries sent by numerous mission societies within the framework of Pope Gregory's Apostolic Prefectures and Vicariates.

Transmitting the Christian message to the African people, playing an active part in accepting and living this message, and making it their own becomes an African narrative. The African Christian faith receives a new expression by Africans: new joy and the power of a living faith.

With admirable clarity and sharpness, Iheanacho analyzes the history of papal African policy and the commitment of Pope Gregory XVI and his successors Pius IX and Leo XIII regarding the foundation and the further development of the Catholic Church in Africa. With the help of numerous new male and female missionary societies, 80 vicariates were established in Africa at the beginning of the twentieth century, starting out from two vicariates. Based on the achievements of three Popes of the nineteenth century, the missionary Pope Benedict XV was able to put into practice his vision of a self-supporting Church in Africa, with its own priests and bishops, who helped prepare not only the Church but also the entire African society for the postcolonial future.

The Popes of the twentieth century called for indigenous clergy and, eventually, indigenous bishops. However, this has not been fully realized, until the years after Vatican Council II through the pontificate of Paul VI. Since then, the Church of Africa has enough clergy of its own and is able to obtain all the necessary bishops from its own ranks. Among them, numerous outstanding bishops and cardinals have been recognized for their excellent activity in the Church of their countries and in all of Africa, as well as worldwide. For example, Cardinal Malula of Kinshasa and Bishop Patrick Kalilombe of Malawi both recognized the signs of the time for their local churches. They showed prophetic courage and commitment to the people of their homeland, by defending the basic rights for Christians and for all people in their country and by even accepting the resistance of its political elite.

The author has put his historical research entirely at the service of a better understanding of the present situation. He shows the challenges to the Church in our time, emphasizing that all documentations and synods are ultimately of little importance, should the majority of the suffering population not being helped to live in dignity and to stand on their own feet.

In the Introduction to Chapter Five, the author writes: "Historians are not prophets, and they get their fingers burnt when they venture to predict the future. As a scientific discipline, therefore, history does not make predictions about the future, for that is outside its domain. Through historical hermeneutics, it is possible to understand the present and to get a glimpse of certain residual elements connecting the past, the present, and the future. Although this remains mostly true of historical perspectives, historians are hesitant and even wary in predicting future events on the basis that the shape of the future and its contours are largely unclear at present. Despite its unknowable nature, certain things may be said about the future from a careful historical analysis of the past and the present." While taking the risk, this book dares to interpret and summarize this development. The author has achieved this in an outstanding manner; he, therefore, deserves thanks and recognition.

What is the present status of the Church in Africa and to what challenges must she find an intelligent and viable response nowadays? How can the Church of Africa meet future challenges in the twenty-first century? What will be her mission in Africa? What is her role within the universal Catholic Church?

The Church must, ultimately, measure herself. Only what she will announce, will really enrich the life of the people of Africa, to become a liberating and joyful experience in their concrete, real situation, showing that the Church of Africa lives the mission entrusted to her by Christ: Go and announce the Good News to all. The African Christian faith received a new expression by Africans, received a new joy and a new power of a faith to be lived. This book is a gift for the Church in Africa and, ultimately, for all Christians and people of Africa. It makes connections, points out means and ways, and explains the present, preparing the people of Africa for their great mission, not only within the worldwide Catholic Church, but also of all humanity.

Iheanacho's area of specialization is Church History, with particular interest in Mission History. The core area of the book, however, is to profile the Vatican's policy of domestication to be realized on the African continent by a local episcopate. The author particularly traces and highlights the various turns and courses taken so far by the Church in Africa.

His vision of the African Church is a Church that neither marginalizes herself, nor shies away from discussing important issues and policies. He would like to see a Church being immersed in the core issues of ecclesial and political affairs.

PAUL STEFFEN

Acknowledgments

Gratitude is to the human heart what engine oil is to a car. It lubricates the heart, frees the soul and provides wings to the body! Those were my sentiments, as I recalled the numerous persons and institutions that assisted me throughout the course of this research.

The University of the Free State, South Africa, comes topmost on the ladder of appreciation. This book, which is the fruit of my postdoctoral research, would never have been possible without the financial grant and gracious support from the University of the Free State.

God does send His angels when we least expect it. Professor Rian Venter and Marina van Biljon are two angels whom God sent to guide me through this. They equally acted as my anchors. Thank you so much for always being there for me! Thanks also to my little friend, Ian (Marina's son). I am grateful to Rev. Marlene Oosthuizen who was my first link to the Faculty of Theology and Religion at the University of the Free State. *A Big Thank You* to: colleagues and staff of the Faculty, and to the wonderful students in the Department of Historical and Constructive Theology for the opportunity to be part of their life story. I am particularly indebted to the library staff of the University for their professionalism and support! Thanks to Professors Wessel Bentley and Philippe Denis for their generosity and assistance.

My debt of gratitude goes to the Missionary Society of St Paul for raising me up so that I can grow. I am particularly grateful to my Superior General, Fr Callistus Isara, and the Vicar General, Fr Anthony Anike, for the permission granted to me and for their understanding. Words do not suffice to express my gratitude to my three confrères who first read the manuscript of this book and for their insights: Frs Massdiile Onyenibeadi, Idara Otu and Nduka Uzor. I cannot forget the brothers who were pillars of support for me during my stay in South Africa: Frs Godwin Garuba, Johnson Ugwu, Macjoe Akpan and Kris Aneke.

A great deal of appreciation goes to my former parishioners and friends at the Ficksburg Catholic Parish, South Africa, for their patience and understanding. They are numerous to mention, but a few persons are worthy of note for their support and assistance: Mme Anacletta M. Ferete, the Chalaka family, the Hardnick family, the Mokoma family, the Moyobo family, José and Susan Pequeno, and Ntate Mohau Rabodila who acted as my "driver" on many occasions. Thanks also to the family of Mr and Mrs Uzoma J. Ekeji (Nwanne di na mba). Many thanks to Mr Ben Mohau who showed me the road to the University of the Free State. Special thanks to Mr Kelvin Le Grange (MSP logistics director in South Africa), Isabelle Le Grange (our mother in South Africa), their children: Cicinho and Kelsey Le Grange. Appreciation to Ms Thuli Ngcobo, Sr Juliana Abioye, EHJ, Yolanda Coutries and Happiness Mofokeng.

Fr Christopher Asama deserves a special mention for his generous spirit and assistance. A million thanks to Bishops Anselm Umoren and Hyacinth Egbebo, Frs Ambrose Akinwade, Mark Odion, Linus Kpalap, Julius Otoaye, Noel Ugoagwu, Evaristus Chukwu and Martin Eke. I must remember the kindness of the following confrères: Frs Nathaniel Oga, Benjamin Okon, Patsilver Okah, George Okeahialam, Christian Unachukwu, Daniel Udofia, Ebuka Umechikelu, Anthony Oleh, Joseph Ibiwoye, Martin Ezeihuaku, Michael Akpan, Felix Ogbuagu, Livinus Torty, Felix Osasona, John Eze, and the entire MSP family. The same appreciation goes to Frs Clifford Ayegwalo, Mike Songu, Abraham Nake. Immense thanks to Mr David Urueste and Anthony Ezenwankwo.

To Frs Luke Buckles and Albert Glade, thank you for giving me accommodation in Rome! I cannot take for granted the generous support of the following: Fr Richard Filima, staff and students of the Saint Patrick Society Formation House in Pietermaritzburg. Mention must also be made of the following institutions for the use of their libraries and for the assistance of their library staff: Pontifical Urbaniana University, Rome; St Joseph's Theological Institute, Pietermaritzburg; St Augustine College, Johannesburg, and The Jesuit Centre in Johannesburg.

My "Thank You" roll call will be incomplete without the following persons: Iheanacho family, His Royal Highness, Eze Peter Onyewuenyi, Commander Jonathan Anioke and family, Mr and Mrs William Mbanu and family, Aunty Stella Obijuru, the Alada family, Frs Lawrence Ike and Francis Obijuru; Mrs Ego Egbe, Mrs Cecilia Okoro, the family of Isaia and Luceta Contaldo and their children: Alessandra, Elisabetta and Luigi. Don Donato Palma, Don Faustin Mundendi and Don Aldo Aliverti (great friends of mine).

I owe special thanks to Professor Paul Steffen for his encouragement and for the Foreword. Many thanks to Marie-Thérèse Murray, for the professional editing of the manuscript. Particular thanks to Mr Matthew Wimer and his team at Wipf and Stock.

Eternal peace to a dear friend, Fr Nonso Onyeme. To my late parents, Pa Cletus Iheanacho and Mrs Nwakaego, to my cousin, Mr Donatus Ikpe, and to Rev. Benedict K. Mokheseng (a dependable ally of the MSPs), may Jesus the Good Shepherd keep you all serene and in peace!

Introduction

At the end of the eighteenth century, the Catholic Church was in a very precarious situation. Its end seemed imminent, with a weakened papacy at the centre. However, in a somewhat dramatic manner, the papacy revived. That revival brought with it the reorganization of old religious Orders, which meant that the missions once again received some attention. The latter part of the nineteenth century was rich in the foundation and formation of new congregations, both male and female, entirely dedicated to the missions. The pontificate of Pope Gregory XVI (1831–1846) gave the much-needed impetus to Catholic missions in the first half of the nineteenth century. According to Stephen Neill,

> Gregory looked far into the future; foreseeing the great expansion that was to come, he prepared the framework within which the missionaries would be able to work by creating a large number of bishoprics and prefectures in all parts of the world[1].

That great Catholic missionary revival was sustained by Gregory XVI's two immediate successors: Pius IX (1846–1878) and Leo XIII (1878–1903). Their long pontificates, covering the entire second half of the nineteenth century, consolidated the process of the Church's missionary work. The missionary reawakening of the 1800s within the Catholic Church in Europe provided a springboard for the missions in sub-Saharan Africa. It witnessed the emergence of new missionary congregations and the reinforcement of old ones, which altogether accelerated modern Catholic missions in Africa.

In the ensuing five chapters and pages, this book traces the historical trajectories of contemporary Catholicism in the sub-Saharan regions of Africa, by highlighting the curves and routes that the Catholic Church has travelled to reach its present state on the African continent. In many ways, those curves and routes were marked by sheer determination and heroism,

1. Neill, *A History of Christian Missions*, 338.

while, at other times, they were characterized by remarkable success on account of the Africans' ready acceptance of the Christian faith. Those trajectories also reveal the underbelly of European interest and onslaught in Africa. The contours display a huge shade of light and darkness in Africa's encounter with Europe as well as the continent's hemorrhage in the hands of Arab slave traders. First, starting in the fifteenth century, the Portuguese exploration of Africa kick-started the infamous transatlantic slave trade. The second phase witnessed the collusion between Christian evangelization and European colonialism. This began in the last decades of the eighteenth century and lasted through the nineteenth century. Sadly, it appears that Africa's encounters with the outside world were often marked by a progressive history of exploitation. This sad historical reality led Pius Okigbo to observe that Africa has been enslaved by everyone in progressive successions, with one period of enslavement beginning where another period ended.[2]

From the evolutionary point of view, the history of African Catholicism is placed within the broader continental history of Africa. In Chapter One, a cursory overview locates and highlights some past and repeated attempts made towards planting the Church in Africa. For roughly three centuries, that aim, which appeared unattainable, remained the primary goal of the Catholic mission apostolate in Africa, as it was worldwide. This was noticeable from 1445, when the first Mass was believed to have been celebrated on West African soil by the Portuguese priest, Fr Polono de Lagos. From available sources, this became henceforth the constant preoccupation of successive popes after Pope Pius II (1458–1468). He first expressed the desire, in 1462, to have the whole of "Guinea" evangelized, together with all the neighboring islands. Guinea was remotely understood as coextensive with the vast African continent at the time of Pope Pius II. Of course, this misconception was largely due to incorrect and inadequate geographical knowledge about Africa. Notwithstanding Portugal's diminishing influence on account of its declining power in Africa, Pope Innocent X, in 1652, remained hopeful that the toils and prospects of the early missionaries would not go entirely unrewarded.

Against the background of the vastness and histories of Africa as well as the cultural diversities and colonial experiences of the continent, Giulio Albanese maintains that "it is better to use the plural when speaking about a continent three times as big as Europe."[3] In view of this observation, in order to consider "Africa" in the plural rather than in the singular, efforts have been made in this book to recognize Africa as "a continent of startling

2. Okigbo, "The Future Haunted by the Past," 28–29.
3. Albanese, "Africa, Quo Vadis?," 149.

contrasts" with various diversities.[4] For instance, those diversities and contrasts are reflected on the tombstone of Bishop Edward Barron, the first bishop of the Vicariate of the Two Guineas. At a cemetery in Savannah in the United States of America, Bishop Barron is honored as "Edward Barron, Bishop of Africa," while another monument in Waterford remembers him as "Bishop of Liberia."[5]

The same diversity is present in juxtaposing the creation of the Apostolic Vicariate of Central Africa in 1846 and highlighting the sacrifices made by the pioneer missionaries in those parts of Africa. This juxtaposition is made in view of the fact that "attention is often directed, in the history of Christian missions in Africa, towards the depletion of the missionary personnel in West Africa as the cemetery of the [W]hite man."[6] With keen attention to details, the generosity of the Church in America towards the restart of Catholic missions in contemporary Africa is equally noted. Similar attention is shown in presenting the differences and aspersions among some founders of missionary institutes. At the time, the various geographical locations within the vast continent of Africa occasioned their altercations. All these vividly demonstrate that the history of the Church in Africa consists of many vicissitudes, as indicated in Chapter Two.

Chapters Three and Four demonstrate how the evolution of the Church in Africa, through the Vatican's general policy of *plantatio ecclesiae*, reached its "omega point" between the 1950s and the 1960s. This became possible because of the emergence of African clergy on the ecclesiastical map and in the administrative structures of the nascent local churches on the continent. The inheritor of previous papal missionary initiatives and directives within the period was Pope Pius XII. He anchored his missionary policy towards the missions in Africa on the "Africanization" of the emerging local hierarchy. He was supported in this regard by Msgr Celso Costantini. As early as 1939, at the very incipient period of the pontificate of Pius XII, Msgr Costantini had urged the pope to accord full elaboration in the concrete realization of the missionary policy already set in motion by Popes Benedict XV and Pius XI.[7] Msgr Costantini was a staunch supporter of the creation of indigenous hierarchies in mission territories. This conviction was impressed upon him by his experiences in China, where he had previously served as the Apostolic Delegate of the Holy See. It seemed that the slacking in the Vatican's enthusiasm after the episcopal ordinations in 1939 of two

4. Russell, *Africa's Twelve Apostles*, 14.
5. Russell, *Africa's Twelve Apostles*, 36, 42.
6. See Chapter 1 of this work.
7. Gori, "Santa Sede e Francia," 207.

first Black African bishops in contemporary history might be attributed to some friction within the missionary organs in Rome. It bordered on time and degree. While Msgr Costantini viewed the process of indigenization as profound and fast, Pius XII favored a slow and gradual process. The perspective of Pius XII arose from the painful experience in China, where the communist government forced the new Chinese bishops to sever ties with the Holy See. Rome regretted its policy of indigenization in China as a result of those ugly consequences. In hindsight, it considered that policy to have been somewhat realized too soon and too rapidly.[8]

Not wanting a repeat of a similar episode in Africa, Pius XII preferred to proceed cautiously—taking one step at a time. However, once those anxieties and precautions were, to a great extent, overcome, the implementation of the policy became accelerated in Africa. It occurred on two fronts, namely the erection of ecclesiastical hierarchies in the soon-to-be independent countries and the ordination of Africans as bishops. Although the policy and its implementation were met with resistance in some missionary quarters and in France, the Vatican never looked back. The success of that policy was boldly acknowledged by Pope Paul VI in his message *Africae Terranum*, issued in 1967 on the tenth anniversary of *Fidei Donum*. The positive outlook of that message was indicative of the fact that the Vatican's fears and anxieties over the future of the young churches in Africa had largely been allayed. The positive turnout of events and development within both the ecclesiastical community and the political spheres in Africa calmed its nerves.[9] Giving outlet to his satisfaction, Paul VI did not hesitate to acknowledge the obvious:

> In fact, the progress of the Church in Africa is truly consoling. The local hierarchy is established almost everywhere. The Church, in fact, did not wait for the nationalist movements to start Africans in positions of responsibility in the priesthood and in the episcopate, thanks to the wise norms imparted by the Roman Pontiffs, especially by our immediate predecessors (*Africae Terranum*, no. 23).

The Vatican's policy of indigenization, realized through the Africanization of the local episcopate, prepared and launched the local churches in Africa into the post-missionary phase. It began to take shape particularly after the Second Vatican Council. This is the fourth phase in the history of Catholicism in Africa. According to Francis Oborji, the fourth phase spanned from Vatican II (1962–1965), through the 1970s and 1980s, to the

8. Gori, "Santa Sede e Francia," 196–197.
9. Hickey, *Papal Missionary Documents*, 20.

convocation of the First African Synod of Bishops in 1994.[10] It was a period of rapid growth when, in Oborji's estimation, the universal Church began to benefit from the fruits of evangelization in the young churches of Africa.[11] This period was also marked by the emergence of prominent African prelates. Notable was Cardinal Bernardin Gantin of Benin Republic. He was the first African bishop to serve in Rome when, on 5 March 1971, Paul VI called him to join the Roman Curia. After being created a cardinal by Paul VI on 27 June 1977, Gantin climbed the ecclesiastical ladder to become the first African to head the College of Cardinals as its Dean from 1993 until his retirement in 2002. Besides Gantin, other prominent African bishops included Cardinals Dominic Ekandem of Nigeria, Paul Zoungrana of Burkina Faso, Hyacinthe Thiandoum of Senegal, Joseph Malula of the Democratic Republic of Congo, and Maurice Otunga of Kenya.[12] The list is by no means exhaustive, but it may not be complete without mentioning conscientious African curial Cardinals Francis Arinze of Nigeria, Peter Turkson of Ghana, and Robert Sarah of Guinea.

The historical trajectory of the Church in Africa is equally colored by other tapestries that must be accounted for, especially regarding future projects, as they may help determine the future direction and shape of the local churches across the continent. This aspect is discussed in Chapter Five. One major issue that the Church in Africa must address is financial independence and self-reliance rather than dependence on foreign assistance. Dating back to 1890, Pope Leo XIII expressed the hope that the financial costs of sustaining African missions were not to continue forever. They were to be of a temporal arrangement until such time when the same African missions could not only fend for themselves financially, but also contribute to the universal purse: "These expenses must be borne for some years, until the heralds of the gospel can establish themselves and take responsibility for their own financial affairs. We hope that we have enough strength to undertake such a project" (*Catholicae Ecclesiae*, no 5). If the continuous financial dependency of Africa may be used as a barometer, it indicates the general lack of development in many parts of Africa since 1890, when Pope Leo XIII first expressed that wish. Africa has remained an impoverished continent on many fronts. The poverty of the continent invariably rubs off on the local church, since most of its members are economically poor and bear, on their skins, the scars of misrule and mismanagement of the continent's resources by African ruling elites.

10. Oborji, "Catholic Mission in Africa," 15.
11. Oborji, "Catholic Mission in Africa," 15.
12. Tomko, "Un Grande Africano," 139–140.

Another important tapestry within the trajectory curve is the apparent paradox that has characterized the history of contemporary Catholicism in Africa. While the Church in Africa has continued to grow numerically, which has positioned it as the future Church and the future of the Church, paradoxically, the same Church in Africa appears to exert less influence within global Catholicism in terms of policy orientation. It has rather gained for itself an international image of a conservative church. This ecclesiastical paradox calls to mind a similar paradox about Africa as brilliantly stated by the prominent African political scientist, Ali Mazrui: "And the basic paradox is that, though Africa is the most centrally located continent, it is the most peripheral in political terms."[13] If the Church in Africa has grown evangelically at the close of the twentieth century but without corresponding theological and economic maturity, and even liturgically beyond the belabored inculturation,[14] the same Church as the future Church and the future of the Church needs to turn the tide to its favor in those regards.

A similar observation can be made about ecological concerns. This is done in the awareness that poverty in Africa has a feminine face and that women constitute the larger bulk of Church membership in both rural and urban areas. Their means of livelihood are threatened by deforestation and soil depletion, due to pollutants. The impact of the ecological crisis on women in rural areas is rendered more precarious when viewed against the background that most of them shoulder a disproportionate burden of Africa's underdevelopment. The women are the ones who carry firewood, and fetch water from faraway rivers and wells. They are the ones who plant, weed and harvest crops to feed themselves and their families.[15] In other words, African women are most vulnerable to the adverse impacts of ecological disasters. This explains why ecological concerns must occupy a front burner in the pastoral considerations of the Church in Africa as the Church of the future.

The brief studies and analysis in this book cannot pretend to preclude further research in knitting together the curves and routes travelled so far by the Church in Africa. As a vast continent, the hues and tapestries of contemporary Catholicism in Africa are complex, on account of varying different locations and factors. Much attention is intentionally limited to Africa south of the Sahara for cultural, economic, political and religious reasons. It is also pertinent to underscore another feature of this book in terms of its aim. What has been accomplished, as far as this book is concerned, remains

13. Cited in Kaggwa, "The New Catholicity," 186.
14. Mugambi, "African Churches in Social Transformation," 211–212.
15. Nasimiya-Wasike, "Christology and an African Woman's," 93.

only but a minimal attempt to contribute towards a continent-wide discussion on African Catholicism and its future direction. However, the book stands out in its insistence that a globalized church offers the Church in Africa the possibility to "connect, compete and collaborate" within the universal Church. It is upon that emphasis that the book anchors its originality in going beyond the mere analysis of past developments.

A word needs to be said about the basic orientation and approach in this book. It is situated within the domain of mission history by means of the historical method. The method entails, among other things,

> investigating, recording, analyzing and interpreting the events of the past for the purpose of discovering generalizations that are helpful in understanding the past, understanding the present, and to a limited extent, in anticipating the future[16].

This explains why an attempt has been made to project the future shape of the Church in Africa. In terms of sources, the book has drawn from a wide range of primary sources, where possible. They are complemented by secondary sources for documentary and literary support. Altogether, both sources give depth to the overall conclusion, since history as a discipline is chiefly oriented towards finding and using material sources alongside rational analysis, in order to arrive at a credible conclusion.

---

16. Hepzi, *History and Development*, 35.

1

Brief perspective on missions in Africa

To date, Adrian Hastings remains one of the great authorities on African Christianity and on the history of the Church in Africa. As he perceptively observed: "A work of history must have its frontiers and yet it is often impossible to adhere to them very rigidly without cutting into a flow of interacting developments unduly."[1] The frontier of this book is essentially the pre- and post-missionary phases of the Church in Africa that can be identified as forming a historic enclosure or a unit. It marks an important period in the history of Catholicism in Africa that spanned from the 1950s to 1994. Be that as it may, the broad title of the book makes it imperative that some significant epochs, which make up the constitutive elements of a historical trajectory of the Catholic Church in Africa, must be accounted for, even if it is done in a somewhat rapid manner.

In view of the impossibility of adhering strictly to the identified frontier, there is no better epoch to begin this book than the fifteenth century. If there are two words to describe that era, those words would be 'dream' and 'hope.' The reason is not far-fetched. It was an epoch when the popes, beginning with Pope Martin V (1417–1431), showed, surprisingly, an unusual and extraordinary interest in the newly discovered regions of Africa by Portuguese explorers. Their paternal attention and pastoral solicitude were cast over territories that dotted the western coastal areas south of the Sahara to the northern tip of the River Congo. Collectively, those areas were known for many centuries to the Europeans as the lands of Upper

1. Hastings, *The Church in Africa*, v.

and Lower Guinea. Those territories provided the theatrical platform for the earliest Catholic missionary endeavors in Black Africa, from the fifteenth century onwards, as underscored by Carlos Stoetzer:

> All of the popes, from Martin V in the XVth century to popes Pius XII, John XXIII and Paul VI, have extended their dedication and love to the missionary work in Africa and supported the heroic sacrifices and the undaunted spirit of the missionaries from the very beginning of the monumental tasks[2].

Through a bird's eye view, this chapter recalls the first encounter of sub-Saharan Africa with the Christian Gospel. In broader continental perspective, that period is generally referred to as the second encounter between Africa and the Gospel. This is the case when North Africa and Ethiopia are grouped together with the remainder of the continent prior to the advent of Islam in both places. In this sense, Joseph Kenny, in his work that covers that period, calls it "the middle period": "The Church of the middle period was much weaker, but left a slight lasting impression."[3] The vestiges of that "slight lasting impression" are traceable in a few places such as the island country of Cape Verde in central Atlantic Ocean and the equatorial island country of São Tomé and Príncipe. In the course of time, both island nations became important transit routes for the transatlantic slave trade. The "slight lasting impression" remained folklore memory in a place called the Warri Kingdom in present-day Nigeria in similar manner that the mission of the same period left its signs in the Congo Kingdom of Afonso I (1507–1543).

As explorers, soldiers, merchants and missionaries had once travelled together in the "Portuguese caravels of Christ,"[4] so too, in a similar fashion, did they traverse sub-Saharan Africa beginning from the late eighteenth century. They became the new faces of Europe and its foot soldiers, under the canopy of "*Pax Coloniae*," especially from the middle of the nineteenth century, when the "Flag" became wedded to the "Cross." Catholic missionary comeback in Africa took place in a changed atmosphere amidst Europe's greater access to the continent. For Catholic missionaries, it was an attempt either to regain lost grounds or to revive old missions that had lain moribund between the seventeenth and the eighteenth centuries. It was bound to be an uphill task on account of many actors and various competing interests. This chapter does not set out to necessarily narrate in detail already well-known facts about those aspects of the history of the Catholic Church

---

2. Stoetzer, "Preface," xiii.
3. Kenny, *The Catholic Church in Tropical*, 75.
4. Taken from the title of Gilbert Renault's book *The Caravels of Christ*.

in Africa. Its aim is rather to connect some indispensable dots in the overall historical trajectories of African Catholicism. This will be done in a very cursory manner, in order to place past events in an appropriate sequence that will allow for situating subsequent events and the projection of likely future trends in the continuous historical curves of the Church in Africa.

A CURSORY OVERVIEW

For over four centuries, effectively between 1460 and 1850, pope after pope dreamed and nursed the hope of flourishing local churches in Africa. The Holy See considered the creation of the amorphous vicariate of the Two Guineas in 1842 to be a significant move towards the realization of a dream that had remained practically elusive until the last quarter of the 1800s. The missionary history of the Church up to this period, dotted as it were by acts of heroism and countless failures, dates back to the period of Portuguese mercantile adventures in Africa. From the first time the Portuguese sailors and missionaries set foot on the coastal areas of the continent of Africa in the middle of the fifteenth century, the vast territories along the western coast, south of the Sahara, and the northern tip of the River Congo were commonly grouped together by the Europeans as Upper and Lower Guinea. Their territories stretched up to the banks of the Orange River in southern Africa.[5]

Of historical importance during the period was the discovery of the mouth and estuary of the River Congo in roughly August 1482 by the Portuguese explorer and navigator, Diogo Cão (1450–1486).[6] That discovery facilitated "the massive arrival of European missionaries and settlers who penetrated the region from the Atlantic seaboard."[7] Through papal bulls such as *In Apostolicae Dignitatis Specula*, *Eximie Devotionis* (1420) and *Aeterni Regis Clementia* (1480), the popes, on their own, confirmed and encouraged Portuguese kings and explorers in their conquest of Africa. However, while lending their support and encouragement to the Portuguese crown, the popes were mindful of the opportunities offered to the Church for the evangelization of the discovered territories and those to be discovered in the future.[8] A case at hand was the fact that missionaries followed suit after the Portuguese's discovery of Sierra Leone in 1415, with formal settlement beginning in 1463. A similar process was replicated in

5. Bane, *The Popes and Western Africa*, 1; Gray, "The Catholic Church and National States," 150.
6. https://www.britannica.com/biography/Diogo-Cao.
7. Gampiot, *Kimbanguism*, 35.
8. Serapião, "The Preaching of Portuguese Colonialism," 34.

Elmina (now Ghana), where the missionaries arrived in 1481 and remained for approximately 241 years. On the other hand, the Capuchins abandoned their missionary apostolate in Sierra Leone in 1723.[9] According to Joseph Kenny, on the heels of the Portuguese docking at Cape Verde in 1445 from the Senegal River, Fr Polono de Lagos was reputed to have celebrated the first ever-known Mass on the soil of West Africa in that same year in Cape Verde.[10] This is one historic fact that is so often lost to historians of African Christianity, especially the second coming of Christianity on the continent.

Until the late 1950s, the Upper and Lower Guineas were of great significance, because they constituted the very epicenter of Catholic missionary activities in the whole of sub-Saharan Africa. Over fifty ecclesiastical jurisdictions in contemporary Africa issued forth from such a vast territory that was amphibious and hazy in its geographical extension, stretching from the desert to the sea, and from Cape Verde (the green vegetation that lay south of Senegal) and the sands of the Sahara, which the Portuguese called "Cape Blanco" (now between Mauritania and Western Sahara).[11] During the course of the missionary endeavors in and around the two Guineas, the popes issued a series of documents and pronouncements to indicate their special attention to the evangelization of the continent. As early as 1444, Pope Eugene IV (1431–1447) appointed Bishop John Manuel of Ceuta as Primate of Africa. His appointment preceded by two years the arrival of the first group of Franciscan friars who landed in Cape Verde in 1446. This was a landmark event in the history of the evangelization of sub-Saharan Africa. In a brief dated 12 December 1462 and addressed to Fr Alphonsus Bolano, Superior of the Franciscans in Guinea, Pope Pius II (1458–1464) expressed his "desire to evangelize Guinea and its neighboring provinces with the islands of the great Atlantic Ocean."[12]

The clearest of all papal solicitudes towards Africa south of the Sahara were demonstrated in two actions of Pope Leo X (1513–1521). First, in 1518, the pope raised Dom Henrique, son of King Afonso I of Congo (1506–1543), to the episcopate at the age of twenty-three years.[13] He made him Titular Bishop of Utica and appointed him as the Coadjutor to Bishop Didacus Pinheiro of the diocese of Funchal. Aware of the reservations raised in some quarters about the episcopal elevation of Dom Henrique, Leo X sought to allay such

9. Fisher, "The Catholic Church in Liberia," 261.
10. Kenny, *The Catholic Church in Tropical*, 1.
11. Isichei, *A History of Christianity in Africa*, 57.
12. Bane, *The Popes and Western Africa*, 6, 9.
13. Bane, *The Popes and Western Africa*, 10; Filesi, "L'Evangelizzazione del Regno," 297.

fears through his brief *Vidimus quae*. In order that the young bishop might not be deprived of professional advice, Leo X judged "it opportune and proper to associate with him some men well versed in theology and canon law." Secondly, in his papal bull, *Exponi Nobis* of June 1518, Leo X authorized the heads of missions in Africa and in all of the Portuguese territories

> to train and ordain to the sacred priesthood suitable candidates from amongst the native Christians and converts and to give those native priests full power to celebrate Mass and administer all the Sacraments to the faithful[14].

With regard to the formation and ordination of a native clergy in Africa, this papal ordinance was, in many respects, both epochal and groundbreaking. Despite many historical setbacks, this policy for the formation of local clergy and the establishment of a native hierarchy in mission areas as quickly as possible, albeit with precipitation at times, remained the mainstay of papal missionary considerations in Africa. Another important feature of the missions of this period is the willingness of the Papacy to keep them "as free as possible from 'protection' and interference by the State."[15] It really did not matter that the Holy See counted on the cooperation and goodwill of the Portuguese Crown for assistance.

It is important to note that, notwithstanding the sporadic nature of the Christian evangelization in Africa at the time, the continent witnessed enthusiastically the early embrace of the priesthood by the natives. This led to the ordination of a sizeable number of indigenous people, particularly from the Cape Verde islands,[16] where the diocese of São Tomé was created in 1533 by Pope Clement VII and its first bishop was Msgr Diego Ortiz de Vilhegas. As an ecclesiastical jurisdiction, the diocese of São Tomé extended from the Gulf of Guinea to the River Gambia, to Cape Palmas (in present-day Liberia), and as far as to the Congo Kingdom and the Cape of Good Hope at the most southern tip of Africa.[17] The Congo Kingdom was detached from São Tomé in 1596, when Pope Clement VIII raised the capital of the kingdom, San Salvador, to the rank of Episcopal See and made it a Suffragan Diocese under the Archdiocese of Lisbon in Portugal. San Salvador of Congo was later put under the jurisdiction of Luanda, when the latter was raised to the metropolitan status of an Archdiocese in 1624.[18] At various times during

---

14. Bane, *The Popes and Western Africa*, 11.
15. Stoetzer, "Preface," xii.
16. Isichei, *A History of Christianity in Africa*, 55.
17. Bane, *The Popes and Western Africa*, 12–13.
18. Robert, "The Development of the Local Clergy," 86.

their pontificates, the popes, up to the eve of European imperialism and colonial fever in Africa, remained in their hope of effecting a continent-wide evangelization of Africa as the continent was then known to them.

Because of the popes' limited knowledge about the continent of Africa, in addition to piecemeal information supplied by wayfaring merchants and explorers, Leo Africanus' curious book, *The History and Description of Africa*, proved to be very handy and insightful. It furnished the popes and their contemporaries with some specifics about the mysterious continent of the Black race that inhabited the tropical inland kingdoms on the southern axis of the Sahara.[19] Another important source of information on Africa, particularly on the Congo Kingdom, *Relazione del Reame dei Congo*, by Filippo Pigafetta, was published in 1591. It was largely based on the narration and an eyewitness account, as the author supposedly heard them from Duarte Lopez, the emissary of King Alvaro of Congo to the papal court during the reign of Pope Sixtus V (1585–1590). There were also intermittent reports by some Carmelite priests between 1583 and 1587. From the second half of the seventeenth century, Italian Capuchins, on account of their longer duration and missionary activities in the Congo, began to send some detailed information to the papal court in Rome.[20] Not unmindful of the peculiar pastoral need of the vast territories in Africa, Pope Innocent X sent some Capuchins to the Congo under the leadership of Friar Anthony Romano. He wrote in his brief dated 22 November 1652:

> As the seed of the Catholic faith planted by God's hand long ago in those parts, needs careful attention of apostolic laborers to bring forth a plentiful harvest of virtue, we have thought it expedient to hire new laborers for this field of the Lord, lest the tender shoots and fragile branches be ruined and despoiled by the wiles of the powerful enemy, or the stalks under the influence of showers of grace, be nipped by the winter frost or smitten by the unlucky star, and so disappoint the hopes of the planters and utterly ruin the whole harvest of God[21].

By the time that Innocent X was concerned by the flickering state of the missions in Africa, Portugal, the main protagonist and mission collaborator with the Holy See, was no longer the lone major player on the African scene. Until the dwindling of its sphere of influence in the middle of the seventeenth century, Portugal was one of the great maritime powers in the world at the time. It had its maritime bases in many places in Africa, Asia and in the New

---

19. Bane, *The Popes and Western Africa*, 11–12.
20. Filesi, "L'Evangelizzazione del Regno," 298–299.
21. Bane, *The Popes and Western Africa*, 28.

World. In the case of Africa, Portugal struggled to maintain its domains with the arrival of other rival competitors from Britain, France, Denmark and The Netherlands, who increasingly encroached upon its continental domination of Africa. Alongside its fierce competitors, all of them fought to make their presence felt, as each sought to carve a niche for itself in Africa, especially in the booming shameful and inhuman transatlantic slave trade.

Together with other factors such as the dreadful *padroado* mission system, Portugal's inability to keep pace with the financial and human resource demands of its increasing territorial onslaughts, the missionary theology of the epoch (seeking more of royal conversions), and ultimately, the slave trade all combined to hasten the failures of those sporadic missions that had initially shown positive signs of establishing Christianity and the Church in sub-Saharan Africa.[22] Three reasons are usually adduced for the decline of the missions of this period: Protestant Reformation in Europe, with the ensuing politico-religious conflicts; the politics of France, Spain and Portugal that were aimed at hemming in the Catholic Church both in Europe and abroad, as well as the difficult climatic conditions and the prevalence of some deadly diseases in coastal Africa.[23] The slave trade was a big distraction for Portugal, which converted Angola into some kind of reservoir for its hounded slaves *en route* to Brazil, thus almost depopulating the interior of Angola, due to incessant slave raids. It is sad to recall that the care of some concerned priests for the plights of the native Americans in the hands of their Spanish and Portuguese overlords, unfortunately, had an undesired effect on Africa, by increasing the demands in North and South America for haunted and imported African slaves.[24]

Although never completely extinct, those missions, however, remained moribund for almost two centuries, relying on life support with occasional visits from some lone and wandering missionaries. For their part, the popes never relented in their pastoral solicitude for Black Africa, as the ordinances of Pope Clement XI made clear in two separate briefs. In July 1707, the pope cautioned one of the Congolese princes against "the illicit and nefarious slave trade with heretics" (most likely with British and Dutch merchants in mind), without mentioning Portugal as one of the slave-trading countries. In another brief, issued sometime in 1712, he forbade missionaries from leaving their mission posts in the Congo until they had completed their mandatory term of assignment, unless "forced to leave on account of

22. Oborji, *Trends in African Theology*, 52; Isichei, *A History of Christianity in Africa*, 72.
23. Russell, *Africa's Twelve Apostles*, 15.
24. Ballard, *White Men's God*, ix-x.

health."[25] The reason for such prohibition was based on reports reaching the pope that some missionaries preferred to work in healthier and milder climatic conditions such as in Brazil, rather than in the Congo and on the Isle of Saint Thomas.

In Clement XI's estimation, "a greater number of laborers" were much-needed in Africa. He considered the insufficient number of missionaries and the lack of commitment on the part of some missionaries to be both inopportune and injurious to the local people, and equally detrimental to the missionary activities in the Congo and the Isle of Saint Thomas.[26] However, all things considered, the checkmating and weakening of the Islamic incursion beyond Mombasa in East Africa remains one of the decisive achievements of the Catholic missions during the Portuguese era in Africa. By so doing, they effectively put a wedge to Islam and confined its spread in the south.[27] The earliest attempt at Catholic evangelization on the Island of Madagascar in the Indian Ocean was made as far back as 1648 by a group of Vincentian missionaries (then known as the Lazarists). That missionary adventure failed. It signaled the beginning of a prolonged history of failures, sufferings and persecutions that would characterize the various Catholic missionary efforts in Madagascar in 1830, 1845 and 1855.[28]

"PAX COLONIAE"

It is an incontrovertible fact that the nineteenth-century Christian missionary movement was "one of the most powerful forces"[29] that transformed Africa in many ways. It is, therefore, impossible and unavoidable to imagine or write the history of contemporary Africa without apportioning a considerable space to the missionaries and their enterprise within the general colonial scheme of things. As Chima Korieh and Raphael Njoku rightly noted in their work, "the Christian missionary movement has received more than a fair scholarly interest."[30] Yet the missionaries were not the only new arrivals on the African scene, as they shared the space with other interested parties on the continent. In many respects, theirs was a symbiotic relationship with their fellow European wayfarers who crisscrossed the breadth and length of Africa, whether they be explorers, soldiers, traders, colonizers or

25. Bane, *The Popes and Western Africa*, 39.
26. Bane, *The Popes and Western Africa*, 39.
27. Ngulu, "The Church in Africa," 17.
28. Brown, "France the Missionary," 657.
29. Korieh and Njoku, "Introduction," 2.
30. Korieh and Njoku, "Introduction," 2.

administrators. Metaphors such as the "Flag and the Cross" or the "Bible and the Sword" are often employed to depict that symbiotic rapport between the missionaries and the colonizers as officials of a foreign occupying power.

The trailblazing of missionaries and colonialists through Africa was greatly enhanced by advances in medicine between the eighteenth and the nineteenth centuries. Charles Marie de la Condamine discovered quinine in 1737, although both Catholic and Protestant (always suspicious of science) missionaries did not enthusiastically use quinine as a prophylactic against malaria almost fifty years after its initial discovery.[31] Another major breakthrough occurred in 1897, when Ronald Ross discovered that the malaria parasite was carried by the Anopheles mosquito. Without any fear of exaggerations, it could be affirmed that quinine helped the Europeans (missionaries and colonialists alike) to energetically colonize Africa, especially the interior. With the quinine then readily available as an antidote to that mythical and fatal African disease, fewer Europeans succumbed to malaria fever and the dreaded yellow fever.[32] Both the missionary movement and colonialism left a deep mark on the African soul. Colonialism, in particular, left an enduring "trauma in the African soul"[33] that has long remained almost unhealed. It led the Ghanaian intellectual and missionary, Dr James Kwegyir Aggrey (1875–1927) to make this curious but interesting proposal: "Certain White people ought for once to be changed into Negroes for a few days in order to experience what we experience."[34] By means of colonialism, the European powers intertwined Africa to Europe "in a relationship of perpetual dependence," which has largely remained undone.[35]

As "*Pax Europeana*" was imposed on Africa and obviously on European terms,[36] the Catholic Church, like other Christian churches, seized the moment to make inroads into the continent. As much as the missionaries would have liked to distance themselves, it remains a historical fact or perhaps, as Roland Oliver described it, "a happy accident"[37] that the Christian churches in contemporary Africa are undeniably the offspring of the missionary labors undertaken during the period of a mutual interaction between colonialism and the missionary movement on the continent. Their mutual and sometimes intricate interaction, in various places and in

31. Ballard, *White Men's God*, 13.
32. Hildebrandt, *History of the Church in Africa*, 194.
33. Baur, *2000 Years of Christianity*, 420.
34. Cited in Baur, *2000 Years of Christianity*, 422.
35. Tekeste Negash, *Italian Colonialism in Eritrea*, 9.
36. Sundkler and Steed, *A History of the Church*, 97.
37. Cited in Pass, *The Faith Moves South*, 134.

certain instances, proved very difficult to disentangle in a clear-cut manner. Emperor Menelik II of Ethiopia was sagacious when, in 1896, he articulated in detail the arrival of the Europeans in the following sequence: "First the explorer, then the missionary, then the soldier."[38] Although it never always occurred in that order everywhere on the continent, that famous saying of Menelik II, nonetheless, gave expression to the views of many Africans, especially those of the local rulers, about European colonialism and the missionary movement. It is important to acknowledge and to note that the missionary movement in Africa, which only developed from the middle of the nineteenth century, had its infancy and fragile roots in the last quarter of the eighteenth century. It was an offshoot of the religious revival in Europe that swept across some Protestant countries, especially England, when many Protestant missionary societies were founded for overseas missions. In this regard, it is right to affirm, as did John Baur, that "the missionary movement in Africa preceded colonialism by almost a century."[39]

Although the advent of the missionaries may have preceded the eventual arrival of colonial soldiers and administrators, nevertheless, an umbilical cord connected the missionaries to the colonizers in two ways, namely facilitation and infrastructure developments brought about by European colonization. In the cyclic web of events, the flag initially followed the cross, but much later, especially after the Berlin Conference of 1884–1885, the reverse became the case. The cross began to follow the flag, as the colonizers increasingly penetrated ever deeper into the interior of Africa.[40] As Africa became the privileged place of competition among European contenders, formal colonization opened up a vast field of missionary activities to missionaries.[41] In this light, "*Pax Coloniae*" may be compared to the *Pax Romana* in Christian antiquity, interpreted by Church Fathers as providential and as *preparatio evangelii*.

Likewise, the "*Pax coloniae*" helped the missions in Africa by implicitly eliciting missionary interests and concerns in Europe on behalf of the missionary movement on the African continent. It helped expand the pool of missionary personnel for the missions in Africa and galvanized material and financial support for the same missions. It was commonplace at the time for humanitarian objectives couched as "civilization" to be intricately interwoven with economic, political and strategic interests. They cumulatively feathered the nest of colonialism in its concrete expression of imperialism

---

38. Baur, *2000 Years of Christianity*, 420.
39. Baur, *2000 Years of Christianity*, 423.
40. Shorter, *Cross and Flag in Africa*, 24.
41. Comby, *Duemila anni di Evangelizzazione*, 257.

in the shape of a formal control of overseas territories. The missionary enterprise, in its turn, understood then as a form of humanitarian work, was identified in 1895 by no less a personage than Lord Rosebery, to be one of the items to be found in the grand basket of "liberal imperialism." In the conjecture of Rosebery, "liberal imperialism," as conceived in the 1890s, implied "the maintenance of the Empire, the opening of new areas for our surplus population, the suppression of the slave trade, the development of missionary enterprise, and the development of commerce."[42]

The idea of Rosebery on imperialism, whether "liberal" or otherwise, was not completely different from that of the French statesman, Jules Ferry (1832–1893). He is generally regarded as one of the fathers of contemporary French overseas imperialism on the basis of his unapologetic support for France's colonial expansion and territorial acquisition. Ferry was persuaded that France ought to have colonies on two grounds, namely economic reasons and "superior races" have the right to dominate "inferior races." His ideas fed the colonial ambition of France.[43] As a matter of fact, 'imperialism' as a concept in contemporary usage, first originated in France in the 1840s, with the impostures of Louis Napoleon (later Napoleon III). Under the disguise of romantic nationalism, Louis Napoleon sought to restore France's purported lost glories and national pride, bequeathed to the French nation by Emperor Napoleon Bonaparte through his many wars and territorial conquests.[44] It was not a mere coincidence that, by 1892, a year prior to the death of Ferry in 1893, France had acquired a vast territory in West Africa, which became known as French West Africa with the consolidation of its presence.

The year 1892 remains remarkable in the annals of contemporary African history, because, from that moment until 1920, the scramble of the continent effectively apportioned thirty colonies and so-called protectorates to European powers.[45] It must be considered, against this background, that, by 1880, only roughly 10% of Africa was under European control and influence, which increased astronomically by the turn of the twentieth century.[46] In the European mindset of the time, Africa was nothing but *res nullius*. It was more or less "a continent without owners, ready to be shared among those who equated might with right."[47] With regard to missionaries, if prior to 1890 they had dreamed and entertained the ambition of setting up missions that would

42. Stanley, *The Bible and the Flag*, 36.
43. Comby, *Duemila anni di Evangelizzazione*, 257.
44. Stanley, *The Bible and the Flag*, 35.
45. Shorter, *Cross and Flag in Africa*, 23.
46. Pass, *The Faith Moves South*, 107.
47. Negash, *Italian Colonialism in Eritrea*, 8.

be independent of colonialism and colonial interference, such hopes effectively evaporated by the end of the nineteenth century.[48] Thenceforth, there ensued between the missionaries and colonizers, a compromised or tolerated understanding, even though both held on to their respective objectives.

On the one hand, political and economic interests were the primary concerns for the colonizers, while, on the other, religious interests remained the overriding focus of the missionaries in their quest to establish Christianity on the continent.[49] Thus, despite the huge financial subventions received from the French government, Fr Augustin Planque, SMA Superior General, defended the independence of the Christians on two different occasions in 1864: "I have said that we cannot sacrifice to the teaching of French our chief aim, that of promoting the Catholic faith."[50] He reiterated that stance somewhat harder in another way: "We are not on the missions on behalf of the French government."[51] It is in this horizon, in the shadow of missions and colonialism, that the history of Christianity on the continent may be described as one of the many vicissitudes of Africa,[52] for the missionary movement, as a matter of historical accident, was circumstantially coupled to colonialism in a marriage of inconvenience.

There were, undoubtedly, occasional points of convergence and divergence between the two, particularly where the colonizers accepted Christian missionary activities for their own convenience. Otherwise, the colonizers tended not to hold a brief for the missionaries, especially when their different goals and interests came into conflict or collided in opposition to one another. When that was not the case, the missionaries considered colonialism favorably as one of the necessities enshrined by the law of history. For that assumption, the legitimacy about colonialism and the domination of another nation by a foreign power was never put to question.[53] As people are normally the children of their time, the missionaries and their mother churches in Europe bore the imprints of their time with regard to colonialism.

Pope Leo XIII (1878–1903), whose long pontificate coincided with European division and colonization of Africa, saw the missions through the optical lens of his time: colonization, civilization, and evangelization.[54] The new missions were particularly comforting to him as he considered them a

---

48. Prudhomme, *Missioni Cristiane e Colonialismo*, 56.
49. Shorter, *Cross and Flag in Africa*, 24.
50. *Augustin Planque*, 107.
51. *Augustin Planque*, 107.
52. Russell, *Africa's Twelve Apostles*, 15.
53. Prudhomme, *Missioni Cristiane e Colonialismo*, 56.
54. Comby, *Duemila anni di Evangelizzazione*, 268.

big compensation for the losses of the Church in Europe, the latter becoming progressively hostile to religion in its anticlerical policies at home, but ironically supporting Christian missions beyond the shores of Europe.[55]

Notwithstanding their occasional skirmishes, the inconvenient marriage between Christian missions and colonialism, as well as the complex relationship between missionaries and colonialists, inadvertently procured some gains and benefits for the unwitting partners. France, the home and epicenter of European anticlericalism, supported the overseas missions of its missionaries, on the basis of its commercial and nationalist interests, since the colonies, their populations and their dependencies meant an increased prestige for motherland. The overseas missions equally brought greater material prosperity and wealth for France in its overseas competition with Britain.[56] As for Portugal, the benefits that accrued from Christian missions were not lost on its anticlerical government in Lisbon, as was apparent in the 1896 instructions of the Marine and Overseas Ministry to Bishop Barros. Among other things, the instruction demanded that missions in Portuguese Mozambique must have the features of Portuguese national institutions, where the Portuguese language must be used and taught and where the Portuguese flag must be hoisted at the mission centers and the missionaries were expected to defend Portuguese sovereignty and national interests.[57]

The dawn of African affirmation in the late 1940s through to the 1960s, with the wave of independence across Africa and the feverish onrush of decolonization (only a lip service, in many instances) brought the missionaries and their work into close scrutiny. Disregarding the blanket accusation of involvement in colonial rule, other criticisms hurled at the missionaries have been hard to erase, particularly, their denigration of African cultures and customs as well as their attitudes of superiority and paternalism.[58] They shared this blame in common with the people of their epoch. The fabulous tales about Africa by the missionaries, in the face of the daunting difficulties encountered in Africa, served to cast these missionaries as heroes before the eyes of their benefactors and supporters in Europe. The missionaries encountered local customs and cultures in their religious proselytism, and colonial administrators or officers came into contact with them in their civil and economic administrations. The missionaries and the colonizers formed

---

55. Comby, *Duemila anni di Evangelizzazione*, 258.
56. Russell, *Africa's Twelve Apostles*, 47.
57. Koschorke et al., *A History of Christianity in Asia, Africa*, 221.
58. Oborji, *Trends in African Theology*, 55.

an alliance in their bid to break African customs, which both viewed as and termed "wicked" and constituting barriers to progress.[59]

Such coupling between colonialism and the Christian missions in Africa led some people to nurse the fear that Christianity might decline or even disappear altogether after independence. On the contrary, as observed by Prudhomme, decolonization did not bring about the disappearance of the Christian missions and Christianity in Africa.[60] Rather, it led to an accelerated growth and development of the local churches immediately after independence. As a matter of fact, the population of African Catholics alone was estimated to be slightly over 222 million as at 2015. That was about 17 percent of world's Catholics.[61] Colonialism, whether for ill or for good, will indissolubly remain one of the main contours of African Christianity, especially south of the Sahara. This is underscored by the fact that the Christianity that thrives in that part of the continent owes its origin to the missionaries of the nineteenth century, because their foundation was essentially laid between 1880 and 1960. It was a very remarkable short period, which, nonetheless, has witnessed phenomenal growth, almost in equal measure to the phenomenal number and presence of missionaries that gave birth to the churches in Africa.[62]

MISSION IN REBOUND AND ITS CONTEXT

Strange as it may seem, the re-launching or revival of Catholic missions in the interior of modern Africa began in the shadow of care for slaves and ex-slaves. In that scenario, there exist three commonalities on dual fronts in the revival of Catholic missionary activities that began almost intermittently and independently of each other in Liberia and in Central Africa. First, Pope Gregory XVI (1831–1846) created both vicariates. For the weary band of three American pioneer missionaries who arrived at Cape Palmas in 1842, Pope Gregory XVI, in 1843, created the Vicariate Apostolic of Upper Guinea that stretched from Liberia in West Africa to Angola in the southern axis of the continent.[63] Three years later, on 3 April 1846, shortly before his death, Pope Gregory XVI created the Apostolic Vicariate of Central Africa. As hazy as the first vicariate, the territorial jurisdiction of the second vicariate stretched from Egypt through Algeria in the north and continued

---

59. Oliver, *The Missionary Factor*, 178.
60. Prudhomme, *Missioni Cristiane e Colonialismo*, 76.
61. Racque, "The Evolution of Catholicism," lines 5–6.
62. Ngulu, "The Church in Africa," 18–19; Oborji, *Trends in African Theology*, 55.
63. Dries, *Missionary Movement*, 43–44.

towards the Red Sea. It also included the areas around the Mountains of the Moon in Eastern Africa and shared boundaries with the two Guineas, where it reached the edge of the Sahara in the west.[64]

Secondly, the reprehensible scourge of slavery left its scars on the African psyche. By 1850, the vast majority of the 15,000 inhabitants of Khartoum, headquarters of the Vicariate of Central Africa, were slaves.[65] Not willing to start their missionary work in Monrovia, under the administration of Protestant missionaries and the government-sponsored American Colonization Society, the Catholic party opted for Cape Palmas, an independent colony of the Maryland Colonization Society which, by its composition, was rather more Catholic in view of its provenance.[66] Once again, like the Central African Vicariate, with the exception of a few natives of Cape Palmas, the vast majority of the inhabitants were American ex-slaves. The view was even expressed in some quarters that the Catholic Church was cornered to consider the mission reprise in West Africa by criticism labeled against it for its apparent indifference to the plights of ex-slaves. In one article, the author was bold enough to identify the Holy See and the Church as "abettors of slavery."[67]

Thirdly, the enormous human sacrifice took its toll on the pioneer missionaries. In the history of Christian missions in Africa, attention is often directed towards the depletion of the missionary personnel in West Africa as the cemetery of the White man. However, no less significant was the high mortality recorded by the Verona Fathers in their missions around Khartoum and the surrounding territories. At one point in time, the Annals of the Propagation of the Faith wrote thus of the missions within the Vicariate of Central Africa: "Each mission station of the Vicariate is marked by several graves, and more tombs mark the road from Shellal to Gondokoro. The day will come when life will rise from these graves."[68] A similar fate fell upon the mission that was headquartered in Cape Palmas with a territory that stretched along a 2,000-league coast, in which there were but few priests and even at that, all but only one succumbed to the dreaded African fever.[69]

The choice and place of Cape Palmas in the reviving of the moribund Catholic missions, which previously had been under Portuguese *Padroado*, deserve prime of place. Prior to the establishment of the American Society

64. Toniolo, "The First Centenary," 99.
65. Toniolo, "The First Centenary," 100.
66. Fisher, "The Catholic Church in Liberia," 267–268.
67. Fisher, "The Catholic Church in Liberia," 265.
68. Toniolo, "The First Centenary," 115.
69. Fisher, "The Catholic Church in Liberia," 274.

for the Colonization of Free People of Color of the United States on 28 December 1816 by the act of the US House of Representatives and under the auspices of Robert Finley, a Presbyterian from New York, the loathing and perplexity of what to do with ex-slaves always haunted the American society. Importantly, the ex-slaves question fired up American interest in colonization, especially in view of the fact that ex-slaves were considered to be a big burden and an overwhelming cumbrance to societal tranquility. Against that background, the idea of sending back ex-slaves to Africa was first floated in 1713 through the social activism of George Keith, Anthony Benezet and Samuel Hopkins. For someone like Hopkins, the question was thought to be so important that, in 1773, he conceived the notion of sending ex-slaves to Africa for the purpose of engaging them as native missionaries on the continent.[70]

A century elapsed before the first set of forty Blacks could set foot on West African soil in 1815 through the pioneering work of Paul Caufee who helped them embark on the journey from Boston to Sierra Leone. Paul Caufee, the son of a rich Massachusetts freedman, personally offset the cost of that travel. Also noteworthy in this regard was the pioneering work of Robert Finley, a Black Presbyterian minister, in Washington who made efforts in 1816 to resettle freed Black slaves in Western Africa. Five years after the Paul Caufee experiment and the attempts by Finley, eighty-six ex-slaves boarded the ship *Elizabeth* on 6 February 1820. That expedition failed as did the subsequent one launched in early 1821. The much-coveted colony of the "Free People of Color" became a reality, with the eventual raising of the American flag on 25 April 1822 on the land that was later named Monrovia, which later became the capital of Liberia, in honor of President James Monroe. He was once directed, in 1800, by the Virginia Legislature to petition President Thomas Jefferson about the possibility of securing land outside the United States of America, where people judged as "obnoxious to the laws or dangerous to the peace of society" might be moved or relocated to.[71] The newly acquired colony on the western coast of Africa for the resettlement of such people that endangered the peace of the American society was naturally under the tutelage of the Protestants and the colony enjoyed considerable support and sponsorship from the American government.

The foregoing fact explains why the small group of Catholic pioneers who sailed from Baltimore on 21 December 1841 chose Cape Palmas for their place of missionary work instead of Monrovia. This is not altogether surprising, since Cape Palmas was a separate colony at the time. It belonged

---

70. Fisher, "The Catholic Church in Liberia," 251–252.
71. Fisher, "The Catholic Church in Liberia," 252–253.

to the Maryland State Colonization Society, which was founded in 1827. This Colonization Society established the short-lived Republic of Maryland, with its headquarters in Cape Palmas, until its eventual absorption by the Republic of Liberia in 1857.

Given its history in the early days of the United States of America in 1634, Maryland prided itself as a safe haven for Catholics. It was meant to be a place where various Christian denominations could live in peace, particularly in view of its "Maryland Act of Religious Toleration," passed by the House of Delegates in 1649.[72] That liberal toleration was replicated in Cape Palmas, as the Maryland State Colonization Society permitted American Missionaries of four different denominations to operate freely in the colony. Those missionaries were from the Presbyterian, Methodist, Episcopalian and Baptist churches. The Catholic group led by Fr Edward Barron only arrived in the colony in 1842. Subsequent to their arrival, the governing board of the Maryland State Colonization Society, in its 1842 annual report, vaunted its policy of religious tolerance and mentioned the arrival of the Catholic missionaries in its colony in the Republic of Maryland:

> The Board have always encouraged the establishment of missions at their settlement, and one of their first acts after the colony was founded was to offer to all religious denominations every facility for missionary labor—and now there are four Christian churches represented by their missionaries in the colony—that is to say, the Presbyterian, the Methodist, the Episcopalian and the Baptist; and the Harriet has just taken out two Catholic priests and a lay assistant to found a mission of that Church in the settlement mission, it is intended to afford to the Catholics of the colony the opportunity of attending the observances of their Church which they have heretofore wanted[73].

In terms of the history of Catholic evangelization in the area and the surrounding environs that later became known as Liberia, these areas were not utterly virgin lands without any prior Catholic presence. For instance, the 1907 edition of *Missiones Catholicae* recalled that mission once opened in the area as far back as July 1634. It was believed that the missionaries may have reached Liberia most likely from Elmina or Sierra Leone. Typical of that mission, like other missions of the same period, it failed to take root on the basis that "not a few natives" were brought to the faith. Another imputed reason is attributable to the difficulties interposed by the Dutch who had laid claim to the territory and obstructed the work of Catholic

---

72. Lasson, "Free Exercise," 427–428.
73. Cited in Fisher, "The Catholic Church in Liberia," 268.

evangelization in the area, especially in Elmina which came under Dutch seizure in 1637.[74] For this reason, after the arrival of the new set of Catholic missionaries in 1842, Fr Barron made the following observation about the pockets of isolated Catholics remaining in the neighboring areas: "At Elmina there was still a Catholic church with a missionary; and, moreover, that at twenty other points there were sanctuaries which had been abandoned by Portuguese and Spaniards."[75]

Bishop Edward Barron, appointed Vicar Apostolic of the two Guineas in 1842, made a similar allusion in his report that accompanied his resignation letter to Rome, dated 7 January 1845. He referred to the scattered remnants of some fading Catholic missions around the area. He also mentioned the presence of some local African priests, although he did not express much enthusiasm on account of their conduct. In this letter to Rome, Bishop Barron stated, *inter alia*:

> Between the Gambia and the other English colony of Sierra Leone, there are several Portuguese settlements; the inhabitants call themselves Catholics but possess no knowledge of our religion. The bishop of the Cape Verde Islands has jurisdiction over those Portuguese settlements. From time to time the bishop sends a priest to the settlements; the priest who is there at present is far from edifying. On my way to Gabon, about forty miles north of the equator, we paid a visit to Prince's Island, a Portuguese colony, where I found several priests. The dean was born in Portugal. The others were native-born and claim to have been ordained in Brazil. They all leave much to be desired[76].

Historically, those pockets of isolated mission stations and others like them around the continent, especially around the coastal areas of sub-Saharan Africa, were hazily and indistinctively distributed across five ecclesiastical jurisdictions, two of which were geographically outside Africa. The five jurisdictions were the diocese of Funchal, a city in Portugal's Madeira archipelago; the diocese of Cape Verde on the West African coast; the diocese of São Tomé on the Gulf of Guinea; the diocese of São Salvador, capital city of the Congo during the period of Portuguese adventure in Africa, and the diocese of Goa in India with jurisdiction over all the African islands along the Indian Ocean. Those vague jurisdictions remained intact from the sixteenth to the nineteenth century.[77]

74. Fisher, "The Catholic Church in Liberia," 262.
75. Fisher, "The Catholic Church in Liberia," 262.
76. Bane, *The Popes and Western Africa*, 49–50.
77. Kenny, *The Catholic Church in Tropical*, 76.

It was from their ruins, dotted with the semblances of former missions, that the reprise of Catholic missionary activities was begun in sub-Saharan Africa in the nineteenth century. Apart from the initiative of the American Catholic Church and its earliest attempts in 1833 to interest itself with the pastoral care of ex-slaves in Liberia, their generous financial contribution to the take-off of that mission is most praiseworthy. This aspect of the commitment of the American Church towards the Catholic rebounding in Africa appeared to have been eclipsed by the coming of other players from Europe when impetus from the American Church slacked. It was financially a poor church in the 1800s, since the large bulk of its faithful was swelled by poor immigrants from Europe. It was also a needy church in terms of pastoral manpower. It remained officially a missionary church until 1908, when it was removed from the sphere of Propaganda Fide during the reform of the Roman Curia by Pope Pius X.

It is significant to recall that, even as late as 1917, only four states had the largest concentration of Catholics in the United States of America: New York (3,088,406); Illinois (1,482,571); Massachusetts (1,406,060), and Pennsylvania (1,185,000).[78] Highly commendable was the altruism of the four dioceses that supported the missionary enterprise of Frs Edward Barron (from Philadelphia) and John Kelly (from Albany), and their Irish-born catechist, Denis Pinder. The diocese of Philadelphia made the highest contribution of $2,400, followed by New York with $711, St John's, Albany, with $350, and Baltimore with $265. Their contribution in many ways underscored the importance of the money factor in frontier missionary work as did the initial grant of $2,425 in 1843 to Bishop Barron from the Lyons Society of the Propagation of the Faith, with the promise of a further disbursement of $9,118 in the future.[79] Worth noting is the personal expense of Fr Edward Barron who gave approximately 20,000 francs of his savings towards the establishment of the mission in Liberia. By every standard, both then and now, it was a mark of great generosity, indicative of his love and commitment to Africa.[80]

It may be right to affirm that the re-launching of the Catholic missionary venture in Africa came at a propitious moment, in view of the fact that such a comeback took place in the context of the gradual change of focus of Rome from the Eastern Churches to the new areas that were

---

78. *Annals of the Propagation of the Faith* (June 1919) as conserved in Archives of Propaganda Fidei, *Nuova Serie*, 620 (1919), 147; Iheanacho, *Maximum Illud and Benedict XV*, 252.

79. Russell, *Africa's Twelve Apostles*, 23; Fisher, "The Catholic Church in Liberia," 267.

80. Russell, *Africa's Twelve Apostles*, 27.

opening up in once considered non-Christian territories.[81] It coincided with the three years (1839–1842), which, in some remarkable manner, marked a very important period in the chronology of the missions. The Holy See became determined to bring the missions under its central command so as to checkmate particularly the pretentious attempts by France and Portugal to exercise unlimited control over the missions.[82] Both that shift of attention and the efforts to bring the missions under the control of the Holy See started timidly with the pontificate of Pope Gregory XVI. It was to him that Bishop John England of Baltimore expressed the need, in 1830, to foster the spiritual needs of African-American Catholics in Liberia. To demonstrate the urgency of that mission, the bishops who gathered at a Provincial Council in Baltimore, in 1833, thought it right to entrust the would-be mission in Liberia to the Jesuits:

> And so, the Fathers, solicitous for the salvation of the negroes, who are migrating to the Liberian Colony of Africa, supplicate the Apostolic See that a mission under the care of the Fathers of the Society of Jesus be established in this region[83].

The Propaganda Fide, in its letter dated 26 July 1834, duly gave its blessings to the bishops' project to embark on that mission, which they wanted to be entrusted to the Society of Jesus:

> It is also agreed that the spiritual care of the negroes, who are migrating from these regions to the Liberian Colony of Africa, should be entrusted to this same Society of Jesus. We have treated about both things with the Most Reverend Father Minister-General of the Society of Jesus, and we have agreed that the Fathers of the Society will be given the entire work, so that your wishes and those of the Sacred Congregation may reach a happy outcome[84].

Unfortunately, things did not work out as both the bishops and Rome had wished. They were not deterred by the inability of the Jesuits to respond to their wish on the ground that they had their hands full with mission to native Americans. No concrete action was taken from 1833 to 1840, when the Propaganda Fide took the initiative and appealed to the American bishops for assistance in foreign missions in Africa. The bishops of New York and Philadelphia asked for volunteers from among their clergy to help in the

81. Camps, *Studies in Asian Mission History*, 28.
82. Tinchese, *Roncalli e le Missioni*, 19.
83. Fisher, "The Catholic Church in Liberia," 265.
84. Fisher, "The Catholic Church in Liberia," 266; Bane, *The Popes and Western Africa*, 46–47.

proposed mission to Liberia. After securing the consent of Frs Edward Barron (Philadelphia) and John Kelly (New York) together with Denis Pinder, a lay catechist, the bishops were elated to inform Rome of the happy outcome. Their message was contained in a letter sent to Pope Gregory XVI and to the Propaganda Fide after their meeting at the Fifth Provincial Council of Baltimore in 1843:

> And now we are pleased to add these things which have been done for the people dwelling in the woods beyond the Rocky Mountains by the missionaries of the Society of Jesus and for the negroes in the western regions of Africa who are being evangelized by our priests at the command of the Holy See[85].

A year after the arrival of Frs Edward Barron, John Kelly and Denis Pinder in Cape Palmas, Liberia, on 31 January 1842, Pope Gregory XVI created for them the Vicariate Apostolic of Upper and Lower Guinea, which included "the whole region called Sierra Leone"[86] and stretched from Liberia in the West to Angola in the South.[87] The momentum and focus of attention towards Africa were continued during the successive pontificates of Popes Pius IX and Leo XIII. In 1848, through the Propaganda Fide, Pius IX approved the amalgamation of two different congregations, the one founded earlier in 1703 by Claude Francis Poullard des Places and the newly founded Congregation of the Immaculate Heart of Mary in 1842 by Francis Libermann. The missionary cooperation between Barron and Libermann paved the way for the men of Libermann to become, as it were, the first group of Catholic missionaries to arrive in Africa within the new scheme of missionary re-launching.[88] Pius IX also approved the first mission of the Oblates of Mary Immaculate (OMI) to the Natal area in 1852. It was a significant step, since it marked the first Catholic mission in Southern Africa. The same is true of the Missionaries of Africa (the White Fathers), founded in 1868, whose first major missionary outreach in East and Central Africa in 1878 coincided with the pontificate of Pope Leo XIII.

The close rapport between Leo XIII and Cardinal Charles Lavigerie, founder of the White Fathers, was one of the defining characteristics of contemporary Catholicism on the continent. Theirs was a personal relationship that helped shape the missionary policies of Leo XIII in Africa. One of those policies was the appointment of Lavigerie as the Apostolic

---

85. Fisher, "The Catholic Church in Liberia," 266.
86. Bane, *The Popes and Western Africa*, 48.
87. Dries, *Missionary Movement*, 43–44.
88. Pass, *The Faith Moves South*, 128.

Delegate for the Sahara and Sudan. It opened the door for the missionaries of Lavigerie whom he sent from Algeria (interpreted by him as "a door opened by Providence"), through the desert to the Great Lakes region of Africa. Cardinal Lavigerie was also made the Archbishop of Carthage and the Primate of Africa. That was in the early days of the Catholic missions in Africa, when the idea of putting all of them under the direction of a single person for the purpose of better coordination was being floated around.[89] In his famous "secret memoir" to the Propaganda Fide on 2 January 1878, Lavigerie enumerated some benefits that would accrue to the missions in Africa if they were brought under a single head. This was to maintain effective control over them. Accordingly, with a single directing authority on the ground in Africa, the missionary actions by the different congregations and institutes would become stronger, more efficient and effective, and would lead to greater success.[90]

A preponderance of old and new missionary congregations were drawn towards Africa. The missions in Africa had their charms and irresistible attraction to win the hearts and minds of a wide variety of missionaries who arrived on the continent. In the estimation of Brockman and Pescantini, "[f]ew missionary works have ever been served by such a collection of ability."[91] Although the missionary activity of the party from Baltimore remains important, it was not strictly the first pioneering work on the vast continent, as some French priests and nuns were already in Senegal as far back as 1758.

It is well known that, with the dawn of the nineteenth century, Africa progressively became a privileged field of missionary activities. Interest and attention on the continent were constantly sustained and reinforced by fabulous missionary tales about missionary heroism in the face of daunting difficulties that were portrayed as stretching the very limits of human endurance.[92] This is not to belittle or explain away the almost insurmountable hurdles encountered and overcome by the same missionaries, a clue of which was articulated by Fr Edward Barron in this manner in one of his three letters to Fr Francis Libermann in 1843: "If you have martyrs, send them to us, so that Cape Palmas, Sierra-Leone and Cape Mount will never be abandoned."[93] In the long list of such missionary "martyrs" of the epoch,

---

89. Comby, *Duemila anni di Evangelizzazione*, 235–238.
90. Lavigerrie, "Le mémoir secret," 130.
91. Brockman and Pescantini, *A History of the Church*, 162.
92. Comby, *Duemila anni di Evangelizzazione*, 264.
93. Russell, *Africa's Twelve Apostles*, 29.

the first place of honor belongs to Anne-Marie Javouhey. In the assessment of Paul Moody,

> The initiative for reviving Catholic mission, and the vision of providing African Churches with their own missionary clergy, can be attributed to a congregation of women, the Sisters of St Joseph of Cluny, and particularly to the woman who founded it in 1805, Anne-Marie Javouhey (1779–1851). She sent them to St Louis, Senegal, in 1819, and she herself went with them to Goree in 1822[94].

As the initiator of Catholic mission in modern Africa in the nineteenth century, Anne Javouhey also contributed immensely to the antislavery campaign.[95] Her missionary undertaking took her beyond the shores of Senegal to Sierra Leone where, as at 1823, she was reported to have been working in a hospital in Freetown.[96] She doubled as

> the first in the history of the Catholic Mission, to send a group of sisters to work as missionaries in Africa opening the great era of the commitment of women as protagonists in the missionary arena[97].

In the same light, her nuns were the very first set of female religious from Europe to set foot on Africa. That giant and significant feat took place during the pontificate of Pope Pius VII (1800–1823) who, after his return to Rome in 1814 from captivity under Napoleon Bonaparte, re-established the Jesuits and sought to revamp the Catholic missionary outreach beyond Europe.

Pope Pius VII created a favorable missionary climate. It led to an epoch-making missionary co-operation between Javouhey and Francis Libermann that gave Africa its first three indigenous priests. They were recruited by Javouhey from Senegal, trained in Paris, and ordained in the seminary of the Holy Ghost Fathers in 1840.[98] Senegal, their country of origin, was first created as prefecture apostolic in 1758 by Pope Clement XIII—the same year that Senegal was captured by the British. In the era that witnessed the beginning of the onslaughts of the French Revolution, Pope Pius VI (1775–1799), in 1779, named Père de Galicourt as the Prefect Apostolic of Senegal, which, in some manner, signaled a new beginning for the

---

94. Moody, "The Growth of the Catholic Missions," 204.
95. Bevens and Schroeder, *Constants in Context*, 223.
96. Bane, *The Popes and Western Africa*, 46.
97. Pierli, "Daniel Comboni," 43.
98. Hastings, *The Church in Africa*, 295.

missions in that part of Africa.[99] The country occupies an important place in the history of the missions in West Africa. Père Barbier founded the first indigenous female congregation of African origin in Dakar in May 1858. It was called the Congregation of the Daughters of the Holy Heart of Mary.[100]

Another person who occupies a prominent place in the history of the missions in Africa is Daniel Comboni, founder of the Missionary Institute of Africa (Comboni Missionaries, 1867) and the Institute of the Pious Mothers of the Negritude (Comboni Sisters, 1872). First appointed as Pro-Vicar of Central Africa in 1872, he was later raised to the rank of Vicar Apostolic, five years later in 1877. His vast Vicariate of Central Africa covered the whole of Sudan, the Great Lake regions of Africa and even westwards to include areas such as Sokoto and Adamawa, both in present-day northern Nigeria.[101] Comboni is most famous for his revolutionary insight articulated in his 15 September 1864 "Plan for the Regeneration of Africa." It is believed that he conceived the plan while praying at the tomb of St Peter in Rome. A keyword to his plan was *(save) Africa through Africans*.[102] On the advice of Cardinal Alessandro Barnabo, Prefect of the Propaganda Fide, Comboni visited some European cities to promote his plan, of which he said:

> Our thought has become set on this great idea and the regeneration of Africa by Africa seems to us the only programme to be followed in bringing about so dazzling a conquest. This is the reason why, in our weakness, we have thought it permissible, humbly to suggest a way along which the lofty goal may more probably be reached. On this very goal every thought of our life will be centred and for it we would be happy to pour out the last drop of our blood[103].

As a historical concept, "regeneration of Africa by Africans" was not entirely peculiar to Comboni, although his biographers tend to suggest that it was an idea that came to him out of the blue.[104] It was rather an ideology that was in vogue even before the late 1800s, when politicians, explorers and missionaries alike became more attracted to it, convinced about the concept and began to peddle with the idea. It was rendered expedient by "the physical obstacles" of the continent, which initially prevented Europeans from establishing a stronghold in Africa. Consequently, in view of the many

99. Bane, *The Popes and Western Africa*, 46.
100. Bane, *The Popes and Western Africa*, 53.
101. Bane, *The Popes and Western Africa*, 53.
102. Pierli, "Daniel Comboni," 43.
103. Pierli, "Daniel Comboni," 26, 43.
104. Wheeler, "Gateway to the Heart," 11.

difficulties that appeared somewhat insurmountable, some missionaries considered the possibility of recruiting local missionaries, to be mirrored after the pattern of the once proposed African force, to be manned by natives, with the aim of advancing "civilization." Europeans who were involved in Africa were convinced that Europeans could not serve in Africa without a terrible sacrifice of life and health. Their experiences, in many instances, duly confirmed that conviction and fear.[105]

Worthy of note is the fact that at least a fifteen-year gap separated the African missionary activities of Fr Edward Barron, who arrived in Africa in 1842, and those of Daniel Comboni, who first saw the shores of Africa aboard the *Morning Star* in 1857. Therefore, it is obvious to affirm that, long before the arrival of Comboni on the African missionary stage, Fr Edward Barron, drawing from his experiences in West Africa, had already conceived the idea and the possibility of training some young African men to become priests, in order to evangelize their people and to meet their other needs. He shared this idea in common with Libermann. In the wise judgment of Barron, the Africans could, through proper education, accomplish much more for Africans than an expatriate missionary might be able to accomplish. His thought was expressed, first, in a letter to Libermann, dated 22 November 1843, and secondly, in his report of 1845 to the Propaganda Fide. He cited the example of the French government who considered it futile to keep its White soldiers and sailors in Africa, when it easily replaced them with "Negroes and mulattoes, leaving only a handful of whites in command of the others." He mentioned in the same report that, while Libermann was in tandem with him on the matter, he helped to fine-tune Fr Barron's proposal with regard to the location of the would-be schools:

> I still think that the easiest and most certain way to evangelize the west coast of Africa would be to get young boys, either at St. Louis or Goree, educate them in Europe and send them back to their own people. From there, they could later strike farther down to the coast. The plan proposed by Pere Libermann seems to me the only one having a fair chance to succeed. He insists on the founding of schools for the native people, from which to draw vocations for the ecclesiastical state. The great difficulty seems to be the selection of a place for these schools. Pere Libermann would like to establish them on the island of Goree. Goree, comparatively healthy as it is, would be an ideal location for a new establishment, which once founded and boasting of several schools under capable management, would certainly show splendid results . . . Moreover, it is useless to expect that

105. Clarke, *Cardinal Lavigerie*, 351–3.

these missions will ever be sufficiently manned by European missionaries, because the climate is so deadly[106].

In terms of terrain and compared with Africa, the missionaries in Asia faced less physical and climatic challenges, but they encountered other difficulties that bordered on mental, cultural and religious constraints.[107] Despite many centuries of continuous commitment with regard to missionary personnel and finance, the Church in Asia has largely remained like a small island in the midst of a vast ocean. By contrast, Africa's terrain, especially in the interior, proved insurmountable for approximately three centuries from the first advent of the Portuguese in the fifteenth century up to the end of the eighteenth century. The interior of the continent was either hot or humid for Europeans. Many who could not withstand the hostile climate succumbed to malaria fever and other illnesses. Msgr Barron experienced first-hand the rigors and climatic hostility of Africa as evident in his report to the Propaganda Fide. Many years later, Pope Pius XII would recall that many of the missionaries "sealed their heroic apostolate with the supreme sacrifice of their young lives but the standard of Christ was still carried aloft to new and uncharted areas."[108]

However, it must be recalled that the adaptation and survival rate of the Europeans increased with much ease at the turn of the nineteenth century. This was largely due to scientific and technological inventions as well as advances in medical science, when it became possible to find a cure for some illnesses that hitherto had no feasible remedy. The promising prospects held out by the missions in Africa and their vitality in the rudimentary stages were once captured by the *Pontifical Yearbook*, when it highlighted the progress and incremental growth of the nascent churches on the continent. It noted that there were roughly 50,000 Catholics in Africa in 1800. Forty years later, that number had risen to approximately 377,000. By the turn of the twentieth century, the total number of African Catholics was put at 750,000 in 1907.[109] All these figures indicated the fertile grounds upon which the missionaries labored in Africa, the receptiveness of Africans towards the Catholic Church, and their collaborative efforts for its growth and expansion on the continent.

---

106. Russell, *Africa's Twelve Apostles*, 31, 34–35.
107. Iheanacho, "*Plantatio Ecclesiae* in Africa," 2.
108. Cited in Bane, *The Popes and Western Africa*, 1.
109. See the "African Report" in K.C. Abraham, *Third World Theologies*, 42.

2

Missions in Africa in the twilight of the nineteenth century

Vast quantities of literature on contemporary Africa are extant, due basically to the socio political situation of the continent, especially between 1878 and 1905. This period provided the background within which the missionaries operated. It also acted as the catalyst that enabled the ever-receptive African humus soil to cause the sprouting of Christian missions around the continent. On the other hand, the same second half of the nineteenth century witnessed remarkable developments in scientific inventions and discoveries, leading to further improvements following the industrial revolutions. For instance, in the 1840s, the American scientist Samuel Morse patented telegraphy with a code through which long and short tones could be made and transmitted over electrically charged wires. By 1860s, the telegraphy had revolutionized communications, marking a rapid start in communication technology. Another scientist, Samuel Colt, invented the handgun in 1833, which meant that the conquest of territories, especially on the African continent, was achieved with greater efficiency.[1]

Three other scientific and technological developments emerged during the middle of the nineteenth century: the *steam engine*, which enhanced movement; the *quinine*, to combat malaria, and geography, for a more coherent knowledge of the world. These innovations in no small measure facilitated, for good and for bad, the presence of Europeans in Africa, first

---

1. Castle and McGrath, *On This Rock*, 225–257.

the missionaries, followed by the explorers and finally, the colonialists. Sometimes, all three arrived together on the scene.

The invention of the steamship meant that people and goods were transported much more rapidly and efficiently than by sailing boat. To buttress this fact, Francesco Pierli used the missionary journeys of Daniel Comboni as an example:

> The industrial revolution, as well, added to the impetus of the missionary enterprise by accelerating and easing communication facilities (transportation, mail, telegraph) from and to all corners of the world. We can realize what this meant by looking at the difference in Comboni's first trip to Africa (1857–58) and his last one (1880–81). The first one from Egypt to Khartoum was through the desert, by camel, and lasted 78 days; the last trip, some twenty years later, could be done by steamship through the Suez Canal which had been opened in 1869, and it took no more than 29 days[2].

With these giant strides in science and technology in the last quarter of the nineteenth century, Adrian Hastings asserted, and rightly so, that "[b]y the 1870s Africa was then, in principle, becoming conquerable by Europe in a way it had not been previously."[3] Indeed, the contrast between power and powerlessness was now so huge that conquest was not only possible, but almost inevitable. Naturally, in their turn, the missions profited from those developments, as missionaries received help and their work was done more easily than in previous epochs. Hence, the second half of the nineteenth century holds the shading contours of churches in Africa, marked by progress in many instances and dimmed by shadows in other ways.

GREAT ATTENTION ON AFRICA BY PIUS IX

The rise of the Catholic Church in Africa from its previous moribund state on the continent, alongside other revolutionary changes that came to Africa, and the presence of other Christian missionaries helped mark the nineteenth century as "the greatest century in the history of Christianity."[4] Such was the conclusion of Kenneth Scott Latourette in his seven-volume *magnum opus*, *A History of Expansion of Christianity*. In his efforts to apply and narrow down the scope of Latourette's statement to focus principally on the missions

---

2. Pierli, "Daniel Comboni," 33.
3. Adrian Hastings, *The Church in Africa*, 398.
4. Latourette, *A History of the Expansion* IV/VII, 442.

in Africa, Walbert Bühlman once wrote: "Nowhere and at no time was an indigenous church so quickly founded and built up as on the continent."[5] That was possible because of the socio-political situation provided the background within which the missionaries operated. As for the Catholic missions in Africa, their rebounding and consolidation took place during the pontificate of Leo XIII, although it was a long process of evolution that predated his reign especially squared in the overall revamping of Catholic missionary activities that began in the waning years of the French Revolution.

As noted earlier, albeit timidly at first, Catholic missions in Africa began to show some signs of a comeback, starting from the early 1800s, when the attention of Rome was beginning to be diverted away from the Eastern Churches towards Africa and Asia. With particular reference to Africa, the ground was prepared by Pope Pius IX and the Propaganda Fide, under the direction of Cardinal Alessandro Franchi, which focused more directly on Equatorial Africa. That part of Africa had remained largely unexplored. Its accessibility as a pathway to the interior of the continent thus paved the way for the International Geographic Conference held in Brussels on 12 September 1876, under the auspices of King Leopold II of Belgium. As a pretext for the realization of Leopold's imperialistic dream, through his promptings, the Conference eventually established the enigmatic "African International Association."

Conscious of not being left behind in the rush into the newly discovered equatorial and central parts of Africa, the Propaganda Fide decided to consult Bishops Comboni and Lavigerie about the feasibility of undertaking missionary expansions into those areas. The Propaganda Fide also sought the opinion of Père Augustin Planque (1826–1907) on the matter. Père Planque became the first Superior General of the *Societas Missionum ad Afros* (SMA) after the death of its founder Msgr Melchior de Marion-Brésillac in 1859. He remained in that position for approximately forty-eight years until his death in 1907. The invitation to Père Planque came in 1876 during his visit to Rome, when Cardinal Franchi invited him to furnish the Sacred Congregation with some proposals that would assist it in its deliberations in a special *Congresso* on Africa, with specific issues on the "International Geographic Conference," the "African International Association" and the possibility of establishing a Catholic missionary presence in Equatorial and Central Africa.

About the seemingly opportunities to be opened up to the Church in the interior of Africa, Lavigerie, in one of his letters dated 1 January 1881, mentioned the enthusiasm of Pius IX, although the old Pontiff was almost on his way to the great beyond. Lavigerie also hinted at the subsequent

---

5. Walbert Bühlmann, "The African Church," 46–47.

instructions by the pope issued to the Propaganda Fide to establish what could possibly be done to realize the missionary projects in Equatorial and Central Africa:

> The attention of the old and holy Pontiff was with sadness on the Catholic world, where the hatred of impiety seemed to hold sway, when for the first time, Cardinal Franchi, Prefect of the Sacred Congregation of the Propaganda Fide, drew his attention to the works of the conference of Brussels and to the new future which was in the making for the peoples of the interior of Africa. Pius IX quickly understood its importance ... Therefore, by his order, the Sacred Congregation of the Propaganda Fide, towards the end of 1877, wrote [to] the heads of the principal missions in Africa, asking them for useful information for the realisation of the injunctions of the Holy Father[6].

Cardinal Lavigerie indicated in the same missive that all those consulted "were unanimous in recognizing the necessity of those new missions and the urgency of their establishment in places where the African International Association was to establish its centers of action." In the analysis of Marcel Storme, he sought to demonstrate that, in reality, not "all the heads of the principal missions in Africa" were consulted, but only three persons; and of those three, two were in Africa and the third person was in Europe at the time. Of those three, only Lavigerie and Planque were unanimous in their approval of the projected missionary venture into the interior. Comboni, for his part, treaded with caution between hesitation that bordered on broad mental reservation and outright disapproval, especially with regard to the fact that some parts of his vicariate were to be carved out for the creation of the new vicariates in the projected areas of the new mission. At least, that much was visible in one of his three letters to the Propaganda Fide on the subject matter of the African International Association. In that letter, written in Khartoum and dated 25 April 1878, he was aggrieved that the "new missions of Tanganyika and Nyanza are found in my vicariate."[7] He cited the brief, dated 3 April 1846, with which Pope Gregory XVI had established, within the parameters of the Mountains of the Moon, the southern limit of the vicariate in central Africa. On the basis of difficulty in communication and very vast distances, he was convinced that the success of the new missionary enterprise into the interior might be unsure, if not altogether impossible. This would lead to a waste of resources in terms of missionary personnel and money.[8]

6. Storme, *Rapports du Père Planque*, 23.
7. Storme, *Rapports du Père Planque*, 152.
8. Storme, *Rapports du Père Planque*, 153.

In his submission to the Propaganda Fide, dated 7 May 1877, Père Planque encouraged the Roman dicastery to seize the opportunity offered by the African International Association to erect new missions in the regions of Equatorial Africa. For its prompt take-off, he suggested that the missions to be created between the Equator and the Zambezi could be entrusted to his own Society of African Missions (SMA):

> The S.C. [Sacred Congregation] could give them the field of exploration and work from the Equator in the North to the Zambezi in the South, on the West, they could extend up to the borders of Luanda and Benguela, and to the East, they could stop at borders of Mozambique and of the Mission of Zanzibar[9].

The delimitation of the new mission areas to be entrusted to the SMA demonstrated the prudence and care of Père Planque, in order to prevent clashes with the Portuguese Padorado clergy and their mission in Angola. It was also to avoid friction with the Spiritans [Holy Ghost Congregation] who were in charge of the apostolic prefecture of the Congo. After carefully navigating through the difficulties of internal Catholic quibbling over territories, Père Planque then alerted Propaganda Fide of the presence of some Protestant groups such as the Nyssa Moravian Missions and the Scottish Missionary Society in the areas of the would-be missions. It was his desire to see that Catholicism took its place among the tribes of the region as quickly as possible.[10] He also informed Propaganda Fide of the understanding between him and Msgr Comboni in terms of territorial agreement. Their understanding was done in reference to the 1846 decree of the erection of the Apostolic Vicariate of Central Africa that had put all those places (at the time unexplored) under the ecclesiastical jurisdiction of Msgr Comboni.

As indicated by Planque, Comboni was willing to "cede" some parts of his vicariate up to the Equator.[11] By this submission, it stands to reason that Comboni was, in principle, not all out against the creation of new vicariates in Equatorial Africa. His main discomfort was having the missionaries of Lavigerie as neighbors. He would rather have the SMAs as his closest neighbors in the earliest stages of the missions in Africa. It must be remembered that the greatness of missionaries and heroism as well as those of their congregations or institutes tended in those days to be based on the vastness of their territories. This phase in the missionary history of the Church in Africa was also largely dominated by a few strong missionary personalities.

---

9. Storme, *Rapports du Père Planque*, 14.
10. Storme, *Rapports du Père Planque*, 14.
11. Storme, *Rapports du Père Planque*, 15.

MISSIONS WITHIN THE GENERAL LEONINE OPTICS

As the curtain was about to be drawn on the pontificate of Pius IX on 7 February 1878, the pontificate of his predecessor coincided with the opening up of the interior of Africa. From the missionary perspective, it was judged favorably by Lavigerie and Planque as providential for the Catholic Church. Advanced age and death did not permit Pius IX, after a very long pontificate, to see the greater development of Catholic missions into the hinterlands of the continent, namely Equatorial and Central Africa. Nevertheless, the already planned action in that regard became a springboard for Pope Leo XIII to continue and even accelerate. As an overall assessment, the progress of the missions in Africa and elsewhere in Asia ought to be squared firmly within the general optic of the Leonine pontificate.

In the estimation of Claude Prudhome, the missions during the pontificate of Pope Leo XIII occupied a central place in the Church's general orientation both in diplomatic maneuvering and in the management of ecclesiastical affairs. Given the fact that missionary priority became, as it were, an essential dimension of the prestige of the papacy under Leo, he saw to it that missionary expansion was not to be disassociated from his diplomatic and political concerns.[12] In that sense, the missions also orbited around the core of the two challenges that confronted Pope Leo XIII at the beginning of his pontificate, namely to end the isolation of the Holy See, by seeking to re-insert it within the European political and social order, and to preserve the Catholic mobilization that had been the pillar of support for his predecessor. In attempting to address both challenges, Pope Leo XIII, to a remarkable extent, made Catholic overseas missions to become a key element in papal policy and in the public perception of the same papacy. In this regard, as opined by Vincent Viaene in his re-echo of the conclusion of Prudhomme, Pope Leo XIII could rightly be considered the first Pope of the contemporary era to attempt to place diplomatic actions side by side with missionary action within a global and aggressive Catholic project.[13] This does mean, as sustained by Prudhomme himself, that the pontificate of Leo provided the opportunity and created the ecclesial space that enabled the Church's *mission ad gentes* to truly become a major preoccupation of the papacy. It seemed to form the core of the general orientation of the papacy and an inseparable part of its policies and considerations.[14]

---

12. Prudhomme, "Stratégie missionnaire," 351, 357.
13. Viaene, "Introduction," 14, 23.
14. Prudhomme, "Stratégie missionnaire," 377.

Leo XIII had a grandiose conception of the papacy, declaring after his pontifical election: "I want to see the Church so far forward that my successor will not be able to turn back."[15] That desire of Leo XIII greatly defined his pontificate, which, to some extent, tended to portray an objective reappraisal of that pontificate. Nonetheless, it remains an incontrovertible fact that no official papal teaching, devoted specifically to the missionary work of the Church, ever surfaced until towards the later part of the nineteenth century. It only materialized with Leo's publication of *Sancta Dei Civitatis* in 1880. In that encyclical, he clearly underscored the universality of the Church's mission of evangelization.[16] As rightly noted by Prudhomme, although Leo did not get the title "missionary pope," his pontificate marked an essential moment in the development of Catholic missions in the contemporary epoch,[17] predicated upon one of Leo's aims to have the Church play a significant role in the affairs of contemporary society. It led him not to adapt a simple or monolithic approach in negotiations, sometimes willing to adapt his policies where and when necessary.[18] He also counted on his personal charm and individual rapports with political leaders. For instance, his personal good rapports with the Mikado of Japan paved the way, in 1898, for the creation of the archdiocese of Tokyo together with three other suffragan dioceses.[19] Similar diplomacy with a personal touch occurred between Leo and Barghash ibn Said, the Sultan of Zanzibar. Both exchanged gifts in 1883, with the pope thanking the sultan for his assistance to the Catholic mission of the Spiritans in his Sultanate of Zanzibar.[20]

Conversely, it must also be acknowledged that, in terms of internal church matters, Pope Leo XIII did not always show himself amenable. He appeared rather ambiguous and even ambivalent, which leaned strongly towards intransigence. A case at hand was when Pope Leo XIII condemned Antonio Rosmini for his adherence to other philosophical systems rather than Thomism, as proposed by the pontiff in his encyclical *Aeterni Patris* (1879). Pope Leo XIII had sought to make the teaching of St Thomas Aquinas the official philosophy in Catholic universities and institutions. He also exerted pressure on Fr Carlo Maria Curci, founder of the Jesuit Italian journal *Civiltá Cattolica*, to retract his article *Regio Vaticano* (Royal Vatican), published in 1883. Curci had, in the said article, suggested that the Church

---

15. Gargan, "Introduction," 1.
16. Patterson, "What has eschatology to do," 288.
17. Prudhomme, "'Stratégie missionnaire," 351.
18. Holmes, *The Triumph of the Holy See*, 194.
19. Murphy, *The Papacy Today*, 27.
20. Njoroge, *A Century of Catholic Endeavour*, 34.

should reform, in order to come to terms with the modern time; his suggestion provoked a big stir in the Vatican. Curci's opinion was no music to the ears of Leo. Curci was even expelled from the Society of Jesus and only re-admitted after his *"mea culpa."* Similar pressure was equally exerted on Bishop Geremia Bonomelli of Cremona to retract for daring to say that the pope ought to forget about the 40,000 square miles of the Papal States in central Italy and make peace with the Italian government.[21]

As "liberal" as Pope Leo XIII could be, there were certain red lines that a person should never cross and the "Roman question" was uncompromisingly one of those red lines. In some ways, they reflected Leo's own share of the pessimistic view of the modern thought at the end of the nineteenth century. That pessimism was present in many ecclesiastical circles such as Lavigerie's genuine alarm about the prospects of the advance of the "African International Association" into the interior of Africa. In Lavigerie's judgment, the Association was propelled not only by commercial interests, but also by atheistic secular and purely scientific motivations. For such reasons, Lavigerie considered it of paramount importance to counteract such moves by seizing the most favorable time provided by divine providence to spread the Gospel and to hasten the apostolic conquest.[22]

In his work, Edward T. Gargan noted that, by circumventing the perception of the "modern society as menaced by the possibility of a final disaster," Leo XIII also subtly tried to extricate himself from that perception through the mission which "he established for himself and for his Church."[23] The means of that extrication was included in the blueprint as articulated by Msgr Wladimir Czacki, Secretary of the Congregation of Ecclesiastical Affairs, prior to Pope Leo XIII's election. According to the Polish prelate, it was incumbent upon the Holy See to consider it its mission and duty to rise up as a moral power in the Europe of the time and, much more than that, "to return to the breast of humanity a principle of justice and political equilibrium."[24] The various works of Pope Leo XIII fit into that parameter and cover a wide range of issues. Those works definitely delineated the spiritual growth of the faithful and the missionary enterprise of the Church as the major issues that took the best part of his time. Especially with regard to the missions, Raymond H. Schmandt emphatically observed:

> His pontificate witnessed a far-flung expansion of Catholicism. The Dark Continent attracted particular attention. One of the

21. Holmes, *The Triumph of the Holy See*, 194.
22. Lavigerie, "Le mémoir secret," 77.
23. Gargan, "Introduction," 3.
24. Viaene, "Introduction," 10.

first papal acts in 1878 involved authorizing the mission of the White Fathers in central Africa. The following year, the prefecture of Senegal and the apostolic vicariate of the Gold Coast were established, followed by the prefectures of Dahomey, Fernando Po, Upper, Lower Niger, the Ubanghi, French Guinea, and the apostolic vicariate of the French Congo. Regular hierarchies were provided for the Church in North Africa in 1884[25].

Against the background of the impetus given by Leo to the missionary expansion of the Church, it is, therefore, not altogether justifiable on many fronts to overtly portray him as "a political pope." A wider overview of his pontifical program and vision demonstrates that such an appellation may, to a large extent, rightly be construed as a false portrait and misrepresentation of the person of Pope Leo XIII. For instance, the religious worldview of Leo XIII, concretized in the universal consecration of the entire human race to the Sacred Heart of Jesus during the jubilee of 1900,[26] was a clear demonstration of his pastoral zeal and commitment to world Christianization. Secondly, a close examination of his eighty-five encyclicals reveals a clear religious orientation, with a global appeal in aspiration and vision. Gian Luca Bacchio is of the view that, with Leo XIII, the use of encyclicals became a privileged means of communication by the popes.[27] Thenceforth, encyclicals became a concrete form of the exercise of ordinary magisterium, which was never used with such great intensity, prior to Leo.[28]

Two outstanding characteristics are discernible in the encyclicals of Pope Leo XIII. First, their exceptional brevity. Secondly, their link to important realities and facts of the history of the time, in which he sought to find a place for the missionary activity of the Church and her subsequent commitment thereafter. Cumulatively, his eighty-five encyclicals fall under two periods of his pontificate. During the first period, from 1878 to 1893, a total of fifty encyclicals were issued, among which were the nine encyclicals entitled "Corpus Leoninum" because of the weight of issues treated in them. This period ended with *Providentissimo Deus*. In the second period, from 1894 to 1902, a total of thirty-five encyclicals were issued. Each of these two periods is further subdivided into phases. The first period has three phases, namely 1878–1882, 1883–1887, and 1888–1893. The second period has two phases, namely 1894–1898 and 1899–1902.[29] Three encyc-

25. Schmandt, "The Life and Work of Leo XIII," 44.
26. Latourette, *A History of the Expansion* VII/VII, 45.
27. Bacchio, *Leone XIII*, 16.
28. Bacchio, *Leone XIII*, 17.
29. Bacchio, *Leone XIII*, 19–20.

licals, namely *Sancta Dei Civitas* (1880), *In Plurimis* (1888) and *Catholicae Ecclesiae* (1890), with particular relevance to the missions in Africa, fall within the first period.

Although the content, tone and orientation of *Sancta Dei Civitas* were rather general, because the encyclical was concerned with the universal mission of the Church, the place of Africa in that universal mission was conspicuous. Addressed primarily to missionaries, their helpers and missionary associations, the document carries an imprint of Leo XIII's missionary vision. He expressed his conviction that the propagation of the Gospel was the first and most important duty of the pope: "the care of propagating the Christian Faith devolves upon the Roman Pontiffs" (*Sancta Dei Civitas*, no. 2). In the language of his epoch, he understood evangelization and mission as "works designed to civilize barbarous nations." He believed that the Catholic missionary effort could profit from the "more complete exploration of places and populations" in bringing the Christian faith to "countries hitherto accounted impracticable." His basic intention was to mobilize the Catholic faithful in Europe to rally round him, in order for "the sacred work of missions" to progress rapidly and unobstructed (*Sancta Dei Civitas*, no. 6).

Although couched in words that may currently be considered both racist and demeaning, however, as far as Leo XIII was concerned, he viewed the twin works of "evangelization and civilization" as "beneficial to those who are called out of the filth of vice . . . brought out of barbarism and a state of savage manners into the fullness of civilized life" (*Sancta Dei Civitas*, no. 10). Without any shadow of doubt, it is very plausible to affirm that Leo XIII's preoccupation with the Church's missionary effort outside the confines of Europe was included in his global plan of Christianization. Through that prism, the missions squared very well within the framework of the major politics of the pope.[30]

The missions constituted one of the major visions that ran concurrently through the pontificates of Gregory XVI (1831–1846), Pius IX (1846–1878), and Leo XIII. While continuing the policies of his two predecessors, Leo XIII accorded missionary activities a decided and merited re-evaluation.[31] Within a heightened sense of universality and accelerated missionary activities, favored by the prevailing circumstances and improved condition in the second half of the nineteenth century, Catholic missions in Africa were included in the more extensive program of the Leonine pontificate. During the Berlin Conference of 1884/1885, the Holy See instructed the papal *nuncio* in Vienna to exert pressure on Austria to use its good office

---

30. Chioccheta, "Le Vicende del Secolo XIX," 24.
31. Metzler, "La Santa Sede e le Missioni," 41.

and international standing to persuade the Conference to decide favorably on Catholic interests, with particular reference to the Catholic missions in Africa.[32] So important were those missions that Martin Bane once estimated that a total of approximately eighty Catholic ecclesiastical circumscriptions were created in Africa at the time of Leo's death in July 1903.[33]

THE ANTI-SLAVERY CAMPAIGN

Slavery as an institution was never a foreign invention on the African continent. On the contrary, traditional African societies, like other societies elsewhere in the world, were involved in buying and selling fellow human beings or making some human beings second-class human beings. They treated such human beings as things and objects by the powers that be and society as a whole. The slavery, as practiced in Africa, prior to the transatlantic slavery with the advent of the Portuguese to Africa, can be described as "domestic" or "limited" slavery. It was practiced on a very small scale and even, in most instances, was not a permanent condition for the slave so sold and bought. Its nature varied from place to place and from time to time, although it was also accepted as an institution whereby profit can be gained. In some instances, slaves were captured in war; at other times, they were bought and used for human sacrifices, and in some cruel traditional practices, slaves were violently buried alive with a dead traditional ruler of a community.[34]

For the hapless victims of such traditional cruelty, their pains and agonies were no less dehumanizing when compared to those who, in a larger scale due to the sheer huge numbers, suffered the indescribable horror and dehumanization during the trans-Saharan slave trade and the transatlantic trade. The only difference, however, is that, given the magnitude of the atrocity and the unprecedented numbers either shipped or marched through the desert in both slave trades, African "domestic" or "limited" slavery paled into insignificance. Africa's first experience with external slave traders may have taken place as far back as the ninth century, with the arrival of the Arab merchants through the Mediterranean regions of the continent in North Africa. They bought slaves in Africa and sold them in Arab countries, in Turkey, Portugal, Spain, or even in India. Unarguably, both traditional African slavery and Arab slavery became, as it were, the main substratum for the continent's second experience of foreign slave traders when the Portuguese

32. Baur, *2000 Years of Christianity*, 199.
33. Bane, *The Popes and Western Africa*, 56.
34. Hochschild, *King Leopold's Ghost*, 10.

first arrived in the coastal regions of Africa in the fifteenth century. They were later followed by other European rivals, especially with the discovery of the New World in the Americas. The Portuguese and their European counterparts, as the newcomers into the African slave markets, were able "to tap into, transform and vastly expand a pre-existing system,"[35] which lasted over four centuries, with catastrophic and devastating consequences for Africa and its people.

In the wake of the nineteenth century, Africa was still plagued by the inhuman slave trade, perpetuated mainly by Arab merchants. "Formally" and yet superficially, Western slave trade in Africa or transatlantic slave trade was abolished by the European powers after two different successive attempts in that regard through the Congresses of Vienna in 1815 and Verona in 1822.[36] Eleven years after the last of those two congresses, Britain first outlawed slave trade in its territories in 1833 and finally freed the slaves under its captivity only in 1838. France followed suit, with the abolition of the slave trade in French territories in 1848, while the United States of America dragged its feet until 1861, when slavery was finally forbidden in the federating states of the Union.[37] Quite interestingly, in South Africa, especially around the Cape Colony, slavery was first forbidden in 1807, but continued unhindered until 1834, when it was definitively abolished in the entire country.[38] In the remainder of the continent, the colonialists had vested interests in not rocking the boat of slavery, which saw them leaving things as they were. Hence, while the Europeans abolished slavery in theory, they tolerated it in practice and, in some cases, they still profited from it through their connivance with the same slave traders.[39] As a matter of fact, the British still gave their support to the Sultan of Zanzibar and the Arab kingpins who controlled the ivory and slave trades along the routes in the Great Lakes region.[40]

It is well known that Brazil had the unenviable position as the last country in the Western hemisphere to abolish slave trade in 1888. Through a legislative act, the *Lei Áurea* (Golden Law), passed by the general assembly on 13 May 1888, couched only in two articles that were extraordinarily simple in stipulation and brevity, slavery became abolished in Brazil. The bill was sponsored by Rodrigo A. da Silva and received royal ascent, with

35. Hochschild, *King Leopold's Ghost*, 10.
36. La Bella, "Leo XIII and the Anti-Slavery," 381.
37. Comby, *How to Understand the History*, 130.
38. Hofmeyr and Pillay, *A History of Christianity*, 4.
39. Shorter, *Cross and Flag in Africa*, 26.
40. Shorter, *Cross and Flag in Africa*, 33.

the approval of Princess Isabel (1846-1921) who stood in for her father, Emperor Dom Pedro II, who was in Europe on an official visit at that time.[41] Ironically, the abolition of the slave trade in Brazil provoked a military coup at the instigation of wealthy slave owners. Strange how an event can sometimes turn out in unforeseen ways! The abolition of slavery in Brazil uncharacteristically led to the demise of the Brazilian monarchy, because the military coup, after toppling the monarchy, established a Republican government in the country. It is worthwhile to cite those two brief articles that finally ended the ominous transatlantic slave trade in Brazil:

> Article 1: From this date, slavery is declared abolished in Brazil.
> Article 2: All dispositions to the contrary are revoked[42].

However, as the transatlantic slave trade was gradually abolished in the Western hemisphere, slavery continued to flourish in other places, particularly in Eastern and Northern Africa, with three cities serving as its pivots or hubs: Zanzibar, Khartoum and Cairo. Thousands of Africans were transported or forced against their will to trek from central Africa to the slave markets in Zanzibar, Khartoum and Cairo. The Arab slave trade in Africa prospered, due to the inaction of the Western powers and by means of their several concessions to the Arabs that bordered on outright tolerance of Arab merchants and slave traders for political reasons. Implicitly, European powers took back with their left hand what they had given with their right hand. In that sense, they continued boosting the trade in human beings, bought and sold at will as merely merchandise.

Referring to the human exploitation of Africans, the English explorer Lovett V. Cameron wrote in 1877: "Africa is losing blood through all her pores. If this state of affairs continues, this country will be depopulated in a very short time."[43] This reality, notwithstanding, the vast majority of people in Europe at the time were misled to assume that the slave trade was over and done with, simply because their own countries had apparently outlawed it. There was silence on the issue, with a mediocre acceptance of the *status quo*. Hardly anything is often mentioned about the Arab slave trade that was a scourge of Africa and that devastated most of the central and equatorial parts of the continent. Perhaps also not to be forgotten is the slave labor that was foisted upon the Congolese by Leopold II of Belgium. It is estimated that this caused the deaths of between eight and ten million Congolese lives.

---

41. Greenwell, "Leo XIII's In Plurimis," lines 9-13.
42. Greenwell, "Leo XIII's In Plurimis," lines 7-8.
43. Russell, *Africa's Twelve Apostles*, 235.

West Africa had long been the native home of Black slaves who were carted away like animals through North Africa to the Middle East and to India.[44]

Both the transatlantic slave trade and the trans-Saharan or Arab slave trade quite regrettably formed part of the historical trajectories of African Christianity. While the former may have been restricted to the Age of Discovery, with the arrival of the Europeans on African shores, the East African Arab-Swahili slave trade was the predominant concern of many missionaries in Africa for the greater part of the nineteenth century. Its discovery horrified David Livingstone (1813–1873), who a year prior to his death wrote in the conclusion of his letter to the *New York Herald*:

> And if my disclosures regarding the terrible Ujijian slavery should lead to the suppression of the East Coast slave trade, I shall regard that as a greater matter by far than the discovery of all Nile sources together ... All I can add in my solitude, is, may heaven's rich blessing come down on everyone, American English or Turk, who will help to heal this open sore of the world[45].

Granted that Livingstone might have been genuinely horrified by the horrors of the Arab slave trade in Africans, he did not disclose in the above citation that a notorious Portuguese slave trader had at one point in time been Livingstone's benefactor. Livingstone hid that ambiguity from the eyes of the world, but only projected his "altruistic Christian civilization." He enjoyed the hospitality of a voracious slave trader during his stay in Angola in 1854, during which he wrote the second version of his diaries, as the first one had been lost in a shipwreck. Perhaps, it was out of pragmatic cohabitation or a marriage of convenience that Livingstone chose not to utter a word about his lodging in the vast estate of a slave trader. So much so for the "for the love" of Africans that Livingstone, the acclaimed "champion" of commerce, Christianity and civilization, equally embodied in himself the contradictions and ambiguities of his time.[46]

The churchmen of the time had similar views and positions. As for the official position of the Catholic Church in terms of its denunciation of the slave trade in Africa, whether in its transatlantic or trans-Saharan form perpetuated by the Arabs, it was a position that took a very long time in gestation. While the papacy, up to the nineteenth century, sometimes made sporadic comments in trying to denounce the enslavement of Americans by the Europeans, it remained strangely mute on the slavery of Africans by either the Europeans or the Arabs. Even more strange, as explicated by

---

44. Renault, *Cardinal Lavigerie*, 367.
45. Baur, *2000 Years of Christianity*, 199.
46. Birmingham, "Merchants and Missionaries," 346.

Philippe Delisle, is the observation that the manual of theology widely used by French Catholic seminaries and theological institutions as late as 1880 still upheld the slave trade in Africa as natural and valid.[47] But the French seminaries were not alone in that regard. In their letter addressed to the Secretary of State on the eve of the American Civil War, the Catholic bishops of the United States of America expressed the view that slavery was "justifiable." The Vatican's all-knowing Holy Office of the Sacred Inquisition, as at 1866, also considered slavery compatible with Christianity.[48]

All of the above were vestiges of die-hard theological prejudices against Black people, notwithstanding the fact that, in 1462, Pope Pius II had declared slave trade to be *magnum scelus* (a great crime).[49] They also failed to recognize the change of position on slavery that had very subtly but gradually begun to shift during the papacy of Pope Gregory XVI. In his papal brief, dated 3 December 1839, Gregory XVI wrote thus: "We have judged that it belonged to Our pastoral solicitude to exert Ourselves to turn away the Faithful from the inhuman slave trade in Negroes and all other men" (*In Supremo*, §1). Although considered to be late in coming and not quite sufficient as a clear and strong condemnation of the slave trade and the policy of servitude by those involved in that inhuman trade,[50] it nonetheless remains significant as serving to launch the Catholic Church on the paths of getting involved with the anti-slavery efforts that were sprouting up almost everywhere in Europe.

From the viewpoint of Gianni La Bella, the anti-slavery activism of the Church occurred in two phases: 1873–1881 and 1888–1890. Mainly the second phase, with Lavigerie as its protagonist and witness in the international arena, was generally known. The first phase is no less important. It provided the intuitions and the genius inherited from Comboni by Lavigerie, which he himself did not always acknowledge, probably on account of the frosty relationship between the two men over mission territories, particularly in Equatorial Africa.[51] The first phase of the anti-slavery commitment of the Church is attributable to the labors and efforts of Daniel Comboni. As the Catholic pioneer in the fight to end Arab slavery in that part of the continent, Comboni exerted himself, for nearly a decade, sparing neither time nor resources in the bid to emancipate slaves in his vast vicariate of Central Africa. He came face to face with Arab slave merchants and the

---

47. Delisle, "La campagne antiesclavagiste," 395.
48. Hillman, *Towards an African Christianity*, 77.
49. Møller, *Religion and Conflict in Africa*, 26.
50. Delisle, "La campagne antiesclavagiste," 395.
51. La Bella, "Leo XIII and the Anti-Slavery," 383.

human merchandise in Khartoum. Due to its geographical setting as the meeting point between the Blue Nile and the White Nile, the city was a slave emporium under the tight control of the Arabs and the Turks. It has been estimated that roughly 25,000 Africans were annually shipped as slaves from Khartoum to the Muslim countries of Arabia, Persia and Turkey.[52]

Painfully aware that the mere ransoming of slaves from their captors was like a drop of water in the mighty ocean of slavery, Comboni went further to lobby the government of Kordofan to pass a law that would abolish slavery in Sudan and its immediate environs. The law was eventually passed, but only remained a dead letter afterwards. Slavery as an institution was deeply ingrained in the Sudanese politics and economy, where many people had their vested interest. Aware of the inherent dangers that such activism posed to Comboni, the priests and their nascent mission, Cardinal Alessandro Franchi, in a letter dated 31 August 1874, instructed Comboni to "proceed with the maximum circumspection."[53] This note of caution and the need to act with prudence was imperative and, as Cardinal Franchi noted in the same letter:

> Where worldly interests, especially those of powerful nations, come into play, even the holiest works encounter difficulties that cannot be overcome with the danger of losing what has already been gained.
>
> Therefore, in conclusion, the prefect of the Propaganda Fide further instructed Msgr Comboni to "take no step, and execute no project without first having informed the Propaganda (Fidei) and received appropriate instruction"[54].

Comboni was aware of the dangers that his anti-slavery activism might pose to his missionary work and even to the lives of his fellow missionaries. He acknowledged that much in one of his letters, but was undeterred, not even by the fact that the anti-slavery law enacted through his influence had remained ignored. He sought other avenues to continue the fight:

> The decree of abolition remains a dead letter, and I believe it will be impossible to make it effective because slavery constitutes one of the main sources of revenue for the governor and merchants of Sudan . . . I am now studying how to put the Catholic mission in such a position that it will be able to force the Pasha to outlaw the abuses connected with the trade. Already there has

---

52. Russell, *Africa's Twelve Apostles*, 232.
53. La Bella, "Leo XIII and the Anti-Slavery," 382.
54. La Bella, "Leo XIII and the Anti-Slavery," 382.

been generated in many of these traffickers a wholesome dread of the priests[55].

It is not out of place to note that, unlike Lavigerie, Comboni's anti-slavery activism was a direct result of a first-hand experience during his many missionary journeys in and around his vast vicariate. While Lavigerie relied, to a great extent, on information sent to him in Algiers from the mission fields by his missionaries in Equatorial and Central Africa, Comboni, on the other hand, was the relentless peripatetic missionary who encountered first-hand the horrors of slavery. As an eyewitness did pen down, and, most probably, with some tincture of exaggeration: "The number of deaths among the slaves is so high that the hyenas cannot eat all the bodies. They are gorged with human flesh."[56] Saturated with such constant and disgusting scenarios, Comboni became physically exhausted by his labors and died prematurely on 10 October 1881. It is reported that Pope Leo XIII, on hearing of the death of the wearied missionary, exclaimed: "Poor Negroes! What a loss you have suffered!"[57] About his experience and his heroic apostolate to slaves, Comboni once wrote in a letter to a friend:

> We feel neither the equatorial heat, nor the drudgery of apostolic life, nor the weariness of long journeys, nor the uncomfortable houses, nor the privation of material things. We have exhausted our supply of linens, shirts and other materials to make garments for the freed slaves. But 'till our last breath our cry will be: "Africa or Death!"[58].

As a complex and multifarious phenomenon, slavery took centre stage during the second phase of the Church's commitment to the anti-slavery campaign and, according to La Bella, both the Holy See and many European powers were not enthusiastically drawn to the cause to begin with.[59] Having taken over the anti-slavery campaign after the death of Comboni, Lavigerie brought to the cause his personal gifts of energy, great intellect and vision as well as what may currently be described as being "media friendly." As a person with "a keen intellect, aided by a memory ready as it was unfailing, a capacity for everything and surmounting everything to his proposed aims,"[60] Lavigerie was well suited to popularize the war against Arab slavery

---

55. Russell, *Africa's Twelve Apostles*, 236.
56. Russell, *Africa's Twelve Apostles*, 233.
57. Russell, *Africa's Twelve Apostles*, 239.
58. Russell, *Africa's Twelve Apostles*, 236.
59. La Bella, "Leo XIII and the Anti-Slavery," 386.
60. Russell, *Africa's Twelve Apostles*, 167.

in the interior of Africa, especially in concentrated areas around Tobora, Uijiji and Tanganyika. His rallying cry was: "*Pour sauver l'Afrique intérieure, il faut souler la colère du monde*" (To save the interior of Africa, there is need to arouse the anger of the world).[61]

The earliest of Lavigerie's attempts to draw the Holy See's attention to the question of slavery in the interior regions of Africa were noted in his "Mémoir secret sur l'Association Internationale Africaine," dated 2 January 1878, to Cardinal Franchi of the Propaganda Fide. On the inevitability of the Church not possibly being proactive in the eradication of slavery, Lavigerie wrote that it was a sacred duty, which the Church could not abandon but must embrace before the "civilized world." He equally argued that the Church could not put its feet into the interior of Equatorial Africa without seeking means and ways to end the horrors of the slave trade in that part of the continent. In order to achieve the desired aim of destroying once and for all that infamous trade in human beings, which he called "the dreadful scourge of our Africa," Lavigerie, in his memoir, insisted on the need to appeal to the sentiments of Christian humanity. He conceded it as factual that the slave trade by sea had been suppressed, but he added immediately that "slave trade by land still exists" in the north and east of Africa, where "the Muslims and their black associates" in the nefarious commerce went about their business unperturbed.[62] He singled out Algeria, Egypt, Zanzibar and Sudan as "les États barbaresques" (the barbaric states), because they were points of departure for the disgraceful and mournful slave expeditions that spared neither women nor infants at the bosom of their mothers.[63] He supported his very vivid description of the Arab slave trade with a mind-numbing figure, with the estimate written in capital letters for the sake of emphasis: "chaque année, QUATRE CENT MILLE nègres sont les victims de cefléau" (each year, FOUR HUNDRED THOUSAND Blacks are the victims of this scourge).[64]

To his eternal credit, as far back as 1878, that is, a full decade before *In Plurimis* of Leo XIII (1888), Lavigerie had implored the Holy See to issue a strong word of condemnation of slavery. He was convinced that any authoritative papal condemnation of slavery would become a golden opportunity for the pope to come out from the undeserved position as the prisoner of his own palace. As judged by Lavigerie, any pronouncement by the pope in condemnation of slavery was to be done "in the name of the Gospel and

61. Russell, *Africa's Twelve Apostles*, 162.
62. Lavigerie, "Le mémoir secret," 131–132.
63. Lavigerie, "Le mémoir secret," 132.
64. Lavigerie, "Le mémoir secret," 134.

in the constant traditions of the Church." Beyond those, it must not remain at the level of mere words, but it must be backed up with action by sending "apostles in the centre of Africa, with the mission to destroy slavery . . . the horrors of which dishonor one branch of the human family." The gravity of the matter required "une bulle pontificale" (a papal bull) to be addressed to the heads of the missions in Equatorial Africa, which would simultaneously declare a great crusade of faith and of humanity against slavery. The same solicited bull must also announce the creation of an army of apostles who would be ready to march even unto death in order "to save the life, the liberty of the poor children of Ham."[65] Finally, from the submission of Lavigerie, any action undertaken in that regard by the pope would go down as one of the greatest events of the nineteenth century and in the history of the Church.[66]

As the saying goes, "In the field of science, chance favors the prepared mind." With ten years' vast experience garnered through extensive study of the letters and reports of his missionaries on slavery hotspots, Lavigerie was well informed on the issue. He seized the moment when the opportunity presented itself in 1888, with the imminent publication of a papal encyclical on the abolition of slave trade in Brazil. Cashing in on his personal rapport with Leo XIII, Lavigerie took the liberty to write to the pope on 16 February 1888 to enlighten the pontiff as to the Arab slave trade. The tone was greatly in line with his thoughts on slavery, as previously expressed in his memoir of 1878. He insisted more forcefully that slavery had not ended everywhere and that a word from the pope in that regard would carry a lot of weight and influence. There is an abundance of literature on Lavigerie's initiative. Suffice it to note that the eminent French Cardinal did not mince words to inform the pope that the problem was widespread across the length and breadth of the continent, so much so that there was not a single ecclesiastical jurisdiction that did not have to deal with slavery and its devastating effects in Africa. His ten years of patient waiting finally paid off when Pope Leo XIII issued *In Plurimis* on 5 May 1888. The pope not only condemned slavery in the strongest terms, but he also used the occasion to underscore the liberating character of the Christian Gospel. He also affirmed that the apostolic force imposed upon the Church the obligation to condemn a grave injustice as glaring as slavery rightly described as "servitude."[67]

65. Baur, *2000 Years of Christianity*, 191. Popular Christian interpretation understood all Africans as descendants of Ham (cf. Genesis 9), and specifically saw the curse on Ham as being alive in Africans. Lavigerie, being a child of his time, identified Africans as the children of Ham; likewise, Comboni also prayed for the "unfortunate children of Ham."

66. Lavigerie, "Le mémoir secret," 136–137.

67. Delisle, "La campagne antiesclavagiste," 396.

To say the least, it would have been too naïve for anyone to expect that a papal encyclical would be binding on all and sundry so as to utter the last word on slavery. Unfortunately, as late as between 1905 and 1906, there were still cases of colonial tolerance of slavery in East Africa, where, for instance, mere commodities such as salt, rubber and ivory continued to be exchanged for slaves.[68] However bad the situation might have remained after the publication of *In Plurimis*, Pope Leo XIII, for his part, was more than eager to associate himself with the anti-slavery campaign that had assumed the visible face of Lavigerie. As a man desirous of "playing big politics" on a bigger international stage, it was more than a privileged moment for Pope Leo XIII, who shared with Lavigerie the same grandiose vision for the papacy and the Church. According to Philippe Delisle, Pope Leo XIII, on the suggestion of Lavigerie, presented himself as the initiator of a new movement to champion the crusade for the final abolition of slave trade in Africa.[69] As they became, as it were, comrades-in-arm, Lavigerie received a mandate from the pope as his legate to fly the flag of the anti-slavery crusade on behalf of the pope. Writing on the development, Russell reproduced the words of Leo XIII as follows:

> It is upon Mons. Le Cardinal that we count most of all for the success of the different African missions. We are well informed as to what you have done in the past so signally for this noble cause and we are confident that you will bring to a successful issue all the inspiring works that you have undertaken[70].

It was a mandate that Lavigerie was too pleased to execute. He travelled around major European cities as the flag bearer of a new Christian humanism imbued with diplomacy together with an opportunity to reconcile faith and humanity, on the one hand, and to foster a spirit of dialogue and cooperation among the different Christian confessions, on the other.[71] Significantly, the anti-slavery campaign became one of the avenues through which Pope Leo XIII learnt in the field about how to be pope in a remarkably changed condition without the irrecoverable Papal States. In trying to position itself as the proactive agitator to end the disastrous Arab slave trade in Africa, the papacy unwittingly carved out a new mission for itself. The papacy began to view itself as being on a universal mission at the service of humanity, backed with a moral stature. This remains one of the benefits

---

68. Shorter, *Cross and Flag in Africa*, 66.
69. Delisle, "La campagne antiesclavagiste," 396.
70. Russell, *Africa's Twelve Apostles*, 161.
71. La Bella, "Leo XIII and the Anti-Slavery," 392.

of the anti-slavery campaign for the papacy, after liberating itself from the menace of territorial acquisition ambitions and from profane political interests. After Leo XIII, the papacy began progressively and systematically to position itself as the defender of peace and the rights of people. As Leo's Secretary of State, Cardinal Mariano Rampolla, perceptively surmised:

> It is a fact that the first in this century to concern itself with the abolition of the trafficking of Negroes was the Civil Power in the Congresses of Vienna and Verona . . . The Popes in this century have done nothing new on this question. The initiative of the present Pontiff is therefore providential and very copious fruits for the prestige of the Holy See and for the salvation of souls can be hoped from it[72].

Besides the Brussels Anti-Slavery Conferences between 1889 and 1890, one of the enduring fruits of the anti-slavery campaign of Leo and Lavigerie is the Sodality of St Peter Claver, founded on 19 April 1894 by Maria Teresa Ledóchoneko in Zoung, Oswald. She was inspired to establish the Sodality after reading Lavigerie's famous speech delivered in London in 1888. He told the Christian women of Europe that they were duty-bound to make "these infamies public" and to raise "the wrath of the whole civilized world." Pope Leo XIII welcomed Maria Teresa's initiative. He approved its establishment and adequately supported it as part of his anti-slavery campaign in Africa.[73] Another concrete fruit was the follow-up encyclical *Catholicae Ecclesiae* of 20 November 1890, in which the pope recalled the principal arguments against slavery as he had previously laid out in the *In Plurimis* of 1888. As concrete measure, through the encyclical of 1890, he instituted a special annual collection to be taken in all Churches on the Feast of Epiphany, in order to support the various anti-slavery projects that were directed towards the final eradication of the slave trade.

On the flipside of the coin, especially among the French missionary circle that made up roughly three-quarter of all Catholic missionary personnel at the time, the anti-slavery crusade of Leo and Lavigerie was not very successful in attracting enthusiastic admirers. The reason was not far-fetched. This was on account of the personality of Lavigerie and his many controversies that bordered mainly on differences in missionary visions and strategies. His frosty relationship with Comboni, as alluded to earlier, saw the veteran Italian missionary preferring to have the SMAs as neighbors rather than Lavigerie's Missionaries of Africa. With regard to the anti-slavery campaign, the first group to disagree with Lavigerie was the Society

72. La Bella, "Leo XIII and the Anti-Slavery," 394.
73. Iheanacho, *Maximum Illud and Benedict XV*, 269.

for the Propagation of the Faith, which refused in 1890 to collaborate in its program of an annual collection in favor of slaves. Its directors were of the view that certain missionary congregations exaggerated the slave question in Africa and probably profited from the anti-slavery campaign. In one of his letters to the directors in November 1888, Lavigerie was at pain to stress that the Society for the Propagation of the Faith could not remain aloft in the crusade against slavery. He acknowledged the generosity of personal and individual alms in support of the missions, but those in themselves were not sufficient to end the scourge, adding that only concerted efforts by everyone, especially the Europeans, could accomplish it. For the directors of the Society, the basis for the foundation of their organization was for peace, while the anti-slavery campaign led by Lavigerie was for war, with the unavoidable consequence of the destruction of the missions in Africa. As far as they were concerned, evangelization was different from the ransoming of slaves and equally different from the campaign to end slavery altogether.[74]

The second group that sought to undermine the efforts of Lavigerie's anti-slavery crusade was the Spiritans. Like Comboni, the tension between the Spiritans and Lavigerie was traceable ten years prior to the launching of the anti-slavery campaign. The background to that conflict was first their collision over the French Congo, where the Spiritans had been operational prior to the arrival of Lavigerie's men, after the submission of Lavigerie in his memoir to the Propaganda Fide in 1878. It must also be acknowledged that Lavigerie took great care to avoid that misgiving by painstakingly going round the missions of the Spiritans in the area when he recognized their presence in Luanda (Angola) towards Gabon in the Vicariate of the two Guineas and in Landana in the Prefecture of the Congo.[75] A similar collision also occurred when, in the same memoir, Lavigerie courted the Propaganda Fide to carve out a large part of East Africa for his own missionaries. The Spiritans and other missionary institutes in the region judged such action as detrimental to their mission fields. In terms of the fight against slavery, the Spiritans cannot be accused of indifference. It is important to note that they were not, in principle, against any effort undertaken either to ransom slaves or to eradicate slavery altogether. After all, even before the formation of the Missionaries of Africa (the White Fathers in 1868), and long after their eventual arrival in East Africa, the Spiritans in 1868 stumbled into a large slave market in Bagamoyo *en route* to Zanzibar. As was the missionary

---

74. Delisle, "La campagne antiesclavagiste," 399–405.
75. Lavigerie, "Le mémoir secret," 110, footnote 2 is important.

practice of the time, they exerted themselves to buy slaves from their captors and to resettle them in the so-called "villages of liberty."[76]

Given the fact that there was no love lost between the Holy Ghost Fathers and Lavigerie, they were not disposed to collaborate in any initiative with Lavigerie at its helm. Their line of argument was similar to that of the Society for the Propagation of the Faith, in which they sustained the view that the anti-slavery onslaught championed by Lavigerie endangered the lives of missionaries, since it put them in the way of direct collision with the Arab slave traders in Eastern and Equatorial Africa. The Spiritans were both suspicious and very critical of Lavigerie's intentions. Alongside other missionary congregations, they suspected Lavigerie of exploiting the anti-slavery campaign to the advantage of the Missionaries of Africa, especially with regard to the funds collected for that purpose.[77] Summarily, it is fair to affirm that the French missionary contemporaries of Lavigerie were not, in principle, opposed to the anti-slavery campaign, which had the strong support and backing of the Holy See. They were rather repulsed by the ebullient and controversial personality of Lavigerie, which sadly alienated a good number of them and acted as a stumbling block. They never overcame that difficulty. As a consequence, they did not join their forces with those of Lavigerie for the common purpose of eradicating the trans-Saharan slave trade in Africa.

TERRITORIAL ADJUSTMENTS AND MISSION JURISDICTIONS

The death of Bishop Jean Remi Bessieux in Gabon in 1876 marked the end of an era and coincided with the greater opening of Africa and the eventual penetration into the interior of the continent by both the missionaries and the colonizers. Bessieux was the only survivor among the missionary band that accompanied Bishop Barron of the two Guineas from France in 1843. He succeeded both Barron and Msgr Benedict Truffet in 1849 as the Vicar Apostolic of almost a borderless vicariate that comprised all the territories between Senegal in West Africa and Angola in Southern Africa. During his thirty-three years of toils from Libreville in Gabon, where he was based, Msgr Bessieux witnessed the progressive expansion of his Vicariate of the two Guineas, by creating a multiplicity of vicariates. The first was in 1848 when the Claretian missionaries, recently founded by Anthony Claret, were

76. Delisle, "La campagne antiesclavagiste," 407.
77. Delisle, "La campagne antiesclavagiste," 408.

assigned the missions in Spanish Guinea.[78] The southern region of the continent welcomed the Oblates of Mary Immaculate in 1852, where thirty-four years prior to their arrival, the Vicariate of Cape Town-Mauritius had been created in 1818. It was almost borderless as an ecclesiastical circumscription, since its widest extension cut across two continents which included Madagascar along the African coast in the Indian Ocean and Australia in Oceania, together with all the nearby territories.[79]

A few years later, in 1858, the SMAs came to Sierra Leone, where a vicariate was created for them to include Liberia and French Guinea. This new vicariate used to be the heartbeat of the old two Guineas. The old Vicariate of Central Africa, before being passed over to Comboni and his Verona missionaries, had been the mission field of Friar Minors from its inception in 1846. It was attached to the Apostolic Vicariate of Egypt and administered by its Vicar, Msgr Aloysius Ciurcia. In 1877, its administration was given to Msgr Daniel Comboni who became the Apostolic Vicar of the vast territory that would later be subjected to a great deal of contention, following the exploration and penetration of Equatorial and Central Africa by European explorers and colonizers. Already as far back as 1868, Lavigerie had worked his way to being appointed Apostolic Delegate of the Sahara and Sudan.[80] With his grandiose missionary ambition, Lavigerie cast his eyes over Equatorial Africa, particularly the eastern axis, where he was bound to encounter and clash with the Spiritans who had been working in the area since 1860.

Those hazy and large ecclesiastical jurisdictions, with the exception of the Vicariates of the two Guineas and Central Africa, were all realized during the long pontificate of Pope Pius IX. Another important fact to note is that, with the possible exception of Spanish Guinea, sub-Saharan Africa was, until 1850, basically divided into two major ecclesiastical jurisdictions, namely the Vicariate of the two Guineas and the Vicariate of Central Africa. The number increased to roughly sixty-one in 1900,[81] three years prior to the death of Pope Leo XIII. Aware of the fact that the French Revolution and the Napoleonic wars practically halted the Catholic missionary efforts in Africa, the biographers of Augustin Planque duly recognized Popes Gregory XVI and Pius IX as the founders of the Catholic Church in contemporary Africa, for both are said to have been

> [s]pecially gifted with inspiration and the apostolic determination to develop the missions. It was they who in the absence of

78. Bane, *The Popes and Western Africa*, 52.
79. Walbert Bühlmann, "Passato e futuro," 580.
80. Bane, *The Popes and Western Africa*, 53–54.
81. Bruls, "From Missions to 'Young Churches,'" 390.

local structures and through the Congregation of Propaganda, directed the African episcopate, made decisions and divided up the territories amongst the various missionary institutes[82].

Sundkler and Steed explain that the diversity and plurality of Catholic missionaries were, without any doubt, marked by their places of origin and the charisma of their various missionary congregations or institutes.[83] Naturally, those different hues and internal characteristics left their impressions on their work, but certainly not without tensions and quibbling in some instances. As the grand missionary strategist that he was, Cardinal Lavigerie, in his memoir, had mused over the idea of creating a single authority in Africa, whose primary responsibility would be to oversee and coordinate the various Catholic mission circumscriptions on the continent. He borrowed this idea from the example of the International African Association, which he admired for its function as a uniting force, around which diverse people with diverse interests came together under the patronage of Leopold II.

The suggestion of Lavigerie was based on the observation that not much inroad had been made by Catholic missions, because they were scattered and badly organized, as "each one follows his own inspiration, his own method, and it must be said, sometimes, without apostolic method and inspiration."[84] He sought to persuade the Propaganda Fide to realize that it had more than enough on its plate, since it had the onerous responsibility to supervise and provide for all the missions of the Church around the globe and not only over those in Africa. On the basis of that hard reality, he considered it practically impossible for the Propaganda Fide to give the required and unalloyed attention to the missions in Africa. Having a person on the ground in Africa and being authorized by Rome, such a person would work under the authority and direction of Rome and would be "specially charged to oversee, to unite, to visit and to inspect the missions among other things." He considered his proposal a panacea to the prevalent practice, whereby all the missionary efforts by the different congregations and institutes were not sufficient. Left to themselves alone, they were not capable of giving the desired result, because they were isolated and sometimes even opposed to one another. The appointment of an overall mission supervisor in Africa would offset some of those notable setbacks.[85]

---

82. *Augustin Planque*, 106. There is a three-volume work on Pius IX by Martina. See Giacomo Martina, *Pio IX 1846–1850*.

83. Sundkler and Steed, *A History of the Church*, 104.

84. Lavigerie, "Le mémoir secret," 130.

85. Lavigerie, "Le mémoir secret," 130.

As hinted at earlier, the push into Equatorial and Central Africa, beginning from 1875, was propitious for the missions, but it also brought in its wake tensions and quarrels among Catholic missionaries over territories. Lavigerie's proposal to the Propaganda Fide to create four new vicariates apostolic in Equatorial and Central Africa was not very pleasant to Comboni and the Spiritans, on the pretext that the interior of Africa was their own "hinterland." They laid claim to those areas through the right of first possession, since they were established on the East African coast since 1860. Almost every missionary institute at the time had a bone to pick with Lavigerie over territory. He drove the SMAs from Oran in north-western Algeria. Comboni feared that Lavigerie might reduce the field of operation for his Verona missionaries. As for the Spiritans, their battlegrounds went beyond East Africa to the Congo. Most of the missions were only at the early stage when Pius IX died in 1878 and left the unresolved issues to his successor. The anti-slavery campaign, a mandate received by Lavigerie from Leo XIII, did not win many missionaries to the cause on a suspicious ground that it was a ploy for Lavigerie to grab more mission territories for his own men.

Although the missions in Africa reached their point of stability during the pontificate of Leo XIII, in many respects, the major concerns of the Holy See and the Propaganda Fide with regard to those missions, bordered mainly on practicality. Their preoccupations, as would be expected, revolved mainly around "the appointment of new ecclesiastical superiors and the subdivision of territories that were seen to be unmanageable units only after laborious fact-finding journeys."[86] This is understandable, since political and ecclesiastical geographical boundaries on the continent were still hazy and fluid in many places. The Holy See and its mission dicastery were often sandwiched between missionary institutes, on the one hand, and colonial administrators, on the other. In most instances, in deference to political sensitivity, with a laborious and tedious diplomatic negotiation, the Propaganda Fide tried to yield to the demands of the colonizing powers. They often preferred missionaries of their own nationalities. Once the intricate question about the nationality of missionaries had been settled, another difficult problem reared its head. It concerned mission territories and jurisdictions of the different missionary congregations that were meant to work side by side with other congregations in the same mission territory.

Intrinsically connected, both thorny questions may be described as two sides of the same coin. The question about the nationality of missionaries, which was settled with the political authorities concerned, could be described as "extra-dispute." The rankling among Catholic missionaries in

---

86. Moody, "The Growth of Catholic Missions," 241.

the same mission field could be described as "intra-dispute." The latter had to do with the internal affairs of the Church and the systematic organization of the missions for better coordination and harmonious pastoral engagement. The aim of its amicable settlement was the elimination of rancor and ill-feeling among Catholic missionaries in Africa. They were jealous and protective of vast areas, many parts of which had not yet been reached by any missionary institute. This resulted in many areas remaining un-evangelized. Protesting against the division of his Vicariate, Daniel Combini once lamented that Propaganda Fide had supported "the insufficiently weighed and undue demands" of Cardinal Lavigerie. He accused the Roman dicastery of having prejudicially given "the principal field of action of my institute" to the "meritorious society founded by the most zealous and eminent Archbishop of Algiers."[87] Comboni's accusation was not all that accurate, because Protestant missionaries were already establishing their missions in Central Africa and around the Great Lakes. Aside from the exaggerations and emphasis of Lavigerie in his submission, there were some isolated mission stations in and around Zanzibar with its annex of Bagamoyo. This mission area stretched over a distance of roughly 1,800 km, that is, from Natal in Southern Africa to Cape Guardafui in Somalia. That long stretch of mission territory, estimated to be roughly five times the size of Italy, was under the administration of the Spiritans with a very limited mission personnel.[88]

The Holy See, through the Propaganda Fide, devised a number of measures to achieve the aim of harmonious co-existence among the missionaries. It adopted the "right of commission," whereby mission territories were shared between missionaries. The old *ius commissionis* mission system remained in vogue until the 1960s, when the Second Vatican Council replaced it with the juridical mission system of *mandatum*.[89] Whereas the old system placed the responsibility of developing a particular mission territory on the shoulders of a missionary institute, the new system underscored mission as the co-responsibility between local churches and sister churches beyond geographical confines. But most importantly, the *mandatum* system placed the burden of evangelization and ecclesial development primarily on the shoulders of local bishops.[90] Following the old system that was devised to settle territorial mission disputes, as at 1881, the Capuchins were in charge of the missions in Tunisia, Libya, Egypt and their Galla mission in present-day Ethiopia. The Vincentians were operational in Abyssinia (present-day

87. Moody, "The Growth of Catholic Missions," 221.
88. Lavigerie, "Le mémoir secret," 109–110.
89. Oborji, "Catholic Mission in Africa," 15.
90. Oborji, "Catholic Mission in Africa," 15.

Ethiopia), while the Spiritans remained in Zanzibar, the Congo, Senegambia and Senegal.

For their part, the Missionaries of Lyons (SMAs) were established in the tropical regions of Guinea up to Dahomey and the Western part of Nigeria. The Missionaries of Verona (the Combonians) retained their missions from the south of Egypt through Sudan in their Vicariate of Central Africa. The Jesuits were assigned Madagascar and the Zambezi area, while Oblates of Mary Immaculate maintained their place in Natal to cover Southern Africa. The Mill Hill Fathers were given the mission in the Cape Colony. It required painstaking patience to accommodate diverse contenders with the peculiarity of diverse concerns. For example, Benguela in Angola was under Portuguese control and required a compromise on the part of the Holy See, in order to bring in missionaries of non-Portuguese nationality. Intense diplomatic negotiation was needed in apportioning some part of Morocco to Spanish missionaries. The *status quo* was maintained in Algeria as the exclusive reserve of the French missionaries, and specifically, the domain of Lavigerie.[91]

The second measure was "on-the-spot settlement" between two missionary congregations involved in a territorial dispute. In 1900, León Livinhac, Superior General of the White Fathers, wrote to Msgr Alexandre Le Roy, Superior General of the Holy Ghost Fathers, about the question of French Guinea, which pitched their two congregations against each other. Livinhac deplored the futility of territorial disputes among their respective missionaries.[92] The last measure was linked to the second, in which the Propaganda Fide deliberately chose to entrust mission planning and execution to missionary congregations in their different geographical areas of assignment. This was to avoid the problems that might have arisen if there had been one single supervising authority of the missions on the ground in Africa, as once recommended by Lavigerie in his 1878 secret memoir to the Propaganda Fide.[93]

The disagreement between the Holy Ghost Fathers under the leadership of Fr Ambroise Emonet and the White Fathers of Cardinal Lavigerie is an epic story. Their prolonged battle raged over the missions in the interior, with counterclaims especially over the French Congo and Equatorial Africa. As far as Lavigerie was concerned, it was nothing short of a "question of right and honor." That dispute was seemingly settled by Rome after a series of

91. With slight additions, see Storme, *Rapports du Père Planque*, 78, especially footnote 2.
92. Moody, "The Growth of Catholic Missions," 243.
93. Moody, "The Growth of Catholic Missions," 233.

meetings between the Propaganda Fide and the two congregations in 1886.[94] However, the dispute continued in another manner, particularly over mission jurisdictions in Equatorial Africa. It warranted the letter of Cardinal Simeoni, Prefect of the Propaganda Fide, to Fr Emonet in 1890. Cardinal Simeoni, in reference to Ubanghi, informed him beforehand that "[c]omplaints could come from Prelates who believe they have jurisdiction on the territory. I would ask your Reverence to reach agreement with them."[95]

There was also the question of the so-called "auxiliary missionaries." One example occurred in 1905 between the Holy Ghost Fathers and the Consolata Missionaries in Kenya (East Africa). Another example was the dispute between the White Fathers and the Monfortian Fathers (the Company of Mary) in Nyassa, aggravated by Cardinal Mieczyslaw Halka Ledochowski, Prefect of Propaganda from 1892 to 1902.[96] Auxiliary missionaries were from a different missionary institute working in the territory entrusted to another missionary order. The arrangement between the institutes concerned was often private, with the "auxiliary missionaries" agreeing not to seek their own missionary jurisdiction. As the experiences of the Holy Ghost Fathers and the White Fathers made clear, the agreement was not always respected.

Another difficulty that ensued in the missions in Africa had to do with mission funding agencies. The Lyons Association for the Propagation of the Faith once complained, in 1868, that Comboni, Lavigerie and the Prefect of Tripoli all simultaneously requested money for their new missions. Some years later, a misunderstanding ensued in 1878 between Lavigerie and the directors of the Holy Childhood Society who protested against the huge financial demands from Lavigerie for the missions in Equatorial Africa.[97] In one instance, finance was a major factor in resolving the problem that arose in the appointment of a successor of Bishop Fedele Sutter in Tunisia in 1881. Because of its political interest in Tunisia, the French government agreed to pay Sutter's annual pension of 6,000 francs, in addition to funding the mission in Tunisia. This led to the appointment of Cardinal Lavigerie as Apostolic Administrator of the Vicariate of Tunis, causing an altercation between him and the Italian Capuchins who had been in that mission for approximately one hundred years.[98]

---

94. *Duquesne Studies, Spiritan Series*, 222–225.
95. Moody, "The Growth of Catholic Missions," 233.
96. Moody, "The Growth of Catholic Missions," 243.
97. Moody, "The Growth of Catholic Missions," 213, 233.
98. Renault, *Cardinal Lavigerie*, 282–283.

Of course, finance was one of the reasons why both the Lyons Association for the Propagation of the Faith and the Holy Ghost Fathers clashed with Lavigerie over the anti-slavery campaign. Not only that the two groups considered it very broad, too direct and too political, the Spiritans, in particular, demanded that the lion share of the anti-slavery fund should actually be given to them. According to them, their missionary congregation had more mission territories. Logically, they were more involved in the evangelization of most of the colonies South of the Sahara. Their missionary undertakings brought them into direct contact with the slave trade that took its toll on their resource in terms of expenses on slave ransom. Their Superior General, Fr Ambroise Emonet, complained once that 100,000 francs disbursed to his congregation to fight slavery was nothing compared to the amount that was needed for both slave ransom and the education of young, ransomed slaves.[99]

It must be remembered that it was in the bid to garner financial support for the missions in Africa that Pope Leo XIII, in his encyclical *Catholicae Ecclesiae* (1890), established a special annual collection on the feast of Epiphany on 6 January. As directed by Leo XIII, the money was designated for the ransom of slaves and in support of the abolition of slavery. He also directed that the money collected should be sent to the Propaganda Fide who, in turn,

> will divide the money among the missions which now exist or will be established primarily to eliminate slavery in Africa. The Sacred Council will divide the rest of the money among those missions which show the greatest need, according to its discretion (no. 4).

From the outset, the money factor was a big issue in the Catholic evangelization of Africa. For instance, the initial launch of the missions in Equatorial Africa around the Great Lakes used up vast amounts of money. On the financial cost of this missionary undertaking, Paul Moody states that "Lavigerie had estimated that the initial Great Lakes advance would cost 400,000 francs." It eventually cost much more than the initial budget. As an enormous undertaking, it ended up "absorbing the equivalent of 10% of the annual funds available to the Propagation of the Faith in Lyon."[100] Similar information is found in Charles Groves in that the disbursements to missionary work in Africa increased (in round thousands) from 448,000 francs in

---

99. Delisle, "La campagne antiesclavagiste," 410–411.
100. Moody, "The Growth of Catholic Missions," 222–223.

1865 to 1,344,000 francs in 1889.[101] These figures only serve to illustrate the important factor of finance in missionary undertakings, especially in rural and primary evangelization, covering expenses on erection of cathedrals and other church buildings, seminaries, dispensaries, schools, maintenance of mission personnel, and many other projects. There is no gainsaying the obvious that the erection of mission institutions, in whatever form, does indeed imply huge capital expenses. This remains a big challenge facing many of the Churches in Africa. The level of economic viability varies from diocese to diocese and from country to country, based on each country's economic development and access to foreign financial assistance. The final chapter of this book shows how a local church that continuously relies on foreign aid and charity for its existence and essential services will always remain an unhealthy church that has not been fully established as a truly local and viable church.[102]

---

101. Groves, *The Planting of Christianity*, 84.
102. Hastings, "In the Field," 94.

3

The broad ambient of plantatio ecclesiae

The accelerated attention accorded to missions in Africa must be placed against the broader background of the accentuation on *plantatio ecclesiae* as a rediscovered missionary concept and praxis within the Catholic Church. It laid dormant for roughly four centuries. Its rediscovery in the second decade of the twentieth century meant a complete missionary reorientation about the final purpose of mission. At the beginning of the twentieth century, the Holy See began vigorously to recall and insist on missionary principles and practical methods that should underpin the works in mission territories.[1] *Plantatio ecclesiae* is a missionary concept that was born old, as far as the history of mission is concerned. In the consciousness of the popes, as demonstrated by Pope Leo X with the episcopal ordination of Dom Henrique in 1518, the aim of missionary work was to establish the local church with all the necessary structures and components. Failure to continue on that tract is generally described as the loss of an apostolic tradition or the much-lauded "apostolic method." One of the ancient documents unearthed to support the position is Clement of Alexandria's *Quis Dives*. Clement comments on the missionary activities of John as one of the twelve apostles:

> When John returned from the Island of Patmos on his way to Ephesus, he also visited neighbouring peoples, either to establish bishops, prepare entire Churches or to set up the clergy (*Quis Dives* 42)[2].

1. Delavignette, *Christianity and Colonialism*, 89.
2. Cited in Seumois, "Local Clergy and Inculturation," 22–23.

It remains an incontrovertible historical fact that the "apostolic method" was operational in the founding and establishment of the old churches in Europe. This was visible in the handwork of legendary local church founders such as Martin of Tours in France, Patrick in Ireland, Augustine of Canterbury in England, and Boniface in Germany. In each and every case, their final goal was the establishment of full-fledged churches with their own native hierarchy and local clergy.[3] In some manner, it seems that the loss of focus about the pre-eminent purpose of mission may be traceable to Europe's discovery and encounter with people outside the familiar confines of the continent. According to Massimo Marcocchi, the Portuguese and Spanish exploration and colonization, which acted as catalysts for the Catholic missionary action beyond Europe, helped the Church exit from its comfortable and traditional European milieu. It was an adventure, with some religious and cultural implications, in which there was no clear-cut distinction between European culture and the Christian Gospel.[4] The inability to draw a line of demarcation meant that the establishment of local churches in mission territories was not perceived as a priority, since indigenous people were not often considered to have the requisites to lead their ecclesial community.

The conspicuous mistrust towards non-Europeans in mission areas was a blatant disregard for the stipulations of the Council of Trent. Tridentine requirement for priestly ordination was specifically about the morality and virtue of the candidate. It never mentioned anything about the race, social class and economic conditions of candidates for the priesthood. With an impressive broadness of vision, some missionaries dug in their heels to insist that the missions beyond Europe could not survive without indigenous components. One such missionary was Alexandre De Rhodes. His twenty-one years of missionary experience in Asia convinced him that the presence and collaboration of the indigenous clergy are simply indispensable. For this to happen, he suggested, in his letter of 6 May 1652 to Pope Innocent X, that bishops were needed as a matter of urgency to ordain indigenous young men to the priesthood. In the estimation of De Rhodes, the local clergy was a constitutive element for the establishment of the Church in any place. The resurfacing of the emphasis on the local content in the implantation of new churches in mission areas remotely began alongside Catholic missionary reawakening in the middle of the nineteenth century. By the end of the century, the Propaganda Fide, in its instruction *Cum postremis* of 19 March

---

3. Guerriero, "Prefazione," 8.
4. Marcocchi, *Colonialismo, Cristianesimo*, 17.

1893, insisted on the formation and ordination of indigenous clergy as the bedrock for the emergence of new churches.[5]

In the course of the twentieth century, however, *plantatio ecclesiae* received greater emphasis so that successive popes began to impress its necessity upon missionaries and their congregations and institutes. In the first half of the twentieth century, all papal missionary documents and pronouncements insisted on *plantatio ecclesiae* as the ultimate aim of missionary activity. They judged it incomplete in the absence of a local hierarchy and an indigenous clergy. The presence of a strong indigenous clergy was considered a basic prerequisite in removing the foreignness of the Gospel and the Church and in consolidating Christianity in any given local community. In Africa, especially from the 1950s, *plantatio ecclesiae* became synonymous with *Africanization* or *indigenization*, upon which the Vatican predicated its missionary policy on the continent. This change of focus occurred in concomitance with the agitation for political independence in many African countries. As with other Catholic mission areas beyond Europe and North America, it was the hope of the Vatican that the emerging particular Churches in Africa could develop with a relative autonomy, attaining their maturity in dependence on their own internal resources both in terms of personnel and finance. In Adrian Hastings' view, the autonomy and maturity of a local church go deeper than having indigenous bishops and priests at the helm. It requires the active support of the faithful, if their local church is to shrug off the unenviable status of being a perpetual recipient of foreign "charity."[6]

This chapter explores a broader perspective of *plantatio ecclesiae* as a missionary concept and places the historical trajectory of the Church in Africa within that context. The missions in Africa that progressively became local churches as from the 1950s benefited from ecclesiological orientation within the Catholic Church's missionary framework and greater openness to peoples of other cultures. It is also true that some factors did not easily favor the practical realization of *plantatio ecclesiae* in some mission territories. For instance, long distances and difficulties associated with such travels necessitated the permanency of missionaries in their areas of assignment. The sense of permanency was also not unconnected with the colonial structure, which was viewed as going to last forever. There was also the problem of local recruitment to the priesthood, which did not witness an immediate and enthusiastic take-off in many places in sub-Saharan Africa.[7] All these factors

5. Marcocchi, *Colonialismo, Cristianesimo*, 26, 50, 58–59.
6. Hastings, *The World Mission of the Church*, 46.
7. Seumois, "Local Clergy and Inculturation," 21.

became almost circumvented with sweeping changes that took place on the continent between the 1950s and the 1960s. Those changes softened the soil for the realization of *plantatio ecclesiae* in Africa and gradually led to the Africanization or indigenization of Catholic national hierarchies in Africa.

HISTORICAL PREVIEW OF PLANTATIO ECCLESIAE

The concept of mission as *plantatio ecclesiae* is simultaneously both old and new in the missionary lexicon. It is old in the sense that the idea of rooting the church in a local environment together with its visible structures has always been part of the missionary understanding from the earliest times. On the other hand, it is relatively new, because its constitutive elements only became better clarified, especially from the middle of the twentieth century. Since then, it became possible to conceive a change of perspective, which was interpreted retroactively as the "apostolic method." In his evaluation of the operative missionary conception before the pontificate of Gregory XVI, Msgr Celso Costantini, the first Apostolic Delegate to China (1922–1933), sought to know the underpinning principle that informed the missionary undertakings of those who were on mission on behalf of the Church. His questions were couched in this manner:

> Let us ask ourselves: What method did the missionaries of the apostolic and post-apostolic era use? Do we use the same methods? We use different methods, that which appears much better to us, but which the experience of four centuries has demonstrated almost sterile[8].

As far as Costantini was concerned, the "apostolic method" was *plantatio ecclesiae*, which was rediscovered in the course of the missionary evolution in the early twentieth century. It is not an overstatement to note that *plantatio ecclesiae* has always been a latent idea in many pontifical documents with regard to *mission ad extram*. Mention has already been made of Leo X's *Exponi nobis* (12 June 1518), where the pope insisted on the necessity to ordain a native clergy for the missions in West Africa and Congo during the Portuguese explorations in Africa. In three of his discourses on the prospects of the Church in China, Pope Paul V (1605–1621) already anticipated the famous 1659 *Instruction* of the Propaganda Fide. The words "*plantetur*" and "*plantata*" appeared in Paul V's directives on the adaptation of the liturgy in China for the benefit of the Chinese. The Pope intended to make a distinction between Christianization and westernization.

---

8. Costantini, *Va e annunzia il regno di Dio*, 265.

The three separate directives by Paul V, namely 12 August 1611, 21 January 1612 and 5 July 1614, indicated a clear orientation of the Church towards a long process of understanding missionary activity as "implantation" in relation to evangelization and the setting up of the local church in a local environment. In his authorization of the use of Chinese for the liturgy, he expressed the hope that "as the religion of Christ it may someday attain solidity once it is planted, and also grow[s] day by day in those areas."[9] A similar idea is evident in Pope Paul V's *Romanus Pontifex* (1615), where he reiterated his previous permission for the limited use of the Chinese language at Mass and the formation of a local Chinese clergy. This is also noticeable in Pope Paul V's *Romanae sedis antistes* (1615), in which he authorized the translation of the Bible into literary Chinese, and the use of Chinese for both the breviary and in the administration of the sacraments.[10]

There is an inherent and visible tension in the long evolution of the missionary conception and understanding of *plantatio ecclesiae*. The tension is pulled in two directions between the *tabula rasa* method and the adaptation method, which is found not only within missionary circles, but also in the directives of Propaganda Fide and even in those of the popes. While, for instance, in its official pronouncements, Rome tended towards the ideal in most cases, in actual practice, it tended to take back with the left hand what it had given or conceded with the right hand through its intransigent demand for Latinization. Up until the discovery of America in 1492, missions within the confines of Europe sought to adapt the Gospel and church practices to the local cultures of the people being evangelized. Recall can be made of the instruction of Pope Gregory the Great to St Augustine of Canterbury, when he set out to evangelize the inhabitants of the British Isle. The same is true of the evangelization of the Germanic tribes that populated many parts of the western axis of the Roman Empire. Such practice went into disuse as soon as Europe made its first contact with other cultures in the modern era.

One obvious consequence of that loss of missionary vision and practice was the entrenchment of a missionary stasis, especially from the sixteenth century,[11] which remained in vogue in some places until the twilight of the nineteenth and even late into the twentieth century in some other areas. The stasis brought about the *tabula rasa* approach as a missionary method that was operative in Latin America and in Africa, where it became particularly

---

9. "Ut in locis huius modi in dies magis plantetur et plantata confirmetur Christi religio." Cited in Seumois, "La Mission "Implantation," 48.

10. Marcocchi, *Colonialismo, Cristianesimo*, 36, 55.

11. Guerriero, "Prefazione," 8.

heightened after the Berlin Conference of 1884–1885. The resultant effect of the *tabula rasa* is that it did not initially permit any manner of adaptation, as the missionaries did not so much seek to discover the possible point of connection between the local cultures and the Gospel. As in Latin America, so also in Africa, where the first instinct was to seek out traces of idolatry to uproot. The ultimate end-product was a "spiritual conquest," which for a long time did not allow for the emergence of a local church whether in Latin America or in Africa. It was even worse in Latin America, where the indigenous people were at first not permitted to receive the sacraments and completely barred from admission to the priesthood, since they were judged as "incapable" of bearing the burdensome demands of celibacy.[12]

In contradistinction to the *tabula rasa* approach, the second method privileged adaptation as the preferred manner of proceeding in missionary undertaking. It seeks to recognize and appreciate the merits in other cultures and traditional values of other people beyond the shores of Europe. It may be out of place to describe it as "respectful" of other cultures during the missionary epochs between the sixteenth and the late nineteenth centuries, because it was particularly practiced more as an act of tolerance, in order to circumvent the cultural differences interpreted as obstacles to evangelization. The Jesuits in Asia are often reputed to have attempted to use this method in Asia, while their confrères in Latin America, particularly in Paraguay, and those in Ethiopia in Africa, during the seventeenth century, were intransigent in their insistence on Latinization rather than the subtle and docile approach.[13] Again, that divergence was contrary to the missionary principles articulated in the 1659 *Instruction* of the Propaganda Fide, which directed that missionaries must adapt to the native cultures where they were to evangelize and practice qualities such as sobriety, gentleness and patience, which the Roman mission dicastery described as "the imitation of the apostles."[14]

The dichotomy between missionary ideal and practice remains a great historical paradox. While the popes and the Propaganda Fide churned out pronouncements and enunciated missionary ideals, the active missionary on the ground in the mission field had few possibilities for maneuvering. He was not permitted by the juridical structure of the post-Tridentine Church to be culturally open and flexible.[15] There was the unfortunate and regrettable case of Fr Joseph Capet who was punished and frustrated out

12. Marcocchi, *Colonialismo, Cristianesimo*, 24–27.
13. Baur, *2000 Years of Christianity*, 169.
14. Marcocchi, *Colonialismo, Cristianesimo*, 53.
15. O'Connell, "The Church in Africa," 5.

of the priesthood in 1848. Capet was audacious to ask for the episcopal ordination of the Chinese and for the de-Europeanization of Christianity. He called for the indigenization of the church, with less foreign leaders at the helm of the local church. He described as "deplorable" the inability of the missionaries to make a clear distinction between the Christian Gospel and the inessentials encased in the European cultural background of the messengers of the Gospel. Capet suffered in the hands of the leaders of the Congregation of the Mission (the Vincentians) over the thorny issues of a local church and indigenous clergy. The Propaganda Fide never intervened on behalf of Capet, even though the same Roman dicastery had, earlier in 1845, directed the missionaries to work towards the ordination of a native clergy. On the contrary, instead of helping Capet, the Propaganda Fide, in a letter of 11 March 1850, instructed its representative in Hong Kong, Msgr Antonio Feliciani, to issue a disclaimer on Capet and to distance Rome from his position.[16]

COMPONENTS AND MODELS OF PLANTATIO ECCLESIAE

There is equally another tension in the Church's progressive comprehension of *plantatio ecclesiae* with regard to two apparent conflicting models of the concept, which in actual sense are only complementary. The first is the official model that may be called the "building construction" model and the second one is the "agricultural model," which is more implied thus in missiology. Official ecclesiastical documents use various expressions such as to stabilize, to constitute, to found, to establish, to order, and to institute. The model conceives the church as an institution or a durable edifice such as a building or a bridge which the missionary was sent to erect or build in a given locality or territory that is coextensive with a specific mission circumscription. Within this parameter of *plantatio ecclesiae*, the edifice (that is, the local church) was expected to be solid in its realization and, as increasingly became the case, its visible solidity was understood to be the native or local clergy expected to continue the work after the missionaries might have gone. Unfortunately, as good and appealing as it might be, the edifice model subtly tended to prolong the work of missionaries, since the edifice was practically assumed not to have been adequately completed. This means that the maturity of the local church was often put off to some later

---

16. Iheanacho, *Maximum Illud and Benedict XV*, 168–177; Tragella, "Le vicende d'un opuscolo," 189–202; Young, *Ecclesiastical Colony*, 144.

date in a distant future. The development of the local church is measured by its external stability.[17]

By contrast, the "agricultural model" uses terms such as "to stabilize, to normalize, to plant and to set up." Like a natural plant, the missionary is ideally expected to plant the seed in an indigenous soil, without materials from the West and without much emphasis on physical structures. The local church of this model is fragile, but steadily works to fashion out its own peculiar religious practices. Its development is more internal than external in realizing its maturity. As a plant, it needs its own organic life to survive. As in the case of the edifice model, it also requires some essential organs to help it subsist and grow in the form of vitality and stability, without necessarily resorting to external help or assistance. Again, those organs are the indispensable emergence and role of the indigenous clergy together with a native hierarchy. Mission is predominantly understood in the "agricultural model" as essentially provisional or temporary. It always exists in an interim state, with the ultimate goal being the disappearance of mission itself as soon as possible with the emergence of an indigenous or local church so as not to construct a religious colony that needs permanent reinforcements, in order to exist in a locality or within a missionary territory.[18] At first sight, the instinct would be to privilege the "agricultural model" over the "edifice model." It is pertinent to remember that both models are complementary. Francis Xavier Clark once intuited:

> The difficulty stems from a fact. Not one thing in purely human experience is simultaneously firm as a building set upon rock, and living as a tree, plant or field growing for harvest. The one has stability not life. The second has life, but is fragile and vulnerable[19].

The complementarity of the two models was attested to in the final declaration of the African bishops at the 1974 Synod in Rome, acknowledging that the local churches had attained some level of maturity, but this did not mean the end of mission and collaboration. They insisted on the continued relation of goodwill and mutual cooperation between the churches both old and new.[20] Their stand came against the background of the declaration of the Protestant churches in the Third World, first in Bangkok in 1973, to be followed a year later in May 1974 by the declaration of All Africa Conference

---

17. Seumois, "La Mission "Implantation," 43.
18. Seumois, "La Mission "Implantation," 43–45.
19. Cited in Seumois, "La Mission "Implantation," 45.
20. Dichiarazione finale dei Vescovi Africani, 290.

of Churches (AACC) in Lusaka. The Lusaka declaration specifically called for a "moratorium" on missionaries and money from the developed world.

To a large extent, the 1970s could be described as the decade of self-awareness by the churches in the developing world. In many of the discussions and debates of the time, the tension between the "edifice" and the "agricultural" models was unavoidably present. For instance, the Protestant participants at the 1974 Lausanne Covenant grappled with the question of whether to continue mission in the developing world or to end it altogether. They were not oblivious of the fact that the reduction in missionary personnel and money from the First World might encourage local initiatives and so help the local churches grow. Like the African Catholic bishops, the Lausanne Covenant, in its final statement, upheld the view that the flourishing of local churches was not a sufficient reason to completely halt the sending of missionaries and possibly also financial assistance where needed:

> A reduction of foreign missionaries and money in an evangelized country may sometimes be necessary to facilitate the national church's growth in self-reliance and to release resources for unevangelized areas... Missionaries should flow ever more freely from and to all six continents in a spirit of humble service. The goal should be, by all available means and at the earliest possible time, that every person will have the opportunity to hear, understand, and receive the good news[21].

A careful consideration of the Lausanne Covenant statement and the final declaration of the African Catholic bishops shows a similarity in their insistence on continued collaboration. In the understanding of the African bishops, the Catholic Church in Africa is but a small unit of the Universal Church, planted and rooted within the African locality. As far as they were concerned, missionaries were welcome to collaborate and assist in further developing the local churches, but under the direction of the local hierarchies. The same was said about external financial assistance, which was appreciated, but also remains within the plan and discretion of the receiving church, although the ultimate aim was the attainment of financial autonomy through the generosity of local or native Christians.[22] It was a summation of their earlier presentation, in which the bishops termed as "a narrow and misleading viewpoint" the idea that missionaries should leave Africa on the ground that their continued presence was a hindrance to the growth and development of the local churches on the continent.[23] Instead of a one-way

21. Cited in Howard, "Editorial: A Moratorium on Missions?."
22. Dichiarazione finale dei Vescovi Africani, 290–291.
23. Sangu, *Report on the Experiences of the Church*, 16.

directional assistance or a unilateral flow of missionaries and money, the bishops called for equal participation in the life of the Universal Church. Such equal participation would take the form of mutual sending and receiving in terms of personnel, finances, technical assistance programs as well as mutual programs of mission education and animation. This mutual complementarity, they argued, would put an end to paternalism of "father-child" relationship and foster instead an equal partnership of sister-churches.[24]

PLANTATIO ECCLESIAE AS A MISSIONARY POLICY

From its earliest inception in 1622, the Propaganda Fide, to its credit, was always animated by the desire to have the Church established in mission areas. The major problem is that the idealism of principles and rhetoric did not often match actual practice. It is certainly not for shortage of pronouncements and documents that the missions beyond Europe had produced very few indigenous priests. For instance, a few years after the establishment of the Propaganda Fide, its first Secretary, Msgr Francesco Ingoli, in a number of memoirs, decried the unwillingness of missionaries to train and ordain native clergy in places such as Latin America and Far East Asia. Against that background, on 28 November 1630, the Propaganda Fide issued a decree to that effect, indicating that there was "an absolute need to promote among the Indians those considered suitable to the sacred orders, and the priesthood included."[25]

In his memoir of 1628, Ingoli defended the indispensable place of a native or local clergy in the foundation of a local church. He debunked as false some of the flimsy excuses invented, in order to deny ordination to the indigenes. In contrast to those who viewed ordination as a favor, Ingoli viewed it rather as a necessity, if the mission must have a future beyond the missionaries. For instance, he countered the accusation against the natives of being drunkards, by pointing out that such things also happened in Europe and yet, people were still ordained despite such shortcoming. In his memoir of 1644, he noted with great pain that, for lack of sufficient priests, parishes in India were left without pastors and dioceses were deprived of bishops in some places for over twenty years, as in the cases of Macao in China and Malacca. In order to circumvent such inconveniences and to remedy the situation, Ingoli insisted on the ordination of the natives as the only permanent solution.[26] Regrettably, the injunctions of the Propaganda

24. Sangu, *Report on the Experiences of the Church*, 36.
25. Marcocchi, *Colonialismo, Cristianesimo*, 45–46.
26. Marcocchi, *Colonialismo, Cristianesimo*, 49.

Fide remained at best mere words even not dead letters in light of the fact that, after more than three hundred years of Catholic missionary activities in India, China, Ceylon and Vietnam, not a single Asian was raised to the bishopric.[27]

Prior to the publication of Benedict XV's *Maximum illud* in 1919, as a modern papal document on the missions, the Propaganda Fide's *Instruction Ad exteros* of 1659 was regarded as the "Magna Carta" for missionaries. It was built upon previous documents issued by the Propaganda Fide such as the "Rules for missionaries" (1626), the decree of 28 November 1630 as well as the three memoirs of Ingoli, submitted in this order: 1625, 1628 and 1644.[28] In a very comprehensive manner, the *Instruction* was a synthesis of all those documents. They collectively were the very source of its enrichment in terms of depth and insight into the core of the missionary problem of the time. Although originally intended for the first three vicars apostolic to the Chinese Kingdoms of Tonkin and Cochin-China, its content, nevertheless, had a universal import and outreach. It forbade the missionaries from being involved in politics and colonial affairs or from assuming nationalistic attitudes in mission areas. They were severely warned not to engage in any kind of commercial activity. On the positive side, it instructed that missionaries were to be equipped with good intellectual and spiritual preparations before embarking on missionary work. Most importantly and above every other consideration, missionaries were to labor assiduously for the creation of an indigenous clergy together with the missionaries' adaptation to the native culture. In many ways, the *Instruction* of 1659 set out in rudimentary forms the missionary principles that would later be formulated into policies in the course of subsequent centuries until they reached the maximum flowerings in the second half of the twentieth century.

It bears recalling that the *Instruction* was only retrieved in 1845 after roughly two centuries in oblivion. The occasion for its re-emergence was the publication of another instruction, *Neminem profecto*, issued by the Propaganda Fide on 23 November 1845. Primarily dedicated to the question of native clergy in the missions, *Neminem profecto* made references to the *Instruction* of 1659. Thenceforth, its significance came to light once again, so that subsequent instructions and directives used it as a template to reiterate the importance of indigenous clergy for the survival of the missions and the need for missionaries to stay away from colonial politics. For instance, the instruction *Quae a presulibus* of 18 October 1883 recalled the prohibition

---

27. Hastings, "In the Field," 84.

28. Marcocchi, *Colonialismo, Cristianesimo*, 45–46, 53; Bühlmann, "Passato e futuro," 580.

about getting involved in the political affairs of the mission country. Another instruction *Cum postremis* of 19 March 1893, in its reference to the *Instruction* of 1659, reminded missionary bishops, especially in India, of the need to solidify the formation and ordination of the indigenous clergy in that country. The stipulations of the *Instruction* of 1659 became, as it were, codified in the following pontifical documents of the twentieth century: *Maximum illud* by Benedict XV (1919), *Rerum ecclesiae* by Pius XI (1923), *Evangelii praecones* (1951) and *Fidei donum* (1957) by Pius XII, and *Princeps pastorum* (1959) by John XXIII.[29] The culminating point of that long evolution was the conciliar missionary document *Ad gentes* of the Second Vatican Council (1962–1965). The common thread that runs through these documents is unmistakably the felt need to root the Church in the native soil and local environment of the mission through the emergence of an indigenous clergy and a native hierarchy.

In terms of content, there slowly but progressively emerged a crystallization of the actual substance of *plantatio ecclesiae*. This happened after a lengthy period of evolution that lasted roughly three centuries. The point of departure can be said to have been between 1611 and 1615, when Paul V variously and consistently used the words *"plantetur et plantata"* in reference to mission and evangelization. As for the Propaganda Fide, with regard to the ideal and theory, it has, since its inception in 1622, always counted the presence of an indigenous or native clergy as the main kernel of *plantatio ecclesiae*. Therefore, it never missed any opportunity to return over and again to that thorny question that hanged heavily over Catholic missions in Latin America, Africa and Asia. Four years after its establishment, it directed a missionary bishop in Japan in 1626 to hasten the preparation and ordination of native Japanese priests. In its 1659 *Instruction* to first vicars apostolic, apart from cautioning them against transplanting the customs and practices of Europe to China, it asked them to "take every care in every way and with every argument to educate the youth in such a way that they will become fit for the priesthood and be ordained."[30]

Returning once again to the same issue in its instruction of 23 November 1845, the Propaganda Fide hinged upon the native clergy as the most important constituent of *plantatio ecclesiae*. It singled out two basic aspects on the matter: indigenous clergy should not be an auxiliary clergy to missionaries, and a serious formation was needed to prepare them for future leadership in the Church, including the episcopate.[31] As a matter of fact,

29. Marcocchi, *Colonialismo,Cristianesimo*, 58.
30. Cited in Müller, "The Main Principles of Centralized," 21.
31. Costantini, *Ricerche d'Archivio sull'Istruzione*, 75–76.

it identified at least fifteen different documents, in which Rome had severally and tirelessly recommended the creation of a native clergy in mission areas as the surest means to build an indigenous church. In particular, it highlighted the frustration of Pope Innocent in that regard who, at a point, even threatened to use "force" by means of canonical measures, in order to get the missionary vicars apostolic to comply with the directives of Rome on the preparation and ordination of indigenous clergy. In its own desperation, the Propaganda Fide, in that instruction of 1845, acknowledged with bitterness the obvious lack of progress on the matter: "Sad experience shows that all the labour spent without interruption on all this has not met with the result that the Apostolic See expected."[32] For some reasons, both tenable and otherwise, attempts to increase the number of native clergy in mission territories met a strong pushback, especially from the missionaries, and their opposition to it lasted well into the twentieth century.

In the first two decades of the twentieth century, as soon as the First World War (1914–1918) had ended, Pope Benedict XV, with his missionary apostolic letter *Maximum Illud*, launched, as it were, a courageous appeal for the missions whose personnel were adversely affected in terms of number and mobilization. For instance, it has been estimated that roughly 1,500,000 Christians in all the German colonies in Africa were at risk of being deprived of the pastoral services of the missionaries of German nationality, who were threatened with expulsion as the war gradually came to a halt.[33] That stark reality was further reinforced by the fact that Africa as a whole could only boast of roughly 145 native priests after the First World War.[34] His overall aim was a comprehensive and practical-oriented reform and reorganization of the Church's missions, especially in Asia and Africa. With hindsight, Benedict XV's *Maximum Illud* is widely acclaimed to have ushered in a new and bold phase in Catholic missionary activity for the whole of the twentieth century. It is also viewed as the first pontifical document to address missionary issues and related problems in their totality head-on. According to Andrzej Miotk, *Maximum Illud* is timeless in its historic importance, which is driven by its historical contextualization of missionary pitfalls and the basis of its biblical inspiration. In the same optic, all subsequent papal missionary documents have sought to emulate Benedict XV, to follow the pace set by him, and to regularly quote *Maximum Illud*.[35]

---

32. Cited in Müller, "The Main Principles of Centralized," 21.
33. Miotk, "The Historical Significance," 17.
34. Cited in Müller, "The Main Principles of Centralized," 22.
35. Miotk, "The Historical Significance," 14; Kroeger, "Papal Mission Wisdom," 94.

With the clarity of his mind and foresightedness, Benedict XV, with Cardinal Willem van Rossum by his side, understood that World War I had exposed the heavy dependence of the missions on Europe. It was from the purview of such a precarious dependence that he became determined to free the missions from the overburdens of European imperialism and colonialism. In their resolve to unhook the missions and to unleash their potentials, both Benedict XV and Van Rossum retrieved the dormant concept of *plantatio ecclesiae* from the annals of mission history. They refashioned it by rearticulating its basic tenets and put it forth as a new missionary guiding principle for the Church's missions in the immediate post-war period, and eventually up to the time of independence in Africa. Although the concept '*plantatio ecclesiae*' never appeared anywhere in *Maximum Illud*, allusions to the concept as well as its basic mainstays were unmistakably ubiquitous in the whole of the document. For instance, as was used in *Maximum Illud*, *plantatio ecclesiae* was presented as being synonymous with the training and ordination of an indigenous clergy that would be both numerically and qualitatively sufficient to shoulder the demands of local leadership in their local churches.[36]

The key idea was developed and woven around the four major contributions of Benedict XV's missionary document, namely centralization of the missions under the direction of Rome; depoliticizing of the missions; de-Europeanization of the missions, and theological shift in the overall ecclesial understanding of mission, which the pope identified and underlined to be the permanent job for the whole Church and not for an exclusive selected group of missionaries.[37] Benedict's clarity of vision and courageous initiative to devote an apostolic letter to the missionary problems of his time eventually paid off over time. That was possible because of the consistency and tenacity with which his successors pursued the outlaid program about the solidification of the training of indigenous clergy and the promotion of some of them to the bishopric. The unbroken chain of command in the implementation of that program ultimately led to the internationalization and the internal diversity of the Catholic world episcopate that manifested itself more clearly in the course of the twentieth century.[38]

Very outstanding in *Maximum Illud* was the introduction of the universal territorial maternity of the Church, which, according to Andre Seumois, was purposefully used to justify the important place and role

36. Seumois, "La Mission "Implantation," 40.
37. Miotk, "The Historical Significance," 24.
38. Schelkens et al., *Aggiornamento*, 96; Iheanacho, "*Maximum Illud* and its Relevance," 87.

of the native clergy in both their emerging local churches and the Universal Church. It became an added component of *plantatio ecclesiae* and very useful in missionary methodology, with the consequence impacting on a missionary change of outlook and orientation towards the emerging churches.[39] It is pertinent to acknowledge that the drafters of *Maximum Illud*, being a pioneer document in uncharted routes in the early twentieth century, found it practically impossible to articulate comprehensively all the intricacies of *plantatio ecclesiae* as a missionary principle. In that regard, further clarifications of the concept and its use only materialized with subsequent papal documents and those issued by the Propaganda Fide. For instance, bearing the imprints of Cardinal Van Rossum, the clarification about *plantatio ecclesiae* loomed very large in Propaganda Fide's letter of 20 May 1923 to superiors of missionary congregations and institutes. It emphasized the primary object or goal of missionary activity as the foundation of an indigenous church. This implied the formation of both an indigenous clergy and physical structures such as church buildings, schools and hospitals:

> It is of the utmost importance that the superiors of the missions entrusted to their congregations should give every attention to the training of an indigenous clergy. This is indeed necessary because the various territories have been entrusted to them with the view of founding and building up the church there. The conversion of non-believers is but the start, the first stone of this building. The formation of the Christian community must follow with its own chapels, or churches, with the foundation (and possibly the endowment) of schools, orphanages, asylums, hospitals and other works. This, however, must be followed, or rather accompanied by the training of an indigenous clergy and indigenous religious communities of both sexes[40].

As two sides of the same coin at the core of *plantatio ecclesiae*, the question of establishing local churches and the formation of a native clergy to lead them was always a perennial problem in the history of Catholic missions beyond the shores of Europe. It did not cease with the publication of *Maximum Illud*. It was even greeted with passive resistance in some places and outright rejection in others, in the belief that Benedict XV was misled in bringing the question to the centre of missionary considerations. Notwithstanding the resistance, the reintroduction and repositioning of *plantatio ecclesiae* by Benedict XV made it possible that the concept acted as a kind of guide for over half a century for his immediate successors. Similarly,

---

39. Seumois, "La Mission "Implantation," 40.
40. Cited in Müller, "The Main Principles of Centralized," 22.

Maximum Illud itself also became like a guidebook for the Propaganda Fide, as can easily be deciphered from many of its directives and policies such as the instructions of 6 January 1920 and 20 May 1923. That of 1920 dwelt particularly on the construction of local seminaries and instructed that the clergy should receive a tripartite formation: scientific, practical and psychological. Scientific entailed courses in missiology, which was then a nascent theological discipline, and non-theological studies such as linguistics and even medicine! Practical stood for adequate preparation in language skills acquisition to enable them to learn local languages for the propagation of the Gospel. Psychological was intended for the formation of character, where the clergy was expected to be alert, attentive, efficient and aglow with pastoral charity. As far as the Propaganda Fide was concerned, all three areas of formation were prerequisites for the effective actualization of *plantatio ecclesiae*.[41]

As for the papacy post-Benedict XV, he bequeathed contemporary papacy with a high sense of missionary responsibility. It was impossible for his successors on the papal throne to turn back the hands of the clock after his pontificate. As a result, from Benedict XV onwards, the Holy See became evermore determined to assert exclusive papal authority over the entire missions of the Church and thus bring them squarely under the direct control of Rome.[42] Their collective charisma and missionary interest were decisive elements that reshaped Catholic missions for the greater part of the twentieth century.[43] In that regard, the first pope to inherit that missionary bequest was Pius XI who was very deeply committed to the missions, with his insistence that superiors of missionary congregations and institutes ought to increase their share in foreign missions, but under the initiative and direction of Rome.[44]

With a reorientation of Catholic missionary theology and praxis already introduced by his predecessor, Pius XI adopted a new approach to native Christian communities in mission areas, by promoting native priests in some countries to the episcopate. By leaving Cardinal Van Rossum as the Prefect of the Propaganda Fide (appointed by Benedict in 1918), Pius XI helped strengthen further the importance of that Roman mission congregation under whose leadership the dicastery was very influential in the implantation of the new policy.[45] Van Rossum was both an initiator and an

---

41. Miotk, "The Historical Significance," 31.
42. Miotk, "The Historical Significance," 27.
43. Iacobelli, "The Vatican's Shift," 92.
44. Latourette, *Christianity in a Revolutionary Age*, 43–44.
45. Schelkens et al., *Aggiornamento?*, 96; Iacobelli, "The Vatican's Shift," 93. For the

executor of missionary policies for Benedict XV and Pius XI, with whom he shared a strong passion for the missions. In a parallel to Raffaello Sanzio's portrait of Leo X and his two influential cardinals, Alexandre Brou, at the death of Van Rossum in 1932, painted a similar picture about the cardinal and the two popes during whose pontificates he piloted the affairs of the Propaganda Fide. Brou was convinced that Cardinal Van Rossum would feature very prominently whenever the history of the missions was written in relation to the two pontiffs:

> That of the missions would portray Benedict XV and Pius XI: of this portrait, the Redemptorist Cardinal cannot be absent, a little behind, as appropriate, because after all, he was especially the executing arm, but all the same, less sacrificed than those of the *Porporati* of Leo X, because his role, subordinate as it may have been, was actually a leading role[46].

The permanence of Van Rossum at the Propaganda Fide was one of the continuities between the pontificate of Benedict XV and Pius XI with regard to the missions. In his own missionary encyclical, *Rerum Ecclesiae* of 28 February 1926, Pius XI took up and treated to a deeper degree some of the issues that were already raised in *Maximum Illud*. He added new elements such as the encouragement for the establishment of indigenous religious orders and congregations as well as the erection of seminaries in mission areas. It was more like reinforcing and building upon the foundations already laid by his predecessor, when he reiterated that the building up of a local or native clergy was judged as an indispensable brick for the establishment and organization of the local church (*Rerum Ecclesiae* no. 19). Although without concretely using the term, Pius XI underscored the aim of mission as *plantatio ecclesiae*. In that sense, missionaries were sent to work for the foundation and establishment of the Church in boundless regions of the world and this, according to him, was not achievable without the native clergy (*Rerum Ecclesiae* no. 21).

As the hurtful experiences in Japan and China still haunted the missionary memory of the Church, Pius XI demanded the formation of the native clergy in mission territories as quickly as possible, adding that their formation must be of a standard as befitting "priests who would one day govern parishes and dioceses" (*Rerum Ecclesiae* no. 25). A very curious *caveat* in the encyclical is found in number 26, where he frowned on the racial

---

work and contributions of the Dutch Cardinal Van Rossum, see Drehmanns, *Kardinal van Rossum*, 85–86; Prudhomme, "Le Cardinal van Rossum," 215–228.

46. The original is in French. Alexandre Brou, "L'œuvre du Cardinal van Rossum," 356. English translation from Iheanacho, *Maximum illud and Benedict XV*, 219.

discrimination meted out against the native clergy who were considered, in some missionary quarters, inferior and belonging to a lower grade of priestly ordination. As if meaning to give a lecture on the common ministerial priesthood of the ordained, Pius XI let it be known that the native clergy were both ordained in the same priesthood and admitted into the same apostolate as the missionaries. He insisted that there should never be any discrimination and any line of racial demarcation between indigenous clergy and missionaries.

Pius XI's injunction in itself speaks volumes about the racial tension that existed among the rank and file of Church personnel in mission fields in Africa and elsewhere. Sadly, as late as 1945 and 1946, when the Propaganda Fide tasked Père Henri Prouvost (MEP) to undertake apostolic visitations on its behalf in French Africa, apostolic visitors could still observe racial tensions between the missionaries and the indigenous clergy. In his report on the visitations, which were undertaken from 15 December 1945 to 15 August 1946, Père Prouvost remarked that the indigenous clergy were regarded as "inferior." He equally noted variously across board some of the disparaging terms used by the missionaries in reference to Black African priests. For instance, they were called "minors" or "juniors" in Cameroon, "servants" in Upper Volta, and "slaves" in Guinea. In Congo Brazzaville, decisions were made without their participation and consultation. Père Prouvost singled out the ill-treatment of Black priests in Gabon, where the bishop refused to treat them with respect as he would treat White missionaries. Finally, in Senegal, even indigenous members of religious congregations were not "members" as such, because their "half membership" did not offer them the possibility of becoming superiors of their various communities.[47] In South Africa, over many years, as Adrian Hastings rightly observed, while the local church was overwhelmingly Black in membership, its leadership remained overwhelmingly White in power.[48] Of course, as in everything human, fine words are hardly matched by actions, since reality is often way different from theoretical insistence on racial equality.

Equally worthy of note is Rome's determination to divide or transfer mission territories from one congregation to another. As a man known to see his order executed without much questioning, Pius XI reminded missionary congregations that the Holy See would transfer or divide mission territories among different institutes and pass over some territories to the indigenous clergy, if and when it deemed necessary (*Rerum Ecclesiae* no. 31).

47. Brasseur, "L'Église Catholique et la Décolonisation," 54; Foster, *African Catholic*, 28–34.
48. Hastings, *A History of African Christianity*, 241.

This last part of the encyclical was meant to signal a warning to missionary congregations and institutes that the era of missionary congregationalism or religious corporatism was over. Unfortunately, missionary congregationalism and religious corporatism became the unintended consequence of the mission system of *ius commissionis* that did not make room for missionary collaboration among Catholic missionaries and also manifested itself in the missionaries' unwillingness to adequately prepare the local clergy that would assume leadership positions in the local churches.

The much-despised religious corporatism operated in such a manner that the corporate spirit of a particular missionary congregation or institute tended to prevail in clear opposition to the overall missionary interest of the Church at large. It created the "stranger" status for anyone who was not a member of a missionary congregation in a mission territory entrusted by the Holy See to that same congregation. What is not often mentioned in the complaint and lamentation against missionary congregationalism and corporatism is the role of Rome in that missionary structure. In the critical position of Vittorio Bartoccetti on the issue, the *ius commissionis* system was put in operation by Rome and it also required a decisive juridical act by the same Rome to put an end to it.[49] Its shortcoming in that regard created a big lacuna in its missionary strategy, which resulted overtime in the absence of a high level of indigenous clergy with the aim of freeing the missions either from the exclusive control of the powerful missionary congregations and institutes or even altogether from the heavy foreign trappings, with which the missions were enrobed. In this light, the insistence of Pius XI on increasing the number of seminaries in missionaries was generally understood as a way of emancipating local churches from Western domination. The creation of seminaries, as a visible sign and organization of the church planted in a local area or community, was also considered to be the very first duty of missionaries.[50]

Like the question of the ordination of the indigenous clergy, the issue of jurisdiction was also a thorny issue for the most part in the history of Catholic missions. The first known case of the Holy See's concession to a missionary congregation, with the exclusive right to work in a vast area alone, is traceable to 1585. The Jesuits, through a papal bull, were permitted to be the only congregation to evangelize China. That bull was only receded through another papal bull in 1633 by Pope Urban VIII.[51] The system of commission as a missionary structure became codified between 1827 and

---

49. Bartoccetti, "L'elemento giuridico," 302.
50. Iacobelli, "The Vatican's Shift," 95; Kroeger, "Papal Mission Wisdom," 95.
51. Wiest, "Learning from the Missionary Past," 194.

1836.[52] Given its historical background, mere pronouncements and pious lamentations as well as entreaties were in themselves meaningless and powerless to effect the desired change in the legal missionary structure of the time, because the blame was not only that of missionary congregations. Due to no fault of theirs, the commission mission system that was sanctioned by Rome seemed to have accorded religious orders and missionary institutes the right to exclusive or permanent title to the mission areas entrusted to them.

In fact, it functioned more like a kind of "charter," whereby the Holy See empowered a missionary congregation with the exclusive right or responsibility to build and administer a would-be church in any given mission area on behalf of Rome.[53] Consequent upon that, it stands reasonable to conclude that the continuous failures on the part of Rome to show a decisive leadership by revoking what it had conceded to missionary congregations and institutes only served to prolong the never-ending tutelage of the indigenous clergy in mission areas, of which Africa was not an exception.[54] Four months after the publication of *Rerum Ecclesiae*, Pius XI returned to the issue of establishing the local church in a letter dated 15 June 1926 and addressed to the apostolic vicars and prefects in China. He reminded them that the core of missionary activity consisted in the establishment and foundation of the local church. The attainment of that desired end or goal was dependent on the formation of an indigenous clergy in the area.[55]

FLOWERING OF THE CONCEPT UNDER POPE PIUS XII

The simplest articulation of the ultimate goal of *plantatio ecclesiae*, as articulated by Benedict XV and Pius XI, was again taken up and further developed by Pius XII, under whom the concept reached its climax with regard to its enunciation in pontifical considerations and papal documents on mission. Pius XII first used it on 30 April 1939 in his address to the leaders of the Pontifical Mission Societies, where he indicated that the final goal of missionary activity was to establish the local church and to provide it with its own hierarchy chosen from among the natives. The clearest of papal thoughts on *plantatio ecclesiae* became evident in another allocution of Pius XII on 24 June 1944, which he delivered to members of the Propaganda Fide and the directors of the Pontifical Mission Societies. In very

52. Comby, *Duemila Anni di Evangelizzazione*, 220.
53. Kalilombe, "The African local churches," 80.
54. Bartoccetti, "L'elemento giuridico," 302–304.
55. Seumois, "La Mission "Implantation," 41.

clear terms, Pius XII declared that missionary activity as such was not only that of the missionaries in faraway mission lands nor that of the Propaganda Fide. This was a major theme that runs through most of Pius XII's missionary speeches and exhortations:

> The great purpose of the Missions is to establish the Church in new lands and to make them take root there so much so that one day it can live and develop without the support of the Work of the Missions. The Work of the Missions is not an end in itself: it waits with ardor for that high goal but withdraws when this has been achieved[56].

The thought pattern of Pius XII on *plantatio ecclesiae* was consistent in various allocutions and exhortations on the missionary activity of the Church. That much was evident in the exhortation to the indigenous clergy, on the occasion of the inauguration of the Collegio San Pietro on the Ganicolo Hill in Rome, on 28 June 1948. As a missionary college, it housed student priests from missionary territories under the jurisdiction of the Propaganda Fide. Many indigenous African priests lived in that college during their years of study in various pontifical universities in the eternal city. In welcoming the students to that inauguration ceremony, Pius XII described the indigenous clergy as "the flower of the missionary apostolate" and acknowledged that,

> [a]lready in many places, in fact, thanks to the tireless and assiduous work of the heralds of Christ, the sacred Missions, have almost achieved that purpose, which is proper to them: the establishment of the Church in new lands. It has developed and deeply rooted those places in a way that it can live prosperously by itself and freely grow without the help of foreign priests[57].

In one of his allocutions in 1950, Pius XII referred to his discourse of 24 June 1944 and reiterated once again that the noble end or purpose of missionary work was "to firmly establish the Church in foreign lands so that it can take deep roots so as to develop by itself and flourish."[58] Besides these discourses, Pius XII also published two encyclicals on the missionary activity of the Church: *Evangelii Praecones* (2 June 1951) and *Fidei Donum* (21 April 1957). He also wrote two letters to the suffering church under communist dictatorship in China: *Cupimus Imprimis* (18 January 1952) and *Ad*

---

56. Pius XII, *Alle Pontificie Opere Missionarie*, no. 2.
57. Pius XII, *In Auspicando Super*, §2.
58. Bate, *Missiology Notes*, 51; Seumois, "La Mission "Implantation," 41–42.

sinarum gentes[59] (18 January 1954). Although specifically addressed to the Chinese Church, the two letters are important in understanding the missionary thought of Pius XII, because he raised the issue of *plantatio ecclesiae*. The pope treated the issue of *plantatio ecclesiae* in all four documents in various ways. He stressed that it was the very basis upon which any reputable missionary activity rose and fell.

From the evolutionary point of view, all four documents and the six other related missionary documents by Pius XII could be described collectively as the very apex of the Church's understanding of *plantatio ecclesiae*. As a concept, *plantatio ecclesiae*, interpreted as indigenization, became the nucleus of the Holy See's missionary policy in Africa from the 1950s, with the purpose of launching the Church into a post-missionary phase of Catholic evangelization on the continent. *Fide Donum* was meant to achieve that goal, because it was specifically written with Africa in mind, with the aim of drawing the attention of the whole Church to the urgent missionary needs of the young Church in an emerging young continent at the time.[60]

Pius XII's major mission encyclical of universal import is without doubt *Evangelii Praecones*, in which he recognized the growing number of "native or indigenous bishops" in various places in the emerging continents of Asia and Africa. He noted with satisfaction the increasing number of indigenous priests that rose from 14,800 in 1926, when *Rerum Ecclesiae* was published by Pius XI, to 26,800 in 1951, while roughly eighty-eight mission circumscriptions had been transferred from missionaries to indigenous clergy.[61] Indeed, while progress had obviously been made towards the indigenization of the Church in mission areas, the pope remarked that a great deal still needed to be accomplished, especially in the erection of local hierarchies. Aware of what still remained unaccomplished, the pope outlined seven principles or norms of missionary activity, which he masterfully wove around a twofold goal of missionary activity: land of mission becomes the home of a missionary; specialized training for missionaries; formation of a native clergy and establishment of an indigenous hierarchy; greater involvement of the laity; interest in social reforms, as dictated and inspired by justice and charity; missionary cooperation, as well as appreciation and Christianization of positive elements in local customs and practices.[62] All these were articulated within Pius XII's vision for the Church and anchored

---

59. In the official rating, *Ad sinarum gentes* is categorized as an encyclical letter.
60. Kroeger, "Papal Mission Wisdom," 97.
61. Metzler, "La Santa Sede e le missioni," 89.
62. Kroeger, "Papal Mission Wisdom," 97.

on the dual principal aims of missionary undertaking that issued forth from *plantatio ecclesiae*:

> The magnanimous and noble purpose which missionaries have is the propagation of the faith in new lands in such a way that the church may ever become more firmly established in them, and as soon as possible reach such a stage of development that it can continue to exist and flourish without the aid of missionary organisations (*Evangelii Praecones* no. 24).

Against the background of the persecution of the Church in China by Mao Zedong's repressive communist government, Pius XII wrote *Cupimus Imprimis* on 18 January 1952, which he addressed to the persecuted Chinese Church. The missionary relevance of that letter concerns the ample space that the pope allotted to *plantatio ecclesiae* in his efforts to explain the role and place of the Church in any given local environment. In explication of Pius XII, the heralds of the Gospel had no other intention, apart from the mission, to bring the light of Christ's teaching to people everywhere. When that has been accomplished, missionaries will take a backseat:

> little by little as the number of native clergy increases among you, enable it to reach full maturity, where the aid and collaboration of foreign missionaries will be no longer necessary[63].

The pope took up a similar argument in *Ad sinarum gentes,* in which he exhorted Chinese Catholics to be loyal to their civil government and to obey it in all matters within its moral and political competence. On the accusation against missionaries as mercenaries of some foreign government, Pius XII recalled the content of his 1952 letter. In his defense of missionaries against the communist calumnies, he reiterated the primary aim of missionary work as that of preaching the Gospel and establishing the local church with its local particularities, which he as the pope earnestly and constantly desired and solicited in his prayers:

> We desire, then, that the day may soon come—for this We send up to God most ardent petitions and suppliant prayers—when Bishops and priests of your own nation and in sufficient number can govern the Catholic Church in your immense country, and when there will no longer be need of help from foreign missionaries in your apostolate[64].

---

63. Pius XII, *Cupimus Imprimis*, §8; see also Connolly, "Pope Pius XII and Foreign Missions," 151.

64. Pius XII, *Ad Sinarum Gentum*, no. 9.

A similar line of thought was particularly evident in his radio message, on 29 April 1951, to the bishops and faithful of South Africa on the erection of a national hierarchy in that country. He underscored the need for the local church to foster indigenous vocation to the priesthood, if it must survive and face future challenges:

> If the Church in South Africa is to meet the challenge of the future successfully, there must be a marked increase in the number of native clergy. When the Church is served and governed by priests and bishops of your own nation, thoroughly trained in the sacred sciences and deeply grounded in the spiritual life, then will the hopes and prayers of the early missionaries be fulfilled; then their long years of toil and sacrifice amid perils and privations, will have received a recompense a hundred-fold[65].

For Africa as a whole, the amiable attention of Pius XII towards the continent was made manifest once again in 1957, when he wrote his last missionary encyclical and dedicated it to the continent, where he saw that the brightest hope for the Church was steadily on the rise. From the missionary perspective, the 1950s were regarded as the "decade of Africa." Among other considerations, the decision of Pius XII to release *Fidei Donum* on Easter Sunday, 21 April 1957, was carefully done with the intention to accentuate the strong connection between mission and Easter-Pentecost, in order to reflect that bright hope on the horizon, which the pontiff perceptively discerned in the emerging young churches in Africa. Eighteen years earlier, in 1939, he elevated two African native priests to the bishopric. They became the first African bishops in the contemporary time. In the early years of the 1950s, he created national hierarchies in all of sub-Saharan Africa as well as apostolic delegations in the different colonial territories in Africa, in order to better coordinate the diversity of Catholic missionary activities on the continent.

Perhaps, it may not be out of place to say that his parting gift to Africa and the last manifestation of his love for the continent remains *Fidei Donum*, which incidentally also became one of his enduring legacies. Archbishop Marcel Lefebvre, in his capacity as Papal Delegate in French Africa, is believed to have made a significant contribution in the writing of *Fidei Donum*. Pius XII showed a great deal of deference to the missionary insight of the French missionary prelate. Lefebvre was one of Pius XII's trusted advisers on missionary issues, especially those pertaining to the missions in Africa.[66] With the document's stress on the catholicity of the Church,

---

65. Pius XII, *All'Episcopato e ai fedeli del Sud Africa*, §4.
66. Mutig, "Archbishop Lefebvre Defies," §19–20 . See also Foster, *African Catholic*,

Pius XII's invitation for diocesan priests to volunteer and serve in mission gave the contemporary Church another category of mission personnel, now known as "Fidei Donum Priests." This would not have been possible without Pius XII's affective attention for Africa anchored in his unwavering conviction: "A Christian community which gives its sons and daughters to the Church cannot die."[67] Hence, he invited every Catholic to be involved in a triple commitment towards the missions: prayer, financial contribution, and an increase in vocations to the priesthood and religious life. He also solicited the assistance of national directors of the Pontifical Mission Societies to help student priests and seminarians from missionaries who were studying in Europe at various Catholic universities.[68] But above all, the most remarkable of those various initiatives has remained the encouragement of Pius XII to diocesan priests to serve in missions that have stood the test of time.[69] This has had the positive effect of pairing some materially poor dioceses with wealthy ones in Europe and America. The result has benefited the sister churches concerned in terms of reciprocity. In recent times, with the scarcity of priestly vocations in the older churches, many priests from

---

263. With the dwindling of his ecclesiastical star, which he himself described as the "fall of my star," Lefebvre noted with bitterness that Pope John XXIII did not value him as much as Pope Pius XII did. He even mused that Pius XII would have made him a cardinal, had the pontiff lived slightly longer.

67. Kroeger, "Papal MissionWisdom," 98.

68. Metzler, "La Santa Sede e le missioni," 91.

69. In their critical study and analysis of the pontificate of Pius XII, Schelkens et al., *Aggiornamento?*, 101–126, did not assign even a paragraph to the missionary initiatives of Pius XII. There is no doubt that there are some controversial aspects of his pontificate such as his distrusting attitude towards the then emerging new currents and developments in theology. The question on the Second World War (1939–1945) and whether or not the response of Pius XII was adequate tend to eclipse other important aspects of his pontificate. Similarly, the pontificate of Benedict XV was, until recently, also beclouded by the questions of the First World War. But, thanks to a wider perspective of research, that pontificate is now being studied from multiple fronts. It is equally important to remember that any pontificate is much bigger than any single issue or policy that may tend to colour judgements and views about any pope within a milieu. Each pope is often faced with a complexity of issues that may require his attention, besides the corresponding policies in addressing issues and challenges. From the missionary perspective, it is possible to affirm this much about Pius XII in relation to his two immediate predecessor. If Benedict XV and Pius XI are regarded as founders of contemporary Catholic missions, Pius XII also shares that privilege and responsibility with them. His pontificate, as far as the missions are concerned, marked the point of arrival and the flowering of all previous papal missionary policies and initiatives. He saw to it that the tempo on the indigenisation of the Church in mission areas, especially in Africa, was maintained and even brought to completion sometime against the protestation of missionary congregations and other political interests.

Africa and Asia now go to serve in those places in return for the generous gestures of the former days.

Within his ecclesial vision and as had become his custom throughout his pontificate, Pius XII revisited the issue of *plantatio ecclesiae*. After drawing up an overview of the great progress it had made in Africa in terms of Catholic missionary outreach and efforts to root the Church on the continent, he drew the attention of the Catholic world to the increasing number of Catholic faithful in Africa. But, as he noted, the number of priests paled into insignificance in comparison to the pastoral needs of the growing population of the lay faithful.[70] Against that background, he asked for the cooperation of the entire Church, while identifying mission as an integral aspect of the catholicity of the Church. This was only realizable through *plantatio ecclesiae*, with the ultimate goal that "the Church should be solidly established among other peoples, and a Hierarchy given to them chosen from among their own sons" (*Fidei Donum* no. 9). In order to safeguard the catholicity of the local church in communion with the Universal Church and forestall the danger of isolationism, Pius XII insisted that the establishment of a native hierarchy was not an end in itself and certainly not the end of mission or missionary activities (*Fidei Donum* no. 11).

---

70. Kroeger, "Papal Mission Wisdom," 97.

4

From missionary tutelage to indigenization[1]

Fourteen years after the end of the Second Vatican Council (1962–1965), the erudite German theologian Karl Rahner sought to give a theological interpretation of that Council. His thoughts were laid bare in an address he delivered on 8 April 1979 at an academic convocation in the Weston School of Theology in Cambridge, Massachusetts. From the theological standpoint, Rahner argued for a triple division of Church history to sustain his basic conclusion that the "world Church" had always been in "potency," until it was finally actualized in Vatican II. Rahner identified the first epoch as the transition from Jewish Christianity to Gentile Christianity, when it expanded on the soil of paganism. The second epoch involved a break that led to a transition from antiquity to the Middle Ages. This, in turn, entailed a substitution of Hellenism with European culture and civilization. The same transition leap continued from its medieval cultural embryo to the time of the European Enlightenment and European colonialism. In the third and final epoch, Christianity made a big leap from a Christianity of Europe (with its American annexes) to a full world religion, which, in turn, enhanced the potentiality of the Church to become a full-fledged "World Church."[2]

---

1. A significant part of this chapter was published in two journals: *Studia Historiae Ecclesiasticae* and *Abuja Journal of Philosophy and Theology*. See Iheanacho, "*Plantatio Ecclesiae* in Africa," 1–17; Iheanacho, "*Maximum Illud* and the African Church," 25–40, respectively.

2. Rahner, "Towards a Fundamental Theological," 717–719.

The actualization of a "World Church," in the affirmation of Rahner, took time in the making, as it entailed a very long historical process. Its origins are traceable to the beginning of the European colonization and the modern world mission of the Church that began in earnest from the beginning of the sixteenth century. According to Rahner, Vatican II was the first major official event whereby the Church sought to actualize her potency as a World Church. At this Council, which took place during the third epoch, the Church no longer appeared as the Church of the West with its American sphere of influence, with mere extensions and tentacles in Asia and Africa. From the evolutionary perspective, there emerged the "genotype" of a "World Church" from a "phenotype" of a European and North American Church. For instance, at Vatican I (1869–1870), there was no representation of an indigenous episcopate from anywhere in the Catholic world, as was the case at Vatican II, even though the proportion of representation was heavily in favor of the Western episcopate, and the African dances were certainly not presented at the Vatican.[3]

No matter how few there might have been, there was, nonetheless, a worldwide episcopate of a "World Church" with all its components.[4] Africa was present at Vatican II, with its one cardinal in the person of Cardinal Laurian Rugambwa of Tanganyika (Tanzania), created Cardinal by Pope John XXIII in the consistory of 28 March 1960. There were also seventy-four other African bishops. At the last session in 1965, many of the young indigenous bishops had become metropolitan archbishops of important ecclesiastical seats in Africa.[5] Such a representation was unimaginable a century earlier at Vatican I, when the whole of Africa was but a virgin land in terms of both the European scramble and the Christian evangelization of the continent. Progressively and without any doubt, as once rightly underscored by David Matthew, the evolution and consolidation of African Catholic priesthood has been one of the mainstays of Catholicism in Africa, and remained one of its essential and defining features.[6]

It will be recalled that the process that led to that world episcopate at Vatican II was timidly and reluctantly proceeded by the ordination of indigenous bishops in mission territories. This was met with pockets of resistance, here and there in some missionary quarters, which reflected deep-seated convictions and orientations that were sustained by racial and cultural prejudices of the epoch. The Church does not exist in a vacuum. It has a historical

---

3. Rahner, "Towards a Fundamental Theological," 720–722.
4. Rahner, "Towards a Fundamental Theological," 720–722.
5. Robert, "The Development of the Local Clergy," 85.
6. Mathew, "Catholicism in Africa," 3.

existence within a milieu. Located within concrete historical situations, the Church shares the ambiguities of each historical epoch. Without consciously intending it, the Church, with its Eurocentric worldview, through its missionary foot soldiers, exported European Christianity together with its culture and civilization. With the aim of mission understood as *plantatio ecclesiae* (planting of the church) and the saving of the souls of infidels, the Church somehow also participated in the European project of conquest and expansion.[7] With particular reference to the Franco-African Catholic world, which, to a large extent, reflects the wider Catholic experience elsewhere in Africa, Elizabeth Foster describes that world as being "forged by conquest, colonization, missions, and conversions, and knit together by Catholic faith, Catholic education, Catholic press and Catholic charities."[8]

Perceptively, colonization, mission, conversion, and education prepared the ground, from which the Catholic Church in Africa emerged in the course of the long nineteenth century. During that time, much of the contours and basic features of the Catholic Church in Africa took shape. They mirrored the contours and basic traits of Catholicism at the time. It was a period when Catholicism was chiefly shaped by "the almost unmitigated triumph of Ultramontanism, the concentration of authority in the papacy and the unquestioned recognition of other papal prerogatives."[9] According to John O'Malley, the missions in Africa and Asia were beneficiaries of the rebounding of Catholicism in Europe during the long nineteenth century, which not only ended at Vatican II, but also acted as the fulfillment of certain aspects of the century. The remarkable flourishing of religious men and women who went on missions from Europe reported back to their base the numerous conversions to the faith, especially in Africa, where those conversions were nothing but unprecedented in the history of Christianity.[10]

One of the positive effects of the Roman centralization on the missions in Africa is noticeable in the growth of the Catholic Church in Africa, which is attributable to the vigorous missionary outreach inspired and animated by the popes. Those missions were personally directed by the popes through the Propaganda Fide until Vatican II, when the Council broadened missionary responsibility with its emphasis on episcopal collegiality.[11] Prior to that broadening of vision, the Propaganda Fide extended its influence in Africa through the missionary congregations that sprang up in the nineteenth

7. Kaggwa, "The New Catholicity," 189.
8. Foster, *African Catholic*, 6.
9. O'Malley, *What Happened at Vatican II*, 57.
10. O'Malley, *What Happened at Vatican II*, 53.
11. Hickey, *Modern Missionary Documents and Africa*, 3.

century and were completely at the disposal of the Roman dicastery in charge of the missions.[12] Notably, in the long nineteenth century, the voice of the pope was heard for the first time ever in Africa through radio transmission. On 24 February 1951, on the occasion of the Eucharistic Congress held in Kumasi, Gold Coast (Ghana), Pope Pius XII addressed the assembly with these words:

> Venerable brothers and dearly beloved of Africa, our heart fills with an unwonted joy as we reflect that our voice is reaching tens of thousands of our devoted children of the Gold Coast gathered together for the first Eucharistic Congress of that region, presided over by our worthy Legate . . . More than beautiful, your cathedral is eloquent; and what a thrilling story it tells of God's incessant love, of missionary zeal undaunted and unquenchable, from the days when the first members of the Society of African Missions prepared the field for the erection of a vicariate apostolic fifty years to the ever memorable year of Jubilee, when it was our privilege and consolation to erect the Hierarchy of British West Africa[13].

In broad terms, this chapter examines the development and growth of the nascent Church in Africa through its teething stage, as it made its journey through missionary tutelage to its coming of age under the leadership of African indigenous clergy. It is believed that the Catholic Church in Africa attained its definitive maturity between 1969 and 1974. One significant event in 1969 was the papal visit of Pope Paul VI (1963–1978) to the continent. He was the first pope to visit Africa. In the course of this pastoral visit, which took him to Kampala in Uganda, he acknowledged in his homily of 31 July 1969, at the closing Mass for the First Plenary Assembly of SECAM (Symposium of Episcopal Conferences of Africa and Madagascar), that the Catholic Church was "well and truly planted in the blessed African soil." He remarked that his visit and presence in Africa bore the imprints of the recognition of the maturity of the African Church. In that same homily, he recalled the history of the missionary labors that gave birth to the local Church, which he described as a history that was replete with "a drama of charity, heroism and sacrifice." As Africans were then assuming its direction, he impressed upon them the responsibility "to continue to build it, hierarchy and then the Holy Spirit (that is, grace with all its charisms), dynamically working together, for a native indigenous apostolate."[14]

12. Müller, "The Main Principles of Centralized," 14.
13. Bane, *The Popes and West Africa*, 63–64.
14. Paul VI, *Homily*, §9.

If 1969 saw the first papal visit to Africa, 1974 became a watershed moment in the history of the local Church in Africa. It equally took place during the pontificate of Paul VI at the Synod of Bishops on "Evangelization of the Modern World," held from 27 September to 26 October 1974. This is in view of the fact that the structures of the 1974 Synod of Bishops in Rome raised the status of the African Church in relation to other churches in the world. Cardinal Paul Zoungrana of Ouagadougou was one of the three papal delegates who presided at the 1974 Synod and Bishop James D. Sangu of Mbeya was one of the Synod *relatores*.[15] Cardinals Zoungrana (1917–2000) and Owen McCann (1907–1994) were the second set of African Cardinals after Cardinal Rugambwa. Cardinal McCann was the first cardinal from South Africa in the history of that local church. Together with Cardinal Léon-Étienne Duval (1903–1996) of Algiers, all three received the red beret from Paul VI on 25 February 1965.[16] The African Church gradually but steadily began to emerge as a force to be reckoned with, particularly on the basis of its numerical strength. It equally emerged that it was impossible to ignore or sideline the young Church. As at 1974, the huge number of African Catholics was put at forty-two million (12 percent of the total population of Africa), distributed in forty-nine archdioceses and 356 dioceses with about 17,180 priests (both indigenous and missionary priests). In real terms, the Church in Africa had a share of roughly 4.1 percent overall global number of Catholic priests of 420,429,[17] with its 220 native African bishops and eight cardinals.[18]

LAYING THE FOUNDATION FOR INDIGENIZATION

Dr Majola Agbedi was among the earliest founders of Ethiopianism. After the severance of ties with the American Baptists and the foundation in 1888 of an indigenous church known as the Native Baptist Church, the prolific Nigerian writer disseminated a pamphlet, which he had written and entitled "Africa and the Gospel." As radical as he could possibly be, he even changed his name from Vincent David to Majola Agbedi to underline the fact that there was no contradiction being an African and a Christian simultaneously. In the pamphlet, Dr Agbedi anticipated by over sixty years the fate that would befall the mainline missionary churches, if they failed to indigenize. Most importantly, and almost with the eyes of a visionary, he was convinced

15. Onaiyekan, "Paul VI and the Church in Africa," 106.
16. Miranda, "Cardinals of the Holy Roman Church," nos. 10, 11 and 16.
17. Sangu, *Report on the Experiences of the Church*, 9.
18. 1975 statistics, as cited by Robert, "The Development of the Local Clergy," 89.

that indigenization of the Gospel in Africa and in ecclesiastical personnel was the only veritable means to render Christianity truly African. Agbedi's remarkable sagacity and the rudiments of movements for the Africanization of Christianity are discernable in that pamphlet:

> To render Christianity indigenous to Africans it must be watered by native hands, pruned with native hatchets, and tendered with native earth.... It is a curse if we intend for ever to hold on to the apron strings of foreign teachers, doing baby for aye[19].

What the Catholic Church was struggling to realize for its scattered missions in Africa between 1950 and 1960 was to implement the great missionary insight of Majola Agbedi. However, before it could proceed smoothly on that course of action, the official Church and its missionaries needed to clarify basic concepts and goals that would underpin and guide their missionary undertaking. This clarification was needed, in order to avoid the mistakes that occurred in Japan and China. The earliest of Catholic missionary enterprises in both empires faded without leaving behind significant traces. Sadly, that happened due to the absence of indigenous priests. The flowering Japanese Church was snuffed out with sustained persecutions that began in 1597. With regard to China, the efforts made by the Nestorian Church in the ninth century or those by the Catholic Church were never successful.

First came the Franciscan friars in the fourteenth century, followed by the Jesuits in the sixteenth century. In all, their missionary undertakings never truly yielded much, since Christianity in the Dragon Empire remained largely a foreign religion of foreigners permitted to reside in China on the basis of their usefulness to the ruling dynasty. In his summation of such colossal failures, Canon Léon Joly published a two-volume work in Paris in 1907 entitled *Le christianisme et l'Extrême Orient: Missions Catholiques de l'Inde, de l'Indo-Chine, de la Chine, de la Corée* (volume I) and *Mission Catholique du Japon* (volume II). As far as Canon Joly was concerned, the missions in those places failed woefully for lack of sufficient number of indigenous priests and, more specifically, the absolute absence of native bishops who could have sustained their local churches when the missionaries were either expelled or martyred.[20] Japan sadly but firmly remained closed to Christianity and to missionary activity from 1624 to the nineteenth century.[21]

19. Cited in Baur, *2000 Years of Christianity*, 127.

20. Joly, *Le Christianisme et l'Extrême Orient*, volumes 1 and 2; Iheanacho, *Maximum Illud and Benedict XV*, 15–16.

21. Lopez-Gay, "The Clergy and the Native Hierarchy," 70.

Those painful experiences and abysmal failures in Far East Asia have always lurked behind in the collective missionary memory of the Catholic Church, so that pope after pope would have preferred not to recall them in their missionary teachings and directives. It is of great importance to note that most of the attention of the Holy See between the First and the Second World Wars was primarily on Asia. For instance, Pius XI inherited an advanced preparation, under the pontificate of Benedict XV, towards raising some Chinese priests to the bishopric. That was finally achieved in Rome on 28 October 1926, when Pius XI ordained the first six Chinese bishops after the first and only one, Bishop Gregory Lopez, was ordained in 1685. Preceding China was India, which, three years earlier, had its first bishop of the Latin rite in 1923, three centuries after the first episcopal ordination of an Indian priest in the person of Msgr Matthew de Castro in 1637.

Then came the turn of Japan, with the ordination of the first Japanese bishop in Rome by Pope Pius XI on 30 October 1927. This was followed by the ordination of the first Vietnamese bishop by Pius XI in Rome on 11 June 1933.[22] According to Paul Brasseur, in his detailed study on the Catholic Church and decolonization in Black Africa, many missionary institutions and publications, especially the French ones, did not so much concern themselves with the essential questions about the creation of somewhat enduring Christian structures and the formation of native or local clergy that was beginning to be considered indispensable. The only notable exception was the magazine of the Missionary Union of the Clergy in Italy. It was founded by Fr Paolo Manna in 1916 and accorded papal recognition particularly in *Maximum Illud* of Benedict XV.[23]

However, within the same optic, two events are important to the history of the African Church, even though one of them is of greater importance for the evolution of the local church. The first was the establishment of the Ethiopian College in Rome in 1919 by Benedict XV in the old monastery of Santo Stefano degli Abissini. Its establishment followed immediately after the creation of the Congregation for the Eastern Churches in 1917. It was also a sign of goodwill and rapprochement on the part of the Holy See towards the Ethiopian Church. In 1931, upon the completion of the construction that was started in 1929 under the auspices of Pius XI, the latter moved the college to its present site near the Vatican.[24] On the basis of the purpose for its establishment, the college housed Eritrean and Ethiopian priests on studies in Rome.

---

22. Iheanacho, *Maximum Illud and Benedict XV*, 4, 287; Metzler, "The Legacy of Pius XI," 64.

23. Brasseur, "L'Église Catholique et la Décolonisation," 52.

24. Metzler, "The Legacy of Pius XI," 64.

The second important development of wider continental relevance and import was the institution of apostolic delegations in colonial Africa, which showed the foresightedness of those responsible for the mission dicastery in Rome. During the missionary phase, those apostolic delegations were intended, among other things, to bring about some uniformity and coordination to Catholic missionary methods in Africa, to ensure discipline among Catholic missionary congregations and institutes, and to act as an efficient and authoritative intermediary between the Vatican and the colonial governments.[25] In the history of papal diplomatic representations in Africa, South Africa occupies the place of honor in that regard. The first apostolic delegation was established in Pretoria in 1922 in the same year as that of Beijing in China. The apostolic delegation in South Africa is historical, due to the fact that, at the time, South Africa was reputed to be an overwhelmingly Protestant country, where for roughly two centuries, especially around the Cape Colony, the public practice or exercise of Catholicism was strongly prohibited.[26] The delegation in Pretoria covered the neighboring countries of Lesotho, Swaziland and Botswana. The first Apostolic Delegate was a Dutch Dominican, Msgr Bernard Jordan Gijlswijk, who was succeeded, in 1945, by another Dutch prelate, Msgr Martin Lucas.[27]

It is also epochal since it was established even before the apostolic delegation of the Belgian Congo, which materialized in 1929, that is, seven years later and even thirty-six years ahead of the delegation for French West and Equatorial Africa. The significance of the delegation in Pretoria in the history of the Catholic Church in Africa is often overlooked, but given the era when it was established, it was truly remarkable, because one would have expected that the Belgian Congo or French Africa would have been the very first ones on the ground that King Leopold II of Belgium had a special preference for Catholic missionaries for his vast Congolese territorial possessions. France's missionaries were everywhere on the continent, supported financially by their home country. Instead, it was the very last place to have an apostolic delegation. The next apostolic delegation after that of the Belgian Congo was the delegation for British East and West Africa, established on 11 January 1930 with the official seat in Mombasa, Kenya and Msgr Arthur Hinsley as the first Apostolic Delegate.[28] This was followed by that of Italian East Africa in 1937.

---

25. Brasseur, "L'Église Catholique et la Décolonisation," 55; Metzler, "The Legacy of Pius XI," 65.
26. Hofmeyr and Pillay, *A History of Christianity*, 9–11.
27. Denis, "Clergy Training," 126, 128.
28. Bane, *The Popes and Western Africa*, 61.

The late establishment of an apostolic delegation for French West and Equatorial Africa requires some explanation. As early as 1940, the Vatican made known its intention of establishing a delegation in French Africa to the French government in Paris after the pattern of its delegation in the Belgian Congo. Diplomatic negotiations were concluded and a French priest of the Missions Étrangères de Paris, Père Henri Prouvost, was appointed to that post and was to have his residence in Gorée, Senegal. All that took place before the invasion of France by Germany in 1940 during the Second World War and brought everything to an abrupt halt. Diplomatic talks between the Vatican and Paris were re-started towards the end of 1944 as the war was gradually coming to an end. However, given the political turbulence and uncertainties of the time, those talks were prolonged for four years. In the course of the negotiations, the French Ministry of external Affairs at Quai d'Orsay gave two conditions to the Vatican for the would-be apostolic delegation in French colonies in Africa. The French government would not welcome an Italian prelate as apostolic delegate as was the case in the Belgian Congo, where Msgr Della Piane (an Italian) was appointed as the papal delegate. Its preference was for a French prelate. The second condition was that it did not want the seat of the delegation to be in Rabat or Casablanca, but in Dakar in Senegal. With all the conditions met, the Apostolic Delegation for French West and Equatorial Africa was finally created on 23 October 1948. Msgr Marcel Lefebvre, C.S.Sp, was appointed as the first Apostolic Delegate with his official residence in Dakar, where incidentally a year prior to his new appointment, he was already assigned there as the Apostolic Vicar of Senegal.[29] As papal representative, Msgr Lefebvre had an oversight function over Church authorities in forty-six dioceses in continental Africa and the neighboring islands that were under French colonial rule. This did not include dioceses in North Africa.[30]

Acutely conscious of the changed political atmosphere in many African countries and the agitations for independence that were particularly rife on the continent after the Second World War, it is not surprising that the Propaganda Fide, a month after the appointment of Msgr Lefebvre, sent him an instruction on his role in relation to Catholics in French colonial Africa. That instruction, dated 22 November 1948, contained the core of the new missionary policy of the Vatican for all Catholic missions in Africa and not specifically for French West and Equatorial Africa. He was reminded that it was his duty as Apostolic Delegate to see to it that the missions in each vicariate and prefecture have structures such as mission schools and

---

29. Brasseur, "L'Église Catholique et la Décolonisation," 55.
30. Mutig, "Archbishop Lefebvre Defies," §18.

hospitals and that they work hard to curtail Islamic influence and expansion. Msgr Lefebvre was also instructed never to forget that the missions, as they were constituted at the time, were only temporary, since the ultimate aim was "to found the Church with an indigenous hierarchy."[31]

That instruction, more than anything else, mirrored the acute awareness of the Vatican of the political evolutions in Africa. As such, the Vatican was in a haste to be ahead of events. From their initial mandate to implement the missionary policies and programs, as devised and directed by the Vatican through the Propaganda Fide, the apostolic delegations smoothly evolved to become papal nunciatures, with full diplomatic status at the attainment of independence by many African countries. It was a very smart move by the Vatican. While helping it to weather the storms of the initial upheavals that came with independences in the late 1950s, it also ensured a smooth transition from the missionary phase to the native era under the direction of an indigenous hierarchy. More so, in light of the understanding by the Vatican, the position of a missionary bishop might become untenable if not altogether vulnerable or undesirable under the worst scenario.

The institution of an apostolic delegation remains indelible in the history of the Catholic Church in contemporary Africa, even if at times this very important historic fact does not always get attention. The same is also true of their evolution into nunciatures. According to Adrian Hastings, while Rome was "Africanizing the episcopate," it was simultaneously building up its formidable network of diplomats to take the place of the apostolic delegates.[32] With their diplomatic muscles, the nuncios eventually displaced the once powerful superiors general of missionary congregations and institutes that used to call the shots. The overall result was that the Holy See (Rome) consolidated its power and ascendancy in the emerging local churches in Africa and made the young and new African bishops, appointed by it, to be loyal and attached to Rome.[33]

That fact was not lost on the prelate Archbishop Bernard Yago of Abidjan at the 1974 Synod of Bishops in Rome. He mentioned, during his intervention, that the local churches in Africa were already being referred to as "papist churches," with too much attachment to Rome. He reminded their critics that the churches in Africa were, at the time, in the early stages of "growth" towards adulthood, still seeking their peculiar features and characteristics. Whatever might have been their shortcomings in the eyes of their critics, Msgr Yago, however, insisted that the young churches in Africa were

31. Brasseur, "L'Église Catholique et la Décolonisation," 55.
32. Hastings, *A History of African Christianity*, 245.
33. Hastings, *A History of African Christianity*, 245.

indeed proud to be "papist" in their filial loyalty to the pope, which should not be misconstrued as servile obedience.[34] That intervention was remarkable in light of the bishops' collective report on the state of evangelization in Africa. One of the suggestions from the African bishops concerned the Vatican diplomatic corps, where they recalled that it was painful to hear the accusation that the Holy See was perpetuating Italian nationalism in the Church through its diplomatic missions and representations. Instead of an overwhelming Italian character in the Vatican diplomatic corps, the bishops asked the Holy See to ensure that its diplomatic representations truly reflected the universal character of the Church. In other words, there should be ample space for priests of other nationalities to be taken up in the Vatican diplomatic service.[35] That suggestion of the African bishops should make every African feel proud.

The apostolic delegates reached their pinnacle in 1950, which happened to be a Jubilee Year, a remarkable year in the annals of the history of Catholicism in Africa. It was the first time that African Catholics participated in a Jubilee Year through their selected representatives who went to Rome for that occasion. They were led from Africa by Msgr Lefebvre, Apostolic Delegate for French West and Equatorial Africa, and Msgr David Matthew, Apostolic Delegate for British East and West Africa.[36] A year later, Pope Pius XII recalled that Jubilee Year of 1950 in connection with the institution of the hierarchy, which he said to have been "our privilege and consolation to erect the Hierarchy in British West Africa."[37] Msgr Matthew, in particular, was exceptionally involved with the promotion of the local clergy and the erection of Catholic national hierarchies in the English-speaking countries in West Africa. For instance, during his tenure, Lagos and Onitsha in Nigeria were raised from Vicariates Apostolic to Archdioceses in April 1950, while in the Gold Coast (Ghana), the Vicariate Apostolic of the Cape Coast became an Archdiocese. In Sierra Leone, the former Vicariate of Sierra Leone became the Diocese of Freetown and Bo. In all of those instances, the bishops concerned became full-fledged resident bishops.[38]

The work of Bishop Matthew was the envy of bishops in French colonies to the extent that Msgr Joseph-Paul Strebler, Vicar Apostolic of Lomé, once suggested to Lefebvre to exert pressure on Rome to also institute hierarchies in French West and Equatorial Africa. He pointed to the examples

34. Bernard Yago, "La responsabilità delle chiese," 178.
35. Sangu, *Report on the Experiences*, 35.
36. Hastings, *A History of African Christianity*, 56–57.
37. Bane, *The Popes and Western Africa*, 64.
38. Bane, *The Popes and Western Africa*, 63.

of the remarkable work done in that regard by the apostolic delegations in Mombasa for British Africa and in Pretoria for Southern Africa.[39] In the Southern African region, national hierarchies were formally erected on 11 January 1951, comprising the Republic of South Africa, Lesotho, Swaziland, and Botswana. The turn of the Eastern African region came two years later on 25 March 1953, when national hierarchies were instituted in Kenya, Uganda, and Tanzania, with four ecclesiastical provinces that covered a total of twenty-eight archdioceses and dioceses. A separate national hierarchy was erected in Zimbabwe (then Rhodesia) on 1 January 1955, and grouped under it were an archdiocese, two dioceses and two apostolic prefectures.[40] Msgr Joseph-Paul Strebler insisted that missionary bishops in French colonies must not wait to have their own hierarchies formally instituted.

Five years after the establishment of hierarchies in Anglophone West Africa, the hierarchies in the French colonies in West and Equatorial Africa were instituted on 14 September 1955, with eleven ecclesiastical provinces, including Tananarive in Madagascar, Dakar, Bamako, Ouagadougou, Conakry, Abidjan, Lomé, Contonou, Yaoundé, Brazzaville, Bangui, and Tananarive.[41] In all these instances, whether in British East and West Africa or in Southern Africa and in French West and Equatorial Africa, those who became resident bishops were all missionaries of European extraction. That notwithstanding, it merits to be acknowledged that it was indeed one of the monumental steps taken by the Vatican towards the realization of local churches in various African circumscriptions, which until then had been at the second phase of ecclesiastical ranking. The first phase was that of a prefecture apostolic and until the formal establishment of national hierarchies in some of those places in Africa, all the bishops were titular bishops, ordained *in patribus infidelium*. Technically and within the juridical set-up, vicars apostolic in mission areas had no ordinary jurisdiction of their own, but they only acted as direct vicars of the pope.

The last parts of sub-Saharan Africa to have the institution of their national hierarchies were the Belgian Congo and British Central Africa. This took place in both areas in 1959. The first was British Central Africa of Zambia and Malawi, with eight dioceses grouped under Lusaka and Blantyre on 25 April 1959. The last was the Belgian Congo that comprised Zaire (Democratic Republic of Congo), Burundi, and Rwanda. The vast Belgian Congo was divided into eight ecclesiastical provinces, subdivided into

---

39. Brasseur, "L'Église Catholique et la Décolonisation," 60.
40. Metzler, "La Santa Sede e le missioni," 109.
41. Brasseur, "L'Église Catholique et la Décolonisation," 60–61.

twenty-nine archdioceses and dioceses.[42] Within a period of seven years, from 1959 with the last institution of national hierarchies in sub-Saharan Africa to 1966, a year after the conclusion of Vatican II, the whole of Black Africa, under the mission jurisdiction of the Propaganda Fide, had seventy-five African native bishops, including seventeen indigenous archbishops, forty-one native bishops and fifteen native titular bishops alongside 2,500 African indigenous priests.[43]

A CHECKERED PATH TOWARDS AN INDIGENOUS CHURCH

All those who can be identified as the founders of the Catholic Church in contemporary Africa can be said to have one thing in common with the rest: their desire to see the emergence of a local church in Africa on the shoulders of its local or indigenous clergy. Some considered it a long-time project, far remote in a distant future, while others thought it was possible and realizable in their time. However near or distant its realization might have appeared, their common desire and vision for a local church united them all. It began with the earliest and bold steps of Mother Anne-Marie Javouhey (1779–1851) and her Sisters of St Joseph of Cluny, founded in 1807, and their collaboration with the Holy Ghost Fathers who set foot in the West African country of Senegal first in 1788 and again in 1799.[44]

The road towards the emergence of an indigenous Church in Africa was painfully slow and long, with many obstacles and daunting failures. That emergence or evolution can be surmised in three phases: 1840–1912, 1913–1936, and 1957–1975. The first phase (1840–1912) was obviously initiated through the courageous efforts and the pioneering role of Mother Javouhey in the training and ordination of local priests for the mission church in Senegal. In 1819, Sister Rosalie Javouhey, possibly a relative of Anne-Marie Javouhey, led the first batch of the Sisters of Cluny to Dakar, where they were to assist Père Terrasse, a Holy Ghost Father, who was alone in Senegal. A second group of sisters joined them in 1823, including their founder, Mother Anne-Marie Javouhey.

In her intuition and indomitable optimism, Anne-Marie Javouhey began to make efforts to recruit local boys to be trained for the priesthood on Senegalese soil. It appears that she did not succeed, due to the lack of personnel to train her students. Not willing to give up so easily, she sent

42. Metzler, "La Santa Sede e le missioni," 110.
43. Müller, "The Main Principles of Centralized," 22.
44. Bane, *The Popes and Western Africa*, 74.

twenty-three of her recruited young African boys to Paris to be trained at the seminary of the Holy Ghost Fathers. Unfortunately, many of the boys died, possibly due to climatic conditions in Europe, which led some of them to suffer from tuberculosis.[45] It is not clear if twenty of them died. Of the initial twenty-three students who were sent to France, only three of them were finally ordained priests on 19 September 1840: Jean-Pierre Moussa, David Boilat, and Arsène Fridoil.[46] Of particular interest is Jean-Pierre Moussa, because Bishop Barron later mentioned him in one of his correspondences, when he wrote about the "beautiful church" on Goree Island "of which a Negro priest, Father Peter Moussa, has charge." He added that "Father Moussa made his studies in the seminary of the Holy Ghost Fathers in Paris."[47] The Holy Ghost Fathers, alongside Mother Javouhey and her sisters, were the avant-garde during the first phase in the training of African local clergy. Of the twenty-five indigenous priests ordained within the period, twenty-three of them were trained by the Holy Ghost Fathers, with the exception of the first South African priest, Fr Eduard Muganda from Marianhill, ordained in Rome in 1898, and Fr André Raponda-Walker of Gabon, also ordained in Rome in 1899.[48]

If the Holy Ghost Fathers or the Spiritans opened and dominated the first phase in the journeys towards the realization of a local church with the ordination of indigenous clergy, the second phase belonged to the White Fathers and the Society of African Missions (SMA). The dominance of the Spiritans of the first phase is understandable, because, between 1860 and 1960, their congregation sent more missionaries to Africa than other missionary congregations.[49] Worthy of note, in the second phase (1913–1936), is that the total number of African local priests rose to 150. The *annus mirabilis* in the annals of priestly ordinations of African native clergy was 1911, because, after that year, priestly ordinations were no longer rare occasions in Africa. For instance, the White Fathers in their Great Lakes Region of East Central Africa (now Rwanda and Uganda) missions began to record the number of ordinations after the first ordination of two priests of that region in 1913. It was no small feat, because the White Fathers, in that region alone, admitted roughly 160 seminarians between 1878 and 1913.[50] This does not mean that such a positive development was evenly distributed across regions

---

45. Bane, *The Popes and Western Africa*, 75.
46. Robert, "The Development of the Local Clergy," 86.
47. Bane, *The Popes and Western Africa*, 75.
48. Robert, "The Development of the Local Clergy," 87.
49. Bevans and Schroeder, *Constants in Context*, 224.
50. Foster, *African Catholic*, 160.

on the continent, as some places still lagged behind. In British West Africa, the emergence of a native clergy never materialized until 1920, when Fr Paul Emechete was ordained as the first Nigerian Priest by Bishop Thomas Broderick.[51] The number of Nigerian indigenous priests rose to ten in 1939, while the Gold Coast (Ghana) even had a slower beginning with only three native priests in 1939.[52]

In the Southern African region, progress was also slow, as the entire region had only a total of thirty-eight native priests from 1919 to 1952. In the opinion of George Mukuka, the reason for such an abysmal result was largely due to the hesitation on the part of religious orders and missionary congregations that evangelized the region. According to Mukuka, their hesitation was not in isolation. It was not unconnected with the racial problem that was generally experienced in the region, especially in South Africa, where some missionaries doubted whether it was opportune to admit Black Africans into the priesthood to serve alongside White missionaries.[53] It is mind-boggling to note, for instance, that the Oblates of Mary Immaculate (OMI), who were the first to arrive on Southern African shores in 1850, never had an African confrère until 1933 with the ordination of Fr Emmanuel Gregory Mabathoana. He eventually became the first Bishop of Leribe Diocese upon its creation in 1952. It is true that Fr Raphael Mohasi had been ordained in 1931 as the first Mosotho Priest from Lesotho.[54] It took the Oblates roughly eighty-three years (almost a century) to make a breakthrough.

In contrast to other regions of the continent, the Belgian Congo showed the most astronomical increase in the number of local clergy from only two native priests in 1920 to approximately seventy-seven in 1939. This increase must be placed against the background of the late arrival of Catholic missionaries in the Congo in 1888.[55] The same was also true of the Belgian Trust Territory of Ruanda-Urundi, whose share of native priests increased most significantly from five in 1920 to approximately 100 local priests in 1950.[56] Contrasting the harmonious transition from a missionary church to an indigenous church with the anarchy that ensued after the independence of the Congo on 30 June 1960, Patrick M. Boyle observed

51. Bane, *The Popes and Western Africa*, 59–60.
52. Groves, *The Planting of Christianity in Africa*, 196–197.
53. Mukuka, "The Establishment of the Indigenous Catholic Clergy," 2.
54. "Mabathoana, Emmanuel Gregory," lines 10, 15–16.
55. Groves, *The Planting of Christianity*, 196; Kachama-Nkoy, "Reflections on the Church," 298.
56. Groves, *The Planting of Christianity*, 319.

that the Congolese Church was already having "an annual ordination rate of 35 to 40 new African priests on the eve of independence."[57] Significantly, by 1961, the Congolese local Church could count as many as 450 diocesan priests among its pastoral workforce, with four Congolese native bishops.[58] This meant, as Boyle rightly asserted, that the

> scattered mission districts of the nineteenth century developed into forty-seven separate dioceses and archdioceses in the 1970s, constituting the largest and most complex national unit of the Catholic Church on the African continent[59].

Prior to the advent of the third and final phase, from 1957 to 1975, the period between the second and the third phases was remarkably characterized by the erection and organization of regional seminaries. From these seminaries, the pioneer indigenous local church leaders would come forth as the vocation boom experienced by the Church was still under missionary tutelage. After the Holy Ghost Fathers opened the first major seminary in Dakar in 1846, the establishment of seminaries in other places across the continent took a sporadic pace. For instance, the White Fathers opened their first seminary in 1889 in Boundville in Congo and another one in Katigondo, Uganda in 1903, followed by another seminary in 1909 for the Rwanda-Urundi missions. On their part, in 1914, the SMAs established a seminary at Ouidah, Dahomey (Benin Republic) for their West African missions, which, in 1919, became the place of formation for students from Lagos, Togo and the Ivory Coast.[60] The Jesuits established a seminary in Madagascar in 1916. The years that followed the publications of *Maximum Illud* by Pope Benedict XV in 1919 and *Rerum Ecclesiae* by Pope Pius XI in 1926, respectively, witnessed the establishment of more seminaries in Africa: Kipalapala (Tanganyika) in 1921; Enugu (Nigeria) in 1924; Pretoria (South Africa) in 1925; Gaba (Uganda) in 1926; Ibadan (Nigeria) in 1930; Mayidi (the Belgian Congo) in 1931; Salisbury (Rhodesia, now Zimbabwe) in 1932; Peramiho (Tanzania) in 1936; Koumi (Upper Volta, now Burkina Faso) in 1939, and Kachebere (Malawi) in 1939.[61]

The establishment of seminaries in Africa progressed steadily from one seminary in a vast mission circumscription to a seminary in a region and to about one or more seminaries in a country. Owing to a multiplicity of

57. Boyle, "Beyond self-protection to prophecy," 54.
58. Kachama-Nkoy, "Reflections on the Church," 298.
59. Boyle, "Beyond self-protection to prophecy," 55.
60. Bane, *The Popes and Western Africa*, 61.
61. Robert, "The Development of the Local Clergy," 87–88.

factors, the vocation to Catholic priesthood had a very late start, but from 1934, a steady pace of development was recorded and particularly from the second half of the twentieth century. As at 1974, the year of the third Synod of Bishops in Rome, Eastern and Central Africa had the highest number of African seminarians in formation, while the overall number of local clergy in 1975 was put at 7,282 priests. With the appreciable progress that the Church was making in Africa, Pope John XXIII, in his missionary encyclical *Princeps Pastorum*, dated 28 November 1959, stressed the importance of allowing native bishops chosen from the local clergy to lead their local churches. Bishops Joseph Kiwanuka of Uganda and Ignatius Ramarosandratana of Madagascar had previously been raised to the episcopate by Pope Pius XII in Rome on 19 October 1939, with another African prelate Msgr Joseph Faye appointed as Prefect of the Apostolic Prefecture of Casamance in Senegal. The experience of Msgr Faye was not a pleasant one, because he was the only African priest in his prefecture among White missionaries. They felt slighted by his appointment by Rome, never hid their disdain for him, and withheld their cooperation and support to the lone African head of mission among them. Elizabeth Foster correctly describes the ordeals of Msgr Faye in the hands of French missionaries as "the trials of an African prelate."[62]

One of the important trajectories of the African Church towards maturity was the establishment of national hierarchies in many places on the continent as from 1950. Although the expatriate missionaries were still tasked with the administration of the metropolitan dioceses, it was nonetheless a milestone in the gradual transition from mission churches to local churches, with their own native or local hierarchies. One important event during this period was the elevation of Bishop Prosper Dodds of Senegal in 1955 to the rank of a Resident Bishop. He became the first African from the amorphous Vicariate of the two Guineas, created in 1842, to be numbered among members of the Catholic hierarchy to head a diocese. It was no small feat, because, prior to his elevation, all other African bishops were either vicars apostolic or auxiliary bishops.[63] No less was the epochal appointment of Bishop Aloys Bigirumwami, first Vicar Apostolic of Nyundo. Msgr Bigirumwami became the first African in 1952 to be nominated Bishop in the Belgian colonies of Rwanda, Burundi and the Congo.[64]

Significant also is the fact that the ecclesiastical propulsion towards indigenization—Africanization or localization (terms in vogue at the time)— fitted very well into the wider agitation for a faster process of decolonization

---

62. Foster, "A Mission in Transition," 265.
63. Bane, *The Popes and Western Africa*, 66.
64. Connolly, "Pope Pius XII and Foreign Missions," 51.

in Africa between 1957 and 1969. That continental wind of change that blew in the 1960s helped, to a large extent, hasten the "localization" of the local Church and simultaneously fanned the flame for self-government. It was a momentous period in the history of contemporary Africa that was suffused with the search for "African authenticity," so that the coming of age of the local Church coincided with the attainment of political independence by many African countries. Within a period of twenty years after the abolition of the missionary *ius commissionis* system in 1969, the transition from mission churches to local churches was accelerated such that most of them were raised to the level of dioceses.[65]

In place of the former missionary system, a new juridical system of *mandatum* was introduced in recognition of the consolidation of the local hierarchy. The new system placed the duty of evangelizing their dioceses and national territories squarely upon the shoulders of local bishops. Francis Oborji affirms that, with the new system, mission became the co-responsibility of local and sister churches beyond their territorial confines.[66] In view of this fact, one appreciates the initial steps towards the establishment of SECAM by young African bishops during the Second Vatican Council. It was initially intended to serve as a body that would allow the young bishops from the continent to speak with one voice. Formally established in 1969, SECAM is presently composed of eight regional episcopal conferences, and has evolved as a continental ecclesial structure whose aim is to "preserve and foster communion, collaboration and joint action among all Episcopal Conferences of Africa and the Islands."[67]

As rightly affirmed by the African bishops in their 1974 report, the coming of age of the local church, although it signified a turning point in the history of the Church in Africa and definitively brought the missionary phase to an end, it did not, however, imply the end of evangelization. They also acknowledged that the remaining task of the continuous evangelization of the continent became the primary responsibility of the African Church and its indigenous pastoral agents; it never precluded the cooperation and support that foreign missionaries could still render.[68] Comprehensively, in his book *The Christian Ministry in Africa* (1960), the prolific Lutheran historian of African Christianity, Bishop Bengt Sundkler, best articulated the evolution from missions at the peripheries to be inserted in the centre of universal Catholicism:

65. Sangu, *Report on the Experiences*, 15, 30.
66. Oborji, "Catholic Mission in Africa," 15.
67. Cited in Pengo, "Missionaries to Yourselves," 5.
68. Sangu, *Report on the Experiences*, 15.

> The story of the development of the Roman Catholic Church and its priesthood in Africa in this century is astonishing, one of the wonders of the dramatic history of world missions... The spread of the Church was guided by a global strategy. Strategy and planning, not improvisation, is the strong impression given by this development[69].

That development was phenomenal in terms of the brevity of the period within which it was accomplished. Cardinal Francis Arinze once explained that, with the exception of Angola and then Zaire (now the Democratic Republic of Congo), most of the African countries south of the Sahara had not yet celebrated their centenary of evangelization, when Pope Paul VI became the first pope to visit Africa in 1969.[70] The second half of the twentieth century belonged to Africa in terms of massive conversion to Christianity and the preponderance in the number of African indigenous clergy and religious. Seventeen years after Paul VI's visit to Uganda, one could speak of an "Africanized hierarchy" of the Church in Africa because, as at 31 December 1986, of the 481 bishops in Africa at the time, 348 were Africans. By 2001, the number of native bishops stood at 474, compared to 142 bishops of non-African origins.[71]

In the interim, the first native African bishop appointed to the archbishopric in Zaire was in 1964. Within a space of four years, an African episcopal majority was an already accomplished task by 1968. A similar development was equally noticeable in other countries: Tanzania (after the ordination of its first native Bishop, Msgr Laurian Rugambwa, in 1952), and Uganda in 1969 (thirteen years after the ordination of its first indigenous Bishop, Msgr Joseph Kiwanuka in 1939), followed by Cameroon in 1970 and Nigeria in 1972.[72] In the same vein, the gradual transition in the administration of local dioceses by African native bishops also began timidly: Lesotho in 1952, Sudan and Cameroon in 1955, Burkina Faso in 1956, Nigeria and Ghana in 1957, Zaire in 1959, and Togo in 1961.[73] There is no doubt that the development of an African priesthood is an essential aspect of the Catholic Church on the continent and remains the most encouraging feature of Catholicism in Africa.[74]

---

69. Cited in Bühlmann, *The Coming of the Third Church*, 151–152.
70. Arinze, "Paul VI and the African Episcopate," 30.
71. Ngulu, "The Church in Africa," 26–27.
72. Hastings, *A History of African Christianity*, 237.
73. Metzler, "La Santa Sede e le missioni," 108.
74. Matthew, "Catholicism in Africa," 4.

THE VATICAN'S POLICY OF INDIGENIZATION AND CONTESTATION

The Africanization or the indigenization of the local Church in Africa, which brought a significant change in its external physiognomies, particularly in terms of leadership, can be traced to three factors: political conditions in Africa during and after World War II; increase in membership, and Church directives and pastoral priorities based on the determination of Rome to part with its former manner of procrastinations and caution. In fact, the local missions at the base level were already Africanized in their rural leadership and organization way before the official policy of indigenization came into full swing as from the 1950s. For Adrian Hastings, Godwin Tasie and Richard Gray, among others, Africanization was not synonymous with the post-missionary era, since long before the start of that process, the cutting edge of primary evangelization in sub-Saharan Africa was primarily and overwhelmingly driven by local African agents in the persons of the village or station catechists, prayer leaders, station church elders, and then local Christian community leaders.[75] Paul Mba Abessole holds a similar view, asserting that the Catholic Church in Gabon, like elsewhere on the continent, was forced by political and religious exigencies to make painful adjustments, in order to face the rapid changes that were taking place in Africa. In his assessment, prior to the acceleration and actualization of the indigenization policy especially from the mid-1950s, the ordination of an indigenous clergy at the time "should not be interpreted as an expression of the will or determination on the part of missionaries to establish an autonomous local church."[76]

In light of the prevailing realities at the time, it is possible to affirm that the policy formulators in Rome had hardly any or no choice but to take notice of the changed conditions of Catholic missions in Africa. In places such as French West and Equatorial Africa, the atmosphere was particularly thin. As early as the end of the Second World War, the White Fathers vicars and prefects apostolic in those places already indicated, in their collective reports, the noticeable change of mentality among their flocks. The slogan "L'Afrique aux Africains" (Africa to Africans) was already gaining ground among the people, so that it was impossible to not be amazed by the highly charged state of political development.[77] It is no wonder that the timid process, which began remotely in 1939 and became considerably stalled for

---

75. Tasie and Gray, "Introduction," 4.
76. Mba, "L'Affranchissement du clergé," lines 12–14.
77. Brasseur, "L'Église Catholique et la Décolonisation," 57.

over a decade, was restarted, as Hastings rightly observed, only when White missionary bishops realized that their presence and authority were being undermined, as they found themselves in increasingly difficult and untenable positions.[78]

Playing catch-up and probably also to be seen as being ahead of events, Rome started to fast-forward its hitherto gradual and cautious process of indigenization, triggering, as it were, a cascade of appointments of native bishops.[79] In some instances, Rome did so with or without the cooperation of the missionaries and their institutes and congregations. Its determination brought about a change in the color of the national hierarchies of the Church in Africa. That change in color was effected through the continental assumption of ecclesiastical leadership by Africans who were elevated as heads of the local churches in their countries and which would have been almost unimaginable in the not so distant past. Yet amidst all the changes that were beginning to take place across the continent, the Holy See's adoption and acceleration of the policy of indigenization was greeted with mixed reactions, ranging from reluctance to a lukewarm attitude and even a formidable pushback in some places. The contestations emanated from some members of the African native clergy and from the missionaries themselves, with the support of European politicians who were convinced that the missionaries had been easily short-changed after many years of toil and sweat in Africa.

The mid-1950s can be described as the hotbed of African cultural and political affirmation. They can rightly also be identified as the hotbed of ecclesiastical affirmation on the part of many members of the African native clergy. For instance, at the cultural level, the first International Congress of Black Writers and Artists (Congrés des Écrivains et Artistes Noirs), held in Paris from 19 to 22 September 1956, attracted leading Black intellectuals of the time. The primary aim of the Congress was to ex-ray problems of colonialism and slavery, especially through the piercing lens of Négritude. Since many of the leading Black intellectuals tended heavily towards Marxism, it is not surprising that the Congress underscored what they identified as the three Ms that affected the history and lives of the Black race.

Those three Ms were Missionary, Military and Merchant, and all three, with their European background, collaborated in different measures to subjugate and rule the Black race. As for the Church, whose representative in Africa was no doubt the missionary, the greatest blame of the Church as they understood it was that it never told the ravaging and domineering powers of the North not to dominate and exploit the peoples of the South.

78. Hastings, "The Ministry of the Catholic Church," 33.
79. Hebga, "Cinquante ans après," 297.

For instance, in Cameroon, the nationalist movement for independence, *L'Union des Populations Camerounaises*, with its Marxist ideology, did not hesitate to identify Christian missions as the long arm of the excesses of European and White colonialism.[80] In its presentation of the work of the Congress in a special edition of its bi-monthly magazine, *Présence Africaine* titled its editorial "Modern culture and our destiny." The editorial described the Congress as "a great event in the conscience of the world" and went further to lament that "the destiny of under-developed peoples is oriented in one direction or the other without any need to consult them." It finally proposed as its goal "to make our culture into a force of liberation and solidarity, and at the same time the hymn of our innermost personality."[81]

Transposed to the question of the Africanization or indigenization of the Church, the Congress became inspirational for a group of young African and Haitian priests on studies in some European universities, particularly in Rome. They came together and put down their thoughts on the administrative structures of the mission churches in Africa in a book entitled *Des Prêtres noirs s'interrogent* (1956), with a preface by Msgr Lefebvre in his capacity as Apostolic Delegate for Black French Africa. In their foreword to the book, the authors re-echoed some of the tenets and expressions of the Paris Congress. Acknowledging their youthfulness, which their detractor might take for their weakness and immaturity to dabble into church and mission administrative issues, the young priests, mainly from the French colonies in Africa, retorted that their youthfulness was rather the source of their strength. Like the editorial of *Présence Africaine*, they also noted with pains the lamentable absence of the Black people in discussions on matters that concerned them. Sadly, that reality did not exclude their local churches, where the missionaries occupied every prominent position and African local priests were simply expected to be seen and to obey without being heard: "for a long time, others thought of our problems for us, without us and in spite of us."[82] Their pain of exclusion may be related to the seminary system, in which many of them were trained. This extract from the Regulations for Gabonese native priests could serve as a symptomatic insight into a general bigger problem. It was drawn up at the time of Msgr Michel-François Tardy, Vicar Apostolic of Gabon from 1926 to 1947:

> In observing the regulations, and in the performance of their work, the native priests will strive to be perfectly docile. They will be able to humbly and loyally submit to the opinions and

80. Brasseur, "L'Église Catholique et la Décolonisation," 60.
81. Présence Africaine, "Modern culture and our destiny," 3–6.
82. "Avant-propos" in *Des Prêtres noirs s'interrogent*, 16.

directives of those who have authority over them ... It is important that the native priest knows how to humbly stay in his place, keeping faithfully in the honest simplicity that suits him[83].

A similar observation was once made by Adrian Hastings that may be suggestive of a wider practice of keeping African local priests in careful check. He noted that, as late as the 1950s, this remark was very much in vogue in reference to African seminarians in formation: "None of you will ever be parish priest."[84] That comment was always made against the backdrop of teaching canon law, since church law at the time had practically no place for assistant parish priests. For that reason, it was considered a waste of time to treat that aspect of canon law on the function of parish priests. Based on the common practice of the time, seminaries in mission areas understood their primary work as that of preparing seminarians who will be ordained to serve as perpetual curates or as assistants to White missionaries. Such entrenched bottle-neck bureaucracy explains the missionaries' considerable initial reluctance to work under local bishops when that became the norm, or even the outright refusal of some White missionaries to live under a common roof with African local clergy.[85] A complexity of attitudes did not envisage the emergence of a local church in the immediate future. As such, missionaries and their missionary societies and institutes sought to protect themselves and their property from the encroaching consequences of the indigenization of the local church and its control in the hands of the indigenous clergy. On the basis of such fact, as explained by Adrian Hastings, it is understandable to note that the tension between African indigenous clergy and the missionaries in terms of the Vatican's policy of indigenization in Africa took place within the complexity of theological, sociological, political, racial and mental changes and challenges of the 1950s and 1960s that were awash everywhere on the continent.[86]

In light of those observations, it bears recalling the opposition mounted by the White Fathers and the Spiritans against the suggestion of the appointment of African priests as vicar generals to work alongside White bishops in diocesan administrations. Both congregations judged the proposal as "premature."[87] Such opposition debunks the myth and hallow about the White Fathers as a progressive congregation in championing the elevation of African indigenous clergy. The proposal rather came from the

83. Mba, "L'Affranchissement du clergé," lines 5–8.
84. Hastings, "In the Field," 85.
85. Hastings, "In the Field," 85.
86. Hastings, "In the Field," 87.
87. Brasseur, "L'Église Catholique et la Décolonisation," 61.

Superior General of the Society of African Missions (SMA) who, in his letter of 11 December 1951, sold the idea to Archbishop Lefebvre. He asked for the introduction of the hierarchy in French Africa within five to ten years, with the appointment of African vicars general. Even R.P. Porrot, after his visit to some missions in French Africa, suggested in 1953 the gradual transfer of a number of positions to African indigenous clergy. He consented that the missionaries could retain the administration of institutions such as novitiates and seminaries, which, he also hoped, would eventually be passed over to the local clergy.[88] It should not be forgotten that the White Fathers proposed the introduction of a probationary year as a way to verify the authenticity of the vocation of African aspirants to the priesthood. What made their proposal appear suspicious was the realization that the canon law at the time did not make provision for such a probationary period in the training of future priests. It was the SMAs who rather expressed their sensitivity to the racial undertones of such a proposal and the psychological effect it might have on African seminarians. The SMA's disapproval was articulated by Msgr Joseph-Paul Strebler, SMA, Vicar Apostolic of Lomé, in his 1950 report to the Propaganda Fide:

> As long as the Church applies exceptional rules to seminarians of color that canon law does not provide for in the case of other races, 'probation' will not be valued, but suffered with grumbling. I share their apprehensions because I know the milieu in which this 'probation' takes place[89].

But the missionaries were not alone in their opposition to the promotion of the native clergy. It remains a mind-boggling fact and inexplicable to some degree as to why some pioneer African bishops such as Bishop Joseph Kiwanuka of Masaka (Uganda) and Msgr Aloys Bigirumwami of Nyundo (Rwanda) were not enthusiastic supporters of native episcopacy. The case of Msgr Kiwanuka is more perplexing. He is believed to have said that the long interval between his episcopal ordination in 1939 and that of another African in 1952 ought to be regarded "as a time set by Rome to prove by experience whether it was safe and opportune to make local bishops in mission territories."[90] In their opposition to further ordination of African bishops, it is assumed that the reasons proffered by them were on the ground that the mere ordination of an indigenous bishop in itself alone was not sufficient for the emergence of a local church. According to the two prelates, much more

---

88. Brasseur, "L'Église Catholique et la Décolonisation," 60.
89. Foster, *African Catholic*, 164.
90. Robert, "The Development of the Local Clergy," 89.

was needed such as a competent vicar general, the director of education, the bursar general as well as qualified personnel to see to the maintenance of church buildings and other property.[91]

However, they were not altogether wrong in asking for a halt to the transfer of the helm of ecclesiastical authority to the indigenous clergy, because the immediate experience was that the emergence of new types of clerical works in the towns such as church and school administrations sucked up the limited pastoral personnel for many of the young churches.[92] This may have accounted for the very slow process in the appointment of indigenous African bishops. The conspicuous examples are Malawi, where there was only one indigenous bishop in 1960 and Zambia that practically had none at all. Even in Uganda, Msgr Kiwanuka was the lone indigenous Bishop until 1962, with the episcopal ordination of Msgr Adrian Ddungu. A similar situation existed in Kenya, where Msgr Maurice Otunga became the first Kenyan to be elevated to the bishopric in 1960.[93] That process became substantially stalled in South Africa, where Africanization seemed to have started early enough with the episcopal ordination of the first Black Bishop in the person of Msgr Bonaventura Dlamini of Umzimkulu in 1954. The country did not see another Black bishop until 1972, when Msgr Peter Buthelezi OMI was ordained as the Auxiliary Bishop of Johannesburg before being transferred to the diocese of Umtata in 1975.[94] Sadly, in the case of Bishop Dlamini, given the racial segregation in place in South Africa at the time, some White Catholics protested against his episcopal ordination, because they could not allow themselves to be shepherded by a Black bishop.[95]

For the advocates of rapid indigenization as opposed to the halting of the process, as Bishops Kiwanuka and Bigirumwami tended to suggest, the shortage in indigenous African pastoral personnel rendered imminent the exit of the missionaries. As far as the indigenization advocates were concerned, the Church in Africa was to find its identity and adulthood within the limits of its resources. They argued that it ought to be done without the seemingly never-ending tutelage of Western missionaries.[96] For the authors of *Des Prêtres noirs s'interrogent*, the subservient position of the indigenous clergy was simply intolerable. In view of that untenable situation and the puerile condition of many of their colleagues, in the estimation of the authors,

91. Brasseur, "L'Église Catholique et la Décolonisation," 60.
92. Hastings, "The Ministry of the Catholic Church," 38.
93. Hastings, "The Ministry of the Catholic Church," 32.
94. Baur, *2000 Years of Christianity*, 296.
95. Bate, "The Church under Apartheid," 153.
96. Kendall, *The End of an Era*, 91.

they took the liberty to pen down their thoughts together in book form, in order to highlight the state of affairs in their various local churches in Africa and in Haiti. As they saw it, the Black race had not been understood and the voices of Black people were kept discreet and even hushed in some instances. Therefore, they had to openly speak their minds, since the fate of Africa was at stake. Their use of Africa was understood as a "substratum of all black countries." Although each country had its own peculiar variations, all Black countries, to a large extent, had similar situations that were determined by some common factors such as colonialism, racism, and subjugation.[97]

Perhaps, a country that best typified that racial divide between Black and White could be said to have been South Africa because of the government-sanctioned policy of apartheid, which the Catholic Church, unfortunately in many ways, mirrored to a fault. It was said at one point in time that the White bishops had very little knowledge about what was going on in the Black communities. The 1972 survey, commissioned by the South African Council of Priests, reported that virtually all those questioned during the survey were of the opinion that the Black members of the clergy did not view themselves as equals in the administration of their churches. This was possible because the church at the time did not have enough room for Black priests to be fully involved in the running of the local churches.[98] The swipe that Jerome Skhakhane directed against the Oblates of Mary Immaculate in the 1970s was indicative of a bigger general malaise of the Catholic Church in South Africa at the time:

> We should be ashamed of ourselves to notice that we even have at one time built churches arranged in such a way as to accommodate on one side the whites, on another the coloured and Asians and finally on another Africans[99].

That observation is not surprising, since the South African bishops themselves had "built a *black* national seminary in Hammanskraal in 1963, only fifty kilometres north of the *white* national seminary in Pretoria."[100]

If South Africa best typified racial discrimination within the Catholic Church in Africa, the Portuguese colonies of Angola and Mozambique supremely typified the ambiguity of the Vatican and its orchestrated policy of indigenization or Africanization on the continent. The Vatican cautiously and selectively applied its indigenous policy in those countries. On the one

---

97 "Avant-propos" in *Des Prêtres noirs s'interrogent*, 17.

98. Bate, "The Church under Apartheid," 153.

99. Cited in Bate, "The Church under Apartheid," 154.

100. Criticism of the South African bishops by Jabulani Nxumalo, as cited in Bate, "The Church under Apartheid," 152.

hand, it did not want to incur the wrath of the Portuguese government in Lisbon. On the other hand, it feared to offend the ultranationalist sentiments of Portuguese bishops who were stationed in Angola and Mozambique. Those Portuguese bishops saw their work more as advancing the glory of their patria than the advancement of the Gospel and implantation of the church. The unholy alliance between the Vatican and Lisbon, with regard to contemporary Catholic missions in Portuguese Africa, was regulated by the Concordat of 1940. This was accompanied by the so-called *Accordo Missionario*. The two documents effectively tied the Vatican's hand of maneuvering in the appointments of bishops in Portuguese overseas territories.

Although the Vatican, in principle, appointed bishops to those places, Lisbon reserved the right of veto in its insistence that bishops for those places must be Portuguese nationals. As far as Portugal was concerned, its African colonies were out of reach for the Vatican. The Holy See accepted and acted accordingly, not so much for the benefit of the missions in Angola and Mozambique, but for the peace and serenity of the Portuguese Church in Europe. Prior to the 1940 Concordat, the Portuguese Church was an outlawed and persecuted entity in Portugal, like its sister church in Spain under the socialist government. The coming to power of the nationalist and fascist governments in both countries "rescued" the Church in those countries but only to reconfigure it to do their biddings. It was General Francisco Franco in Spain, while the strongman in Portugal was António de Oliveira Salazar. During his tenure as Prime Minister (1932–1968), the 1940 Concordat was signed between Portugal and the Holy See.[101] It elevated Luanda and Lourenco Marques (now Maputo) to archdioceses.

Another immediate and visible effect of that Concordat was the creation of Msgr Teodosio Clemente de Gouveia (1889–1962) as Cardinal in 1946 by Pope Pius XII. His elevation to the cardinalate served two purposes. The first one was political so as to please Lisbon. According to Adrian Hastings, it was "a political gesture of goodwill towards Portugal in the wake of the Concordat."[102] The second purpose was rather personal as a sign of appreciation for his active role in facilitating the process towards the signing of the concordat. At times, De Gouveia boasted that it was through his efforts and diplomacy that the Holy See decided to abide by the terms of the Concordat and to sign it. The Portuguese decorated De Gouveia with the medal of the Grand Cross of the Order of Prince Henry for his labor in the advancement of Portuguese national interests in Mozambique, where

---

101. Serapião, "The Preaching of Portuguese Colonialism," 34; Birmingham, "Merchants and Missionaries," 346.

102. Hastings, *A History of African Christianity*, 60.

he was the Archbishop of Lourenco Marques (now Maputo) from 1940. In deference to the demands of Lisbon, the Vatican recognized Portuguese patriotism in its overseas colonies in agreeing that the members of the secular clergy of Portuguese nationalism, together with the bishops, were to serve the Portuguese White communities.

Within the constraints of that accord between the Vatican and Lisbon, the pastoral needs of the Black communities were to be served by members of the regular clergy (missionaries and religious orders) from other European countries. This is the background to the later fallout between the White Fathers and the Portuguese colonial administrators in Mozambique in 1971, with the tacit support of the Portuguese bishops who accused the White Fathers of abandoning their missions in the country for lack of "Christian pastoral zeal." The Concordat stipulations explained why the Portuguese bishops in Africa were not admitted to the first plenary session of SECAM at its inauguration in Kampala in 1969, because they were said to be members of the Episcopal Conference of Portugal, with its official headquarters in Lisbon. A year later, at the second meeting of SECAM in Abidjan in 1970, the other bishops criticized the Portuguese bishops for their acquiescence of the manifest atrocities committed by Portugal against Angolans and Mozambicans in their struggle for political independence.[103]

In terms of implantation and indigenization of the Church in Angola and Mozambique, it remains a sad story that almost 400 years of Catholic presence in those Portuguese possessions in Africa, the Catholic Church had nothing but a foreign status. It was a church of settlers and colonizers rather than a local church. The admission and training of the natives for the priesthood in contemporary time began in roughly 1882 and, as at 1970, Angola had only 140 indigenous priests and only one indigenous Bishop, Msgr Eduardo Muaca. It was especially in Mozambique, with independence in 1975 and the ascent of the Marxist-Leninist nationalist leader, Samora Machel, that what Vatican all along had dreaded the most that might happen in post-independence Africa, eventually became a reality. Against the backdrop of the role played by Portuguese bishops and their disproval of the self-determination of Mozambican nationalists, and the inaction of the Vatican to denounce the atrocities of Portuguese colonial repressions, Samora Machel expelled most of the Church's pastoral personnel from Mozambique.[104]

The consequence was disastrous, since the local Catholic community was ill-equipped for such an exodus that affected approximately one third of their missionary and pastoral manpower, including four of the nine bishops

---

103. Serapião, "The Preaching of Portuguese Colonialism," 37.
104. Baur, 2000 Years of Christianity, 331–332

who had been in Mozambique until the time of their expulsion from the country. The overbearing presence of the Portuguese clergy and the furtherance of their nationalist sentiments did not permit them to make a difference between the political colonial interest of Portugal and the religious and ecclesiastical interest of the Church. That much is displayed in the conspicuous absence of the native character in the mission personnel, because the first Mozambican priest was only ordained in 1953 and their number was a meager twenty-seven indigenous priests in 1975. Consequent upon the turn of events in the country, the Vatican was only forced by circumstances to begin to appoint indigenous bishops of Mozambican nationality, something it had previously feared to do so as not to anger Portugal.[105] It was a heavy price for the Vatican to pay for its failure to be proactive since, while it had brought other missions in Africa under its control and supervision, it deluded itself by according diocesan status to the missions in Angola and Mozambique dependent on Lisbon, while the remainder of the missions elsewhere in Africa were regarded as vicariates or prefectures. The missions in Portuguese territories were poorly served and weaker than in most of the other places on the continent.[106]

The racial issues were by no means limited to the Catholic Church in South Africa. Compared to the excesses of Portuguese bishops such as De Gouveia, his successor Custodio Alvim Pereira, Francisco Nunes Teixeira of Quelimane and Felix Niza Ribeiro, the racial preferences of the South African bishops becomes insignificant. With the notable exception of Bishop Sebastiao Soares de Resende, the first Bishop of Beira, even himself was a subtle nationalist, the other Portuguese bishops were as notoriously nationalists and colonialists as the colonial officials of the Portuguese government in Africa. It is astonishing that the Vatican, under Pope Paul VI, never took notice and never bothered to rein in the nationalist excesses of the bishops to the detriment of both the missions and the legitimate aspirations of the people for self-rule, to which the bishops paid no attention in their scorn for Africans. Nobody best captured the absurdity of the missionary situations in Angola and Mozambique than the then Archbishop Emmanuel Milingo of Lusaka. He once decried the financial inducements and entitlements that secured the silence of the bishops. They were rendered numb to the oppression of their flock by a colonial power that happened to be the bishops' country of origin: "With these privileges, the Catholic Church is muzzled.

---

105. Baur, 2000 Years of Christianity, 333–335.
106. Hastings, *A History of African Christianity*, 60.

No priest will be allowed to work in Portuguese Africa unless he promises not to say anything against the government."[107]

The failure on the part of the Vatican to call Pereira to order may be considered one of the failures of the pontificate of Paul VI in relation to Africa. As Luis Serapião rightly observed, a great deal goes wrong when men of God unashamedly assume roles as men of the State, as indeed some of the bishops in question actually did. For instance, in 1965, Bishop Ribeiro expelled the White Fathers from the minor seminary in Tete and passed the administration to the Jesuits of Portuguese nationality. This was done for political reasons, because the White Fathers had been in charge of the minor seminary since 1950.[108] At a point in the 1960s, Custodio Alvim Pereira expelled some of his Mozambican seminarians who accused him of being more of a Portuguese representative than a bishop of the Catholic Church. For the seminarians whom he did not expel, he drew up a rule where, according to him, they ought to realize that

> [t]he native people of Africa have the obligation to thank the colonialists for all the benefits which they receive from them... The slogan *Africa for the Africans* is a philosophical monstrosity and a challenge to the Christian civilization, because today's events tell us that it is communism and Islam which wish to impose their civilization upon the Africans[109].

It is obvious that, in many instances, the indigenous clergy was up in arms against both ecclesiastical and political forces. It was one of the reasons that Engelbert Mveng once described the courage of the authors of *Des Prêtres noirs s'interrogent* as "the first distinctive statement by African theologians" in pursuit of an independent local church. Their courage is often regarded as the remotest push by African indigenous priests for the proper Africanization of their local churches. It put in motion a lengthy process that slowly gathered momentum as time progressed and reached its *terminus ad quem* with the first African Synod of Bishops in 1994.[110] As curious as it could be, Fr Gérard Bissainthe, one of the contributors to the book, was a participant at the 1956 International Congress of Black Writers and Artists in Paris. At the time, he was a young Haitian priest with a leftist orientation in his writings. Fr Bissainthe was, at one point in time, the leader of Jeune Haiti, an anti-communist movement. His presentation at the Congress was on "Christianity in the face of the cultural aspirations of the

107. Serapião, "The Preaching of Portuguese Colonialism," 37.
108. Serapião, "The Preaching of Portuguese Colonialism," 38.
109. Cited in Serapião, "The Preaching of Portuguese Colonialism," 36.
110. Mveng, "The Historical Background," 20–31.

Negro peoples" and his chapter in *Des Prêtres noirs s'interrogent* is entitled "Catholicisme et indigénisme religieux." To a great extent, as noted by Bénézet Bujo, *Des Prêtres noirs s'interrogent* can be regarded as the "founding charter of African theology."[111] With a single purpose, it brought together some young African francophone scholars who would later emerge as both pioneers and leading figures of the nascent discipline of African theology between the 1970s and the 1980s. It included the likes of the Congolese theologian Vincent Mulago, with his insistence on the need for missionary adaptation; the Beninese theologian and future Bishop Robert Sastre on "Roman liturgy and negritude," as well as the prolific Rwandan philosopher Alexis Kagame, who was celebrated for his literary prowess.[112]

As it turned out, it was in *Des Prêtres noirs s'interrogent* that the phrase "fundamental African theology" appeared to have made its debut as an expression. It was coined by the Cameroonian theologian Meinrad P. Hebga, in his own contribution entitled "Christianisme et Négritude." He argued that Négritude was compatible with Christianity. On the basis of that compatibility, he called for the rethinking of Christian problems by means of African categories, particularly with reference to the skin color of Jesus, Mary and the Jewish extended family system that, in some way, was akin to African culture:

> And ourselves, African priests, are we so sure that we always defend ourselves well from a vague complex of poor relations in the Church of God? Now, we must be sowers of Christian enthusiasm. Hence the need to rethink, each one of us, this problem of fundamental African theology... Negritude can be assumed by Christianity without getting lost in it or denying itself[113].

Although less known in most of Anglophone Africa at the time, *Des Prêtres noirs s'interrogent* was important enough to cause a major stir in French Africa. It had both political and religious undercurrents. There was some measure of inquietude among the bishops, particularly those in French Africa, who, in one of the plenary meetings under the presidency of the Apostolic Delegate, on the suggestion of the bishops in Cameroon, directed that the local clergy should guard against the possibility of making a compromise with movements that had political and radical agendas. In the same line of thought, indigenous priests were instructed to remember

---

111. Bujo, "Vincent Mulago," 15.
112. Bujo, "Vincent Mulago," 14.
113. Hebga, "Christianisme et Négritude," 190–191; Hebga, "Englebert Mveng," 40 and footnote 3.

the Catholic Church as one and as such there was no place for particularistic spirit and exaggerated nationalism.[114]

The Propaganda Fide issued an instruction *Consideranda* in 1956. Primarily addressed to missionary congregations and institutes, it recalled the stipulations of *Maximum Illud* in directing missionaries not to prize their congregations and institutes above the overall interest of the Church, especially with regard to the indigenous hierarchy. It also insisted that missionaries were not to put their countries before the good of the Church's missionary apostolate. In the same vein, it demanded that indigenous priests must guard against actions that might be detrimental to the missions or that might jeopardize the progress and growth of the missions.[115] As the Latin adage goes, virtue lies in the middle. Both the Holy See and its missionary dicastery, the Propaganda Fide, needed to tread cautiously in the application of their policy of indigenization in Africa. But even at that, it did not escape close scrutiny and critics, especially in France, where it was interpreted as a political undertaking by the Vatican in its bid to form an alliance with nationalist movements for independence in Africa.

One of the influential manuals of study widely in use in the francophone domain was the *Code de morale internationale*, produced by l'Union de Malines and published in Paris in 1937. L'Union de Malines assembled a group of Catholic theologians and sociologists from different European countries to articulate a common understanding about the place of Christianity in the superstructure of colonization. According to the ideologues, "coloniser, c'est civiliser; civiliser, c'est émanciper." In other words, based on their understanding at the time, to colonize was to civilize and to civilize was to emancipate. Civilization, with its related components such as evangelization and education, was used as a justification for the colonial enterprise. That understanding formed the basis of vitriolic criticisms from François Méjan (1908–1993) directed against the Vatican's policy of indigenization in Africa. Méjan was a lawyer by profession and a civil servant who had been on service in French Africa. His disapproval and criticisms of the Vatican's policy were published in his book *Le Vatican contre la France d'Outre-Mer*. From the standpoint of Méjan, the missionary policy of the Vatican was a novelty, because it was based on the de-westernization of the missions in Africa and geared towards the elevation of the indigenous clergy, which, in his judgment, fanned the flames of their aspiration for independence. It was also a novelty, because the Catholic Church had not previously implemented such a radical policy in a place such as South America, where the Catholic

---

114. Brasseur, "L'Église Catholique et la Décolonisation," 55–56.
115. Brasseur, "L'ÉgliseCatholique et la Décolonisation," 56.

missions had been working since the arrival of Christopher Columbus in 1492. Méjan thus posed this question: "Why is the Church now doing in Africa what it did not in South America?"[116]

The diatribes of Méjan against the Vatican emanated from the fact that he could not bear seeing a White missionary work under an African bishop. That much he did not hide and considered it opposed to the teaching of Leo XIII and against missionary practice and tradition. He quibbled that a White missionary could not be made to work as an auxiliary to the local clergy. It was equally an impossible demand to require missionaries not to work for the interests of their countries of origin. The Holy See, he argued, abandoned Western civilization to its own detriment if it continued to insist that the Church needed to be indigenized in mission territories. Méjan viewed the acceleration in the appointment of young African clerics to the bishopric as a big mistake on the part of the Church.

Not only was the speedy promotion of indigenous priests against the hitherto common practice, but in his judgment, the Church was playing into the hands of African neo-nationalists and would stand to regret its policy, as in the case of South Vietnam, which brought about the subordination of the Catholic local hierarchy to nationalist politics. The consequence of that policy might as well end in popping up some Hitler in Africa, as was the case in Germany. Méjan was emphatic that the Vatican, through its indigenization policy, contributed to the global anger against the White man, which had progressively led to the shrinking of the once vast overseas colonies of Europe. And with regard to France, the Church had shown the worst of ingratitude for not recognizing and returning the favors, advantages and benefits, which the Church had always received from generous France until then.[117]

Wladimir d'Ormesson, a French diplomat at the Vatican, expressed a similar sentiment. In thanking Méjan for the boldness and clarity of his thought in articulating the unspoken truth about the ingratitude of the Vatican towards France, d'Ormesson wrote this much:

> We are showered with ingratitude on all sides. We have spread civilization far and wide and now this civilization pushes us away in the very name of the doctrine that gave rise to it . . . it is a bitter cycle[118].

---

116. Méjan, *Le Vatican contre la France*, 11.
117. Méjan, *Le Vatican contre la France*, 10–21.
118. Cited in Foster, *African Catholic*, 5.

The preface writer of the book was Bernard Lavergne, professor in the Faculty of Law at the University of Paris. He cited the words of Luc de Clapiers, marquis de Vauvenargues and eighteenth-century French writer, so as to make his point about the timeliness of the book and the courage of its author to state the truth as it was:

> There is need to have great resources in spirit and in heart to savour the truth when it hurts, or to practice it without offence. Few people have enough strength to bear the truth and to say the truth[119].

As events turned out, the French did not have the final word on the polemics relating to the Vatican's indigenization policy in Africa. Beside the authors of *Des Prêtres noirs s'interrogent*, some Africans also wanted an immediate end to the missionary tutelage of the local churches in Africa. While the French were vexed about the supposedly speed with which the policy was implemented, the Africans were rather dissatisfied with the slow pace in progress. As noted earlier, many places on the continent either had only one native bishop or were yet to register any indigenous episcopal ordination by 1960. One of those who fired the salvo was Bishop Joseph Malula (later Cardinal Malula). Following his episcopal consecration on 20 September 1959, less than a year before the independence of Zaire from Belgium, Bishop Malula declared that he wanted to see the emergence of "A Congolese Church in a Congolese State," implying their desire to see the evolution of an African Church in an independent Africa as quickly as possible. In his praise for Msgr Malula, Elochukwu Uzukwu described the bold assertion of the Congolese ecclesiastic as "more an exception than the rule," given the time it was made.[120] The insistence of Malula on "a free Congolese Church" may be explicable by the affirmation of Adrian Hastings:

> only when local bishops form a majority in the country and at the meetings of the episcopal conference, it is really clear in theory and in practice that theirs is the decisive responsibility[121].

The preponderance of White missionary bishops in the national hierarchies, as they were constituted in Africa at the time, made the realization of a clear majority by a few African indigenous bishops among them an impractical possibility. Even after Congo (Zaire at the time) had had many of its bishoprics occupied by indigenous bishops, Cardinal Malula returned

---

119. Bernard Lavergne, "Préface," 7.
120. Uzukwu, "The Birth and Development," 3.
121. Hastings, "The Ministry of the Catholic Church," 33.

to the same issue, although reframed differently, at the 1974 Synod of Bishops in Rome. Since Africa was to be Christianized by Africans, it meant that a postcolonial continent that had suffered political, economic and cultural dominations, demanded respect for its autonomy and its responsibility. Again, since the past was the past, a post-missionary Church in Africa must ask itself how it could "indigenize" and "localize" on African soil.[122] One of the criticisms against African advocates of "indigenization" is their half-hearted attempts to seriously rethink their commitment beyond mere rhetoric and their apparent "dislike" of anything Western. For instance, unlike some African countries, Zairian schools at the time of Cardinal Malula maintained a decided character. In the explanation of Patrick Boyle, that Western character was part of the inheritance of the Congolese Church from the missionaries and the indigenous bishops who strenuously worked to preserve it. By so doing, they stamped an orientation to Zairian education that has remained endured, because the social and political prestige of mission schools lies in the fact that they had trained most of the country's leaders of the independence era.[123]

Many critics of the post-missionary African Church leader hold the view that Africanization of Christianity went beyond the replacement of European bishops and White missionaries with African indigenous clergy. Such critics also went beyond the mere translation of liturgical and biblical texts from foreign languages into African languages. It ultimately required a change of mindset in terms of vision and orientation.[124] As the number of expatriate bishops in Africa dwindled very significantly in the late 1970s, the focus of the contestation regarding indigenization slightly shifted towards the agitation for the restructuring of ecclesiastical institutions that were inherited from the missionaries. Walbert Bühlmann identified three phases in the controversy on the paths towards indigenization of the African Church. In the first phase, the outcry was not very discernible, but it was characterized more or less by passive or active resistance by the indigenous priests who were very few or even non-existent in some places. The missionaries controlled everything during this phase. The second phase was characterized by the slow emergence of the native priests as a distinct group, but they remained in the minority. They lamented their oppression under the missionaries and complained that the missionaries prevented them and their local churches from developing. The last stage in the contestation saw the occupation of key diocesan posts by the indigenous clergy who had

---

122. Malula, "Per cristianizzare l'Africa," 130.
123. Boyle, "Beyond Self-Protection to Prophecy," 55–56.
124. Salamone and Mbabuike, "The Plight of the Indigenous," 212, 216.

emerged as a strong group in many places. The final phase also witnessed the calming of the tension that had previously existed between the local clergy and the missionaries. Where the missionaries had been previously resisted in the first and second phases, in the last stage of the controversy, they were welcomed most especially for their financial support.[125]

It became somewhat paradoxical in 1974 at the Synod of Bishops in Rome, when Bishop Jean-Baptiste Gahamanyi of Butare (Rwanda), during his presentation, questioned the rationale why the established churches of Europe and America should abandon the poor churches of America! He acknowledged the inability of their local churches to support their pastoral personnel such as priests and catechists. He reminded the synodal assembly that missionary apostolate was more than the simple establishment of local churches with their native hierarchies and indigenous clergy. For that very reason, he argued that it was not possible for bishops and priest in wealthy countries not to remember their confrères in the poor countries of Africa.[126] Such a mindset served to reinforce the presumption and pretentiousness in some missionary circles at the time, which strongly subscribed to the view that Christianity in Africa could not survive without foreign assistance, especially from Europe and America. No less a great Christian figure in the twentieth century, Bishop Stephen Neil was convinced that he did foresee the survival of African Christianity without missionaries and financial help from the West.[127]

A few African theologians loathed the attitude of begging with cap in hand by the local churches. One of such theologians was the Cameroonian ex-Jesuit priest, Fabien Ebuoussi Boulaga. In his 1974 article entitled *La dé-mission*, he demanded the immediate withdrawal of missionaries from Africa: "Let Europe and America give priority to their own evangelisation. Let us plan the orderly departure of missionaries from Africa."[128] Six years later, Walbert Bühlmann proved, from the standpoint of statistics, that the call in the late 1970s by Africans for the withdrawal of missionaries from Africa was indeed made in good faith, although not without some controversial undertones. He noted that there were roughly eighty million people in the United States of America alone (equal to approximately one-third of the total population of Black Africa). Translated in actual fact, it meant that eighty million Africans were pastorally served by 5,000 missionary priests

---

125. Bühlmann, *The Coming of the Third Church*, 274.

126. Gahamanyi, "I sacerdoti e i catechisti sono poveri," 173–174.

127. Kendall, *The End of an Era*, 88–89; Mbiti, "Foreword," xvii.

128. Isichei, *A History of Christianity*, 326, 332; Pouconta, "Meinrad Pierre Hegba," 76.

and 10,000 nuns. The important question to ask was: How did people in the United States of America at the time feel about those eighty million people without any church affiliation in America?[129] In order to remedy that anomaly and imbalance, the venerable Kenyan theologian had, a decade earlier in his famous speech in Milwaukee, as the Secretary General of the Presbyterian Church of East Africa, insisted on a radical change of mindset in reference to what he called "the Vasco da Gama mentality." It was a mentality "that went out to explore the world and help the heathen and the poor." As far as Gatu was concerned, that mentality was "still haunting the many of western churches."[130] Perhaps, he should also have added "some of the churches of Africa."

In 1967, the Cameroonian theologian Meinrad Pierre Hegba sustained a similar line of thought with his article entitled "Émancipation d'églisetutelle?." He expanded and published it in 1976 with the title Émancipationd'église sous tutelle. Essai sur l'ère post-missionaire. Hegba understood the tutelage of the local churches as "spiritual neo-colonialism" and their "emancipation" required the rethinking of administrative structures and capital-intensive social projects such as schools and hospitals. According to him, if judged expedient, a local was at liberty to discard personnel-and-resource-draining projects. Such rethinking and discarding of projects that local churches could not shoulder would translate to their eventual emancipation from financial preoccupations bequeathed to them by the missionaries.[131] A corroboration of Hegba's thought can be found in the musing of Bishop Patrick Augustine Kalilombe on the prospects and difficulties of the Lilongwe diocese under his pastoral leadership as the first Malawian to occupy that post in the diocese in 1974.[132] Lilongwe became a Diocese in 1959, with the appointment of Msgr J. Fardy as its first Bishop.

As a dynamic and visionary leader, Msgr Kalilombe soon realized the insufficiency of the Africanization of the episcopate without a corresponding radical restructuring of church apparatus. As he aptly articulated, "a local church running with the help of other churches is always a dependent church." Although local contribution amounted only to 16,388 kwachas of 96,650 kwachas needed annually to run his diocese, he was convinced that local means need to be found, in order to augment the diocesan financial resources; necessary adjustments were also imperative. In his determination

129. Bühlmann, "Mission in the 1980s," 98.
130. Kendall, The End of an Era, 91.
131. Pouconta, "Meinrad Pierre Hegba,," 71.
132. For a brief biography of Msgr Kalilombe, see https://dacb.org/stories/malawi/kalilombe-patrick/

to end the dependency syndrome, he considered it anomalous that the local church alone, amidst all the agitations for political, economic and cultural independence in Africa at the time, should still remain dependent for its existence on the charity of other churches from abroad. He concurred with the prevalent idea of his time that the African local churches, despite their indigenization in terms of the composition of the national hierarchies, had largely remained copies of their European and American prototypes. To keep those copies in existence, foreign resources and supports were constantly needed, because the "local churches" had only been "transplanted" churches, together with the corresponding methods and structures. He judged that all those needed total overhauling in cognizance of the local reality and exigencies.[133]

The thoughts of Hegba, Kalilombe and the others indicated the progression to another level with regard to the thorny question of indigenization. It soon became evident that much more than the appointment of African indigenous clergy to the bishoprics in the local churches was indeed needed. In his book *Missions on Trial* (1980), Walbert Bühlmann synthesized the debates and the predominant views on the 1956 issue, when *Des Prêtres noirs s'interrogent* was published by a group of thirteen young African and Haitian priests in Europe. Beside individual nuances, the core of the opinion remained essentially the same. Kalenga Matembele, a Congolese priest, taking the liberty to "speak in the name of African Catholic priests from different countries," seemed to have succinctly captured the kernel of their grievances against Rome and the missionaries beyond the question of Africanization of the episcopate. In a nutshell, everything came down to the fact that the real "implantation of the Church" had not taken place in Africa, since the "local church" was, in fact, only "a faded copy of the European church." While it appears that the Roman Church had, in principle, permitted the Africanization of the local church, it felt its structures threatened with its insistence that everything had to proceed according to the imported pattern.[134]

In the final analysis, the Church remained, to a large extent, one of the organizations and institutions on the continent that were still dependent for their survival on outside help in terms of personnel, money and ideas. The contestation about Africanization or indigenization was one big issue that defined the Catholic Church and gave its peculiar face and identity. It is not surprising that the controversies around it lasted for over twenty-five years. The liberality, with which some episcopal conferences in Africa discussed the almost unspoken issue of priestly celibacy, can also be

133. Kalilombe, "The African Local Churches," 85–89.
134. See Bühlman, *Mission on Trial*, 48–53.

interpreted as part of the defining feature of the young churches. The boldness and forward-looking, with which a few episcopal conferences on the continent made their voices heard on the topical matter of the day, are quite remarkable. In comparison to later developments, the then young churches of Africa seemed to have shown an unusual courage and openness with regard to priestly celibacy after the argument of Adrian Hastings who, in 1964, defended the priestly ordination of "tried and tested married men."[135]

Four years later, in July 1968, subsequent to the article of Hastings, the bishops of Zambia sought permission from Rome to ordain some married men. The hierarchies of Gabon, Chad, Central African Republic, Congo-Brazzaville and Cameroon followed suit in July 1969 in asking for the green light to ordain married men whose ordination, the bishops concluded, was the only possible way "to answer the most elementary pastoral need." Although Cardinal Paul Zoungrana considered the issue an "imported question," it did not stop the matter from being discussed widely prior to the 1971 Synod of Bishops in Rome. Three African bishops, namely Cardinal Malula of Kinshasa, Msgr Peter Sarpong of Kumasi, and Msgr Joachim N'Dayen of Central African Republic, raised their voices in support of the ordination of married men.[136] Typical of Rome, as Kalenga Matembele rightly observed and lamented on the celibacy question: "Our views were asked but were not listened to."[137] Perhaps, that hard realization had the effect of forcing and shaping the local young churches of Africa into their conservative mould that seems to have become the subsequent trademark and the collective identity of the Catholic Church in Africa.

135. Hastings, "The Ministry of the Catholic Church," 40.
136. Hastings, "The Ministry of the Catholic Church," 41.
137. Bühlman, *Mission on Trial*, 51.

5

A populous church—Quo vadis?

Historians are not prophets, and they get their fingers burnt when they venture to predict the future. As a scientific discipline, therefore, history does not make predictions about the future, for that is outside its domain. Through historical hermeneutics, it is possible to understand the present and to get a glimpse of certain residual elements connecting the past, the present, and the future. Although this remains mostly true of historical perspectives, historians are hesitant about, and even wary of predicting future events on the basis that the shape of the future and its contours are largely unclear at present.[1] Despite its unknowable nature, certain things may be said about the future from a careful historical analysis of the past and the present.

In light of the above, the 1972 phenomenal book by Karl Rahner, *The Shape of the Church to Come*, is instructive. Occasioned by the 1971 National Synod of the Church in Germany, Rahner called on the Church to a critical self-examination of its mode of being and operation, to jettison a ghetto mentality and to better engage the world with courage and responsibility.[2] From the history of the Catholic Church in Africa, one noticeable thread that has been running through it is its search of a *persona* and a theology. This perennial search was deciphered by Adrian Hastings in 1989, after the announcement, on 6 January 1989, of the convocation of the First Africa Synod by Pope John Paul II that was to take place in Rome.[3]

1. Hogan, *The Irish Missionary Movement*, 172.
2. Rahner, *The Shape of the Church to Come*.
3. Hastings, *African Catholicism*, 19.

The Church in Africa has remained constantly in flux from the missionary phase to the post-missionary era between the 1970s and early 1980s. This state of flux continued even after the First and Second African Synods in 1994 and 2009, respectively. In search of its *persona*, the shape of the Church in Africa to come begins presently with a critical self-examination of its brief history. This quest for the identity of the future Church in Africa already featured in the first session of the First African Synod, when, in the course of his presentation, Cardinal Hyacinthe Thiandoum of Dakar asked: "Church of Africa, what must you now become so that your message may be relevant and credible?"[4]

PROGRESS AND PITFALLS POST-MISSIONARY ERA

Collectively, particular churches in Africa passed from the missionary tutelage to the tutelage of Rome. The Roman tutelage became heightened during the pontificate of John Paul II, under whom the local churches took refuge in conservatism. In the late 1960s, the Roman curia under Pope Paul VI fired the first salvo in that direction, when Rome was alarmed by the bold proposals emanating from Africa on the heels of the immediate post-Vatican II years. As most of them emerged from countries that still had a significant presence of White missionaries at the head of national hierarchies, Rome thought it expedient to accelerate the appointment of local African clergy to take their place. Such acceleration was needed, in order to diffuse the pressure from those bold proposals, especially in relation to the request for permission for the priestly ordination of married men to assist in the pastoral care of the emerging churches. Besides Rome's outright rejection of those requests from Zambia, Cameroon, Central Africa Republic and South Africa, the Zambian episcopal conference was singled out for reprimand. They were sternly warned to desist from further discussion on the matter. The clipping of wings of the young churches appeared somewhat completed by the late 1970s, with the elevation of many African priests to the bishoprics across the continent. For some obvious reasons such as financial support, coupled with their determination to give a good account of themselves, pioneer African bishops did not consider it prudent to rock the boat.[5]

True to its character, Rome often concedes with one hand and holds back with the other. In his speech to six cardinals and forty bishops from Africa in Rome for SECAM'S meeting on 26 September 1975, Paul VI sought to inquire from the bishops if there was still any residue of foreignness about

---

4. Thiandoum, *The Church in Africa*, 12.
5. Hastings, *African Catholicism*, 132–133.

the Church in Africa. He added a *caveat* that any theological research "in a manner suited to the African mentality" must not be permitted to derail the work of evangelization, since there is no "freedom or autonomy outside" the ecclesial community:

> Is the Church in Africa dependent on an imported form of Christianity which makes it foreign to its own populations? Is it not necessary to seek new and more appropriate ways, in the theological as in the pastoral field, to integrate by perfecting the traditional cultural values of your peoples, however prudently and with wisdom? ... There can be no freedom—or autonomy, as they say—of theological research which is outside the "communia Ecclesiae"[6].

The experience and historical progression of the local church have been drifting in this direction, specifically between autonomy and tutelage. Within that binary, the Roman control of the particular churches in Africa became accentuated, as the influence of missionary congregations and institutes rescinded. It is, therefore, safe to assume that such control was realized with an increase in the number of African bishops. The process of "Romanization" of the Church in Africa, after Paul VI, became a *fait accompli* with the long pontificate of his successor. The pontificate of Pope John Paul II coincided with the definitive end of the missionary period in Africa. By the time of the First African Synod in 1994, Africans constituted roughly 90 percent of the Catholic bishops on the continent and a good number of them were appointed by John Paul II.[7] Intermittently, during the pontificate of John Paul II, the Church in Africa became progressively a church to be lectured and rarely heard. Compared to the early years that witnessed some bold initiatives, the Church in Africa seemed to have been intimidated into silence.[8] By contrast, John Paul II treaded with caution in his dealings with the Church in the United States of America. Although viewed as problematic on account of its resources and challenging contentions, American Catholicism was one of the significant realities during the pontificate of John Paul,[9] which, in his judgment, was "the source of much recent criticism of traditional Catholic morality."[10] The same standard of measurement was not always used in the case of Africa. For instance, the modest aspiration of SECAM in 1986 to get around the seemingly less problematic question

6. Paul VI, "To the Participants at SECAM," §6, 12.
7. Oborji, "The Mission *ad gentes*."
8. Hastings, *African Catholicism*, 136.
9. Riccardi, *Il Potere del Papa*, 364.
10. Hanson, *The Catholic Church*, 92.

of "inculturation" earned the continental episcopal body some reprimand from Rome.

That reprimand must be placed within the context of the Roman curia, where some officials acted as heavy counterweights to the power of national episcopal conferences and continental episcopal groupings such as the Latin American Bishops' Conference (CELAM) or SECAM. The predominant fear among those curial officials was about the so-called "progressive theologians" who, in the reasoning of the men of the curia, if not checkmated, posed the danger of hijacking the proceedings and directions of episcopal conferences.[11] The position of that segment of the curia was further reinforced by John Paul II's policy of "personal interventionism," which was one of the major distinguishing characteristics of his pontificate concerning internal church affairs and style of ecclesiastical government.[12] With regard to SECAM, as shown by Jean-François Bayart, the critical audacity of the African episcopal continental grouping within the first ten years of the pontificate of John Paul II was effectively curtailed because of the temerity of the bishops towards some kind of auto-definition of their local churches as different from European and American churches with Western background and culture.[13] The issue in question was the 1986 audacious assertion of the Theological Commission of SECAM at the end of its meeting in Abidjan, where it dared to make a distinction between the pope's role as presiding over the Church in "charity" and not in "culture":

> The work of inculturation will only be done by the Churches of Africa themselves. And if the Pope presides, it is by charity and not by culture. It is among other things for not having understood this distinction that there have been, during the history of the Church, the ruptures of the Byzantine, Slavic and Germanic worlds ... Our Churches were founded by missionaries from the Latin world, but that does not mean that we have become Latin ... It must therefore be recognised that today, the admission of cultural pluralism on the part of the West is purely theoretical; there is no effective admission of such pluralism[14].

With a scathing remark, the late Cameroonian theologian Jean-Marc Éla once observed that the rhetoric about indigenization or Africanization of the episcopate was more like window-dressing.[15] From his standpoint,

11. Hanson, *The Catholic Church*, 91–92.
12. Hanson, *The Catholic Church*, 91.
13. Bayart, "Les Églises chrétiennes," 7.
14. Cited in Bayart, "Les Églises chrétiennes," 7.
15. Éla, *African Cry*, 102–103.

the passing over of the mantle of leadership of the local churches to African clergy was not accompanied with the required true autonomy that would have stopped them resembling mere extensions of Rome. This can be gleaned from their slowness for bold initiatives and discreetness in the expression of themselves.[16] It remains ironical that, after the re-establishment of the married diaconate in 1964 at Vatican II, the Church in Africa was the only local church to make the least use of it.[17] It is equally pertinent to note that the emergence of Small Christian Communities (SCCs), between 1960 and 1970, was one of the defining features of contemporary African Catholicism, especially in the francophone and eastern regions of the continent. The first datable event in that regard was the Sixth Plenary Assembly of the Zairian Episcopal Conference (present Democratic Republic of Congo) that took place from 20 November to 2 December 1961. During their plenary session, the Congolese bishops approved a pastoral plan for the establishment and promotion of what they called "Living Ecclesial Communities." In their collective presentations at the 1971 and 1977 Synods of Bishops in Rome, the African bishops highlighted the privileged place of the SCCs as indispensable tools of evangelization and a unique way of living the reality of ecclesial communion. For their part, the establishment and pastoral guide of the SCCs occupied the attention of the bishops of East Africa during the AMECEA meeting in Nairobi, Kenya, in 1976, where they stated that the "systematic formation of Small Christian Communities should be the key pastoral priority in the years to come in Eastern Africa."[18] It could be asserted that the 1970s and the 1980s were the era of SCCs in the annals of the history of contemporary African Catholicism.[19]

This broad sketch forms part of the backdrop of the historical perspectives of the Church in Africa during the first sixty years following the Vatican's indigenization program. While it does not capture every possible issue in the course of the past sixty years, it becomes, nonetheless, the basis for any future projection concerning the future of the Church in Africa. It remains only but a future whose roadmap is yet to be invented and distinctly drawn. As Thomas Sankara of Burkina Faso once said: "In order to bring about a radical change, it is necessary to have the courage to invent the future."[20] At the Abidjan Conference in February 2007, a fellow Burkinabé, Bishop Anselme Titianma Sanon of Bobo Dioulasso, courageously delineated

16. Éla, *African Cry*, 103.
17. Hastings, "The Ministry of the Catholic Church," 40.
18. Healey, "Historical Development," lines 60–61.
19. Majawa, "African Christianity," 220.
20. Cited in Albanese, "Africa, *Quo Vadis*," 152.

three key areas for the ecclesial future. According to Bishop Sanon, those key areas should engage the attention of the Church in Africa if it intended to take its place as an equal member alongside other sister churches under the bigger umbrella of the Catholic Church. In some ways, he was asking the Church in Africa to have "the courage to invent the future," by setting aright its present and future priorities. From his standpoint, the Church in Africa must live the teaching and spirituality of the Second Vatican Council; mature to become relevant and self-reliant, and contribute intellectually to the universal context.[21] In other words, if its previous mode of existence had been "parasitic," passive and the object of ecclesiastical "charity," the church of the future, as envisaged by Bishop Sanon, ought to stand up for itself, to make its voice heard loud and clear, and to rely on its own resources however meager those resources might seem.[22]

IN SEARCH OF AN IDENTITY PRE- AND POST-1994

One of the enduring legacies of Karl Rahner's ecclesiological insight is the distinction between the "worldliness" and "sinfulness" of the Church.[23] In her comments about Rahner's distinction, Karen Kilby explains that the "worldliness" of the Church is shaped by temporality, while its "sinfulness" refers to the departure of the Church from the ideal as a result of its being subject to change and occasional missteps like any other human institution.[24] Its worldliness is the inescapability of being embedded and a contingent of the Church in a particular place and time because those, to whom the Church must preach and reach out, have contexts within which they live. For pastoral reasons, according to Kilby, in her explication of Rahner's ecclesiology, the Church is, therefore, "always in the world, always already worldly, always in the midst of things, and only deceives itself if it thinks otherwise."[25] In this regard, the truths of the Christian faith are equally "perceived, received, known and articulated in historically particular ways."[26] Consequentially, the *locus* of the particular church within the universal Church, in terms of its geographical location and situation, shapes it and imprints its unique identity. As any botanist can tell, "the shape of a tree is the fruit of its interaction with its environment . . . The tree exists in

21. Majawa, "African Christianity," 217
22. Majawa, "African Christianity," 217–218.
23. Kilby, "Karl Rahner's Ecclesiology," 196.
24. Kilby, "Karl Rahner's Ecclesiology," 197.
25. Kilby, "Karl Rahner's Ecclesiology," 198.
26. Kilby, "Karl Rahner's Ecclesiology," 197.

itself, but it is only alive in multiple interactions with what is not itself."[27] The Church, as elsewhere, does exist like a tree and interacts with its immediate surroundings in Africa.

The Church in Africa finds itself in a continent that has been struggling with identity crisis in various manners: traditional, cultural, religious, political and economic. The African identity crisis arises from the historical context of different competing realities, including traditional culture and religion, Western civilization, Christianity, and Islam. In *Things Fall Apart*, Chinua Achebe articulated the multifaceted struggles of Africa for adjustments and auto-affirmation. Africa's efforts in that regard have not always been successful but characterized at times by some wobbling that has given rise to "Afro-pessimism," which considers Africa not only as a continent with problems but as the continent that is a problem for the world. This fact became more manifest since 1989, after the fall of the Soviet Block, when Africa progressively became relegated to the margin in the remaking of a new "world order."[28] All the discourse about "inculturation" and a "self-sustaining" local church must be understood within the wider discourse about Africa and its place in the world. While Pope Benedict XVI might assert that "Africa constitutes an immense spiritual 'lung' for a humanity that appears to be in a crisis of faith and hope,"[29] it is worthy of note that Vatican ecclesiastical bureaucrats are sometimes perplexed about what to do with its teeming population of African Catholics.[30] Their perplexity is rooted in the perennial Vatican's worries about "compatibility" and "communion," often tinctured with suspicions towards "African Christianity" that ought to develop within the framework of "legitimate pluralism."[31]

Rahner's preoccupations with the 1971 German Synod of Bishops might illuminate the horizon of the envisaged future of the Church in Africa in terms of self-understanding and self-affirmation. As far as Rahner was concerned, it did not suffice to repeat unquestionable statements of faith or assertions lifted from the decrees of Vatican II. He judged all those to be too general, and as such, it was pre-eminently important for the German Church to understand itself before proceeding to consider other issues. Essentially, the quest for self-understanding would bring about four important questions. Who are we? Where do we stand as a Church? What are we to do?

---

27. Radclife, "The Shape of the Church to Come," lines 4, 7–8.
28. Bediako, "Africa and Christianity," 303.
29. Benedict XVI, *Homily*, §4.
30. Allen, "To bongos and bass guitar," line 13; Racque, "The Evolution of Catholicism," line 33.
31. Maurice, "Le Symposium des Conférences," 473.

How can the future church be envisioned?[32] All four questions converge into one central issue principle. It concerns a critical self-introspection about the "who" and the "essence" of the Catholic Church in contemporary and future Africa as well as in its relation to the universal Church. First, creative imagination and vision are required to understand that the Church is embedded in Africa. The fates of both are intimately united. And to borrow from Ludwig Rütti,[33] the Church journeys with Africa towards the promised future. It does so in a manner that the Christian faith becomes of service to the continent in its journey towards self-affirmation and self-reliance in confronting the widespread dependency syndrome in Africa. In reference to the Church's self-reliance in the African context, it invariably implies its identity, its mission, and its self-realization.[34]

At its Eighth Assembly held in Lagos, Nigeria, from 12 to 19 July 1987, SECAM expressed the determination to facilitate a "concerted study on questions of interest to all the Churches in Africa and Madagascar, and to promote solidarity." They were identified by SECAM's then outgoing president, Cardinal Joseph Malula, as four significant challenges to the Church in the African context, namely the church's cultural identity, justice, social advancement, and ecumenism. It equally considered dialogue with African Traditional Religion and Islam and the difficulties in attaining African unity.[35] The search for its true identity as a local church has been a constant preoccupation for the leaders of the Church in Africa. It was manifested in the mid-1960s, when six African members on one of the committees of the Propaganda Fide in Rome realized to their dismay that they had hardly any or no knowledge about the problems of the different local churches within the African ecclesial context as a continent.[36] With the establishment of SECAM in 1969, local churches began a collective long journey in seeking their common identity. This meant that their concerns for a common African identity dominated much of African theology for approximately forty years. During that period, a shared identity was variously sought by means of terms such as 'adaptation', 'incarnation', 'indigenization' and 'inculturation.'[37]

At the 1974 Synod of Bishops, some leading African prelates such as Bishops Hyacinthe Thiandoum of Dakar, Joseph Malula of Kinshasa, Jean

---

32. Dederen, "Karl Rahner's The Shape." Dederen identifies only three questions. A fourth one has been added for the purpose of this research.
33. See Colzani, "La teologia della missione," 52.
34. Nwaigbo, "Self-reliance in the 21st Century," 36.
35. Maurice, "Le Symposium des Conférences," 475.
36. Maurice, "Le Symposium des Conférences," 472.
37. Kaggwa, "The New Catholicity," 190–191.

Zoa of Yaoundé, and James Sangu of Mbeya all spoke passionately about "adaptation." As far as they were concerned, this catchword would impart a defining mark or character on particular churches on the continent. According to Raymond Hickey, it was at the same synod that the term 'evangelization' largely replaced 'missionary apostolate', which had acquired a somewhat pejorative connotation in the immediate postcolonial context of the 1970s. As a concept, 'evangelization' was understood to be wider in scope to include all aspects of the Church's missionary apostolate in both the emerging young churches in the global south and the older churches in the global north.[38] That change in concept and understanding also occurred within the second epoch of the Church's missionary transition from 1945 to 1989, when the adaptation model replaced the model of implantation.[39]

Against the aforementioned background, the African bishops, at the 1974 Synod, shifted slightly from "adaptation" judged by them as "inadequate" and opted for "incarnation," which later gave way to "inculturation." Subsequently, inculturation became the presumed panacea for the problem of identity for the Church in Africa.[40] This is understandable, since the presence of the African bishops in 1974 represented collectively a new local church in Africa that was coming of age and that, as explained by Hickey, "was seeking visible symbols of its identity within the catholicity of the Church."[41] Despite the fact that the Church in Africa and its theologians came to appropriate "inculturation" as a catchword in relation to the identity of the local church, it bears recalling that the term itself was not proposed by Africans. The American anthropologist Melville Jean Herskovits is credited to have coined the term 'inculturation' in the 1930s to denote "the cultural education of a person."[42] It was borrowed from the field of anthropology by P.B. Segura in 1959, when he applied it theologically in his essay, "L'initiation, valeur permanente en vue de l'inculturation." In 1962, in his essay "L'Église ouverte sur le monde," Joseph Masson used the term again in a theological sense. It later gained widespread usage from 1975 after the Missiology Congress held at the Pontifical Urban University, Rome, and after the Thirty-second General Congregation of the Jesuits (1974–1975), which took place in Rome.[43]

38. Hickey, *Modern Missionary Documents*, 19.
39. Kaggwa, "The New Catholicity," 190.
40. Kaggwa, "The New Catholicity," 190–191.
41. Hickey, *Modern Missionary Documents*, 20.
42. Carreño, "A Truly African Church," 53.
43. Kaggwa, "The New Catholicity," 191; Winters, *Priest as Leader*, 27.

Situated in vast a continent of roughly 11,596,00 square miles, that is 22% of the earth's total landscape and three times bigger than Europe,[44] particular churches in Africa are different from one another on account of their missionary history and cultural heritage as well as their political, and socio-economic background. Despite the variegated nature of the local churches' experiences and peculiarity, one noticeable common denominator, since the beginning of the post-missionary phase of the history of contemporary African Catholicism, is the quest for self-definition and identity. In his speech at the First Plenary Assembly of SECAM on 28 July 1969, Cardinal Paul Zougrana of Burkina Faso surmized:

> Our very being must not be conferred on us from outside; the Gospel is a germ of life and the Church in Africa must develop itself up according to its own apostolic priorities[45].

One of the resultant offshoots of those "apostolic priorities" is that African theology became too narrow on culture that tended almost towards antiquarianism, as well as elitist, selective, artificial and idealistic in its longing for elements of a mythical traditional Africa of the past.[46] It may be described as romantic enthusiasm for an imaginary African "golden" past.

In her critique of the Congolese bishops, especially their proposal of marriage by trial, Bernadette Mbuye Beya cautioned that "inculturation" must never be confused with irrelevant traditionalism that is irrelevant to contemporary Africa.[47] One of the criticisms against the Church in Africa is its overt concern for self-definition and identity, which, during the course of the 1980s, became almost synonymous with "inculturation." The inherent danger tended to be the exclusion of other things, as if to give the impression that other important issues did not seem to have mattered. In fact, as Walter Aelvoet, Director of the African News Bulletin—*Bulletin d'Information Africain*—once observed:

> The churches in Africa were almost exclusively concerned with 'inculturation'—that they hardly concerned themselves about human rights, justice, and peace, freedom, democracy and the wretched material conditions in which human beings have to live[48].

---

44. Sangu, *Report on the Experiences*, 15.
45. Linden, *Global Catholicism*, 250; Kazingufu, "Synods in the Life," 18.
46. Kaggwa, "The New Catholicity," 192.
47. Kaggwa, "The New Catholicity," 194.
48. Cited in de Gendt, "African Christianity," 109.

The continental episcopal body SECAM showed itself susceptible to the distractions of "inculturation," which may have had some effects on its slowness towards development in other areas in terms of sharing ideas, advocacy and actions.[49]

Notwithstanding its perceived retardation and lack of steam, Kibanga Muhilh asserts that, in some important ways, SECAM provided a platform for some of its silent or dormant members: "The fact of pronouncing together on problems of African societies relieves certain episcopates who, for one reason or another, are almost confined to silence in their country."[50] The constant preoccupations with self-identity and "inculturation" were in no small measure a big distraction for the Church in Africa.[51] Those preoccupations naturally reached their *terminus ad quem* at the First African Synod, where a disproportionate amount of time and space was allotted to discussions on "inculturation." Apart from the twin question of justice and peace, "inculturation" was the second most discussed theme as a major interest for the Synod,[52] which meant that other crucial problems afflicting both the Church and the continent were rather touched lightly. Aside from all the flowering presentations, the Synod did not put much in place in terms of effective structures and mechanisms for the implementation of synodal deliberations and conclusions.[53]

Notwithstanding its shortcomings, the First African Synod cannot easily be dismissed with the wave of a hand as a mere talking show. It remains an important milestone and a reference point in the history of African Catholicism. In the estimation of Paulin Pouconta, that Synod was the culmination of the long march of the local Church's quest for its true place in the universal Church, and its specific mission.[54] This must be placed within the parameter of what the Synod fathers underscored in their final message, acknowledging that the universality of the church "is not uniformity but rather communion in diversity compatible with the Gospel" (*Final Message* 7). The cornerstone of the synodal definition of the Church in Africa is that the local churches on the vast African continent constitute the "Family of God in Africa" (*Final Message* 24).

---

49. Linden, *Global Catholicism*, 270.

50. Maurice, "Le Symposium des Conférences," 476.

51. Mugambi, "Theological Method," 98.

52. Carreño, "A Truly African Church," 51; Shorter, *Christianity and the African*, 116.

53. Henriot, "The Second African Synod," 11.

54. Pouconta, "Meinrad Pierre Hegba," 87.

This ecclesial self-understanding may not have been all that revolutionary. Nevertheless, it served as a springboard for both the rediscovery and the repositioning of the Church in Africa for the future. The question of its mission formed the basis for the Second African Synod of Bishops that took place in Rome from 4 to 25 October 2009. This Synod can be described as a complementary synod to the First African Synod. Francis Oborji observes that, while the First African Synod offered an opportunity for auto-definition and auto-awareness of the Church's mission of evangelization on the continent, the Second African Synod was complementary in providing the means for auto-critical examination of the Church to articulate concrete terms, scopes and strategies for effective evangelization.[55] Relevant theological questions needing answers include: What has really changed after the First and Second African Synods? How would the Church in Africa harness its numerical strength to reposition itself in the global Catholic community?

According to Jesse N.K. Mugambi, although there have been remarkable strides, the Church in Africa is yet to bring its influence to bear on the international scene despite its numerical strength. In order to be able to do so, it must be critical of itself through self-reflection and must grow out of self-congratulation. This was the case with the Latin American Church and its theologians in the mid-1960s, when they made an introspective self-criticism leading to a shift in their theological themes and pastoral orientations that impacted on the universal Church.[56] It is undeniable that the Church in Africa has registered an astronomical growth in the number of its faithful. Roughly a quarter of the world's Catholics are projected to come from Africa by the year 2030.[57] One notable lack of influence of the continent church could be observed in the appointment of the cardinal prefect to the Congregation for the Evangelization of the Peoples. If the vast majority of Catholics, as projected, may come from Africa, it is surprising that no African cardinal has been made head of that important missionary dicastery. In the course of the 400 years of its establishment, Propaganda Fide has seen the emergence of two Asian prelates as its cardinal prefects, whereas no African has attained that height. Against this background, the sad reality is that, even though the Church in Africa may have the numerical strength, but without ideology and strategic planning in ecclesiastical politics, it may remain a Church without influence where it matters most.

It can be adduced that numerical strength may not necessarily mean adulthood nor translate to global influence. This apparent lack of

---

55. Oborji, "Catholic Mission in Africa," 19–21.
56. Mugambi, "Theological Method," 93–94.
57. Ngulu, "The Church in Africa," 29.

commensurate influence in relation to its numerical strength is best illustrated by the perceptive observation of David Barrett: "If might were right, the elephant would be king of the forest."[58] *La Croix* once acknowledged this fact with dismay, when it noted that African Catholicism may be thriving, but it sadly "remains on the margins of global theological thinking."[59] Although the First African Synod made "inculturation" its central theme, as if it were connatural with the local church, a great deal more still needs to be done, since theological thinking is certainly much more than "inculturation." More so, within the local church, core issues have largely remained untouched, as can be deciphered in this candid perception by Joseph Ogbonnaya:

> But thus far, inculturation has been liturgical only, with the Eucharist celebrated in various native languages of Africa; in the use of local instruments used in sacred music; and in liturgical vestments sewn using African textile materials. In other areas of life, attempts at inculturation have been heavy on words and light on action[60].

In light of Ogbonnaya's observation, one area is ecclesiastical structure and administration. As an offspring of missionary Christianity, the Church in Africa shares a few heritages in common with other Christian churches on the continent and displays certain commonalities with them. In that continental spectrum, African Christianity remains an heir to hierarchical, authoritarian, and bureaucratic ecclesiastical structures bequeathed to it by the missionaries. This may not change in the foreseeable future.[61] Within the context of the Catholic Church, the much-lauded "inculturation" has practically not been able so far to replace those inherited structures with a viable alternative. "Inculturation" has largely maintained the emphasis on the need for the liturgy to be ritually contextualized, while carefully obviating the polemics about changes in ecclesiastical structures. Perhaps, it could be that such a move may not meet the dual criteria of "compatibility" and "communion," as set by the Vatican. More importantly, it could be that those structures actually meet the needs of African ecclesiastics, particularly from the point of view that their ecclesiastical powers, as inherited from the missionaries, are somewhat reinforced by the traditional African tendency for authoritarianism that is manifestly present in African contemporary

---

58. Cited in Oduyoye, "A Letter to My Ancestors," lines 41–42.
59. Racque, "The Evolution of Catholicism," lines 31–33.
60. Ogbonnaya, "The Church in Africa," 83–84.
61. Turaki, "Evangelical Missiology," 277.

politics.[62] Interconnected with administrative and structural dependency is the question of financial dependency *vis-à-vis* self-reliance. The latter could be designated as the derived demand of the former, albeit the level of financial dependence varies from diocese to diocese and from country to country.

It has been the collective aspiration of particular churches in Africa to attain some reasonable level of financial autonomy. As far back as 1974, the Kenyan bishops, in their submission presented in the collective report of the African bishops at the Synod, stated categorically their "aim to form a community that is self-supporting, self-ministering and self-propagating."[63] The Kenyan bishops' aspiration was corroborated by their Tanzanian colleagues in the same report, with the acknowledgement that "[a]ny Christian community which does not evangelize the people in her surroundings is like a fire which does not give warmth."[64] There certainly has not been the absence of any form of goodwill on the part of African bishops. Rather, what has been in short supply is the determination to match their goodwill with action. This is hampered by the insufficiency of financial resources to embark upon evangelization, sustain existing ministries, and maintain administrative and organizational machineries, which can be quite bogus in some dioceses. In applying the sociological model to the church, as Ferdinand Nwaigbo has succinctly shown, the Church, in its operational apparatus, is an organization or an institution created and structured by the work of human beings. In this regard, as a society, self-reliance and financial stability are necessary conditions, if the Church must provide for ministers and attend to other needs.[65] The vast majority of specific churches in Africa are poor and depend almost exclusively on Rome and other foreign churches for their financial support, even for the training of seminarians and the ongoing formation of priests. Realistically, the costs of their training and other expenses are well beyond what any poor diocese in Africa can afford.

In light of this reality, it is not an overstatement to affirm that it is in relation to financial capability that the Church in Africa mirrors effectively the continent where it is situated. Naturally, the fragility of the Church in Africa and its poverty cannot be dissociated from those of the continent whose social and economic crisis appears to worsen on a yearly basis.[66] The Church in Africa is poor, simply because it finds itself in a poor continent

---

62. Mugambi, "Theological Method," 86; Linden, *Global Catholicism*, 199.
63. Sangu, *Report on the Experiences*, 13.
64. Sangu, *Report on the Experiences*, 34.
65. Nwaigbo, "Self-reliance in the 21st," 37, 40.
66. Luneau, "The Expectations," 84.

where poverty is widespread, and the dependency mentality has long been a deeply enshrined phenomenon among political leaders. It often leaves them clueless and without a sense of creativity on the internal generation of revenue and proper management of available resources. It is a syndrome deeply enshrined in the psyche of many African leaders which spurs them to go cap in hand and keep knocking on the doors of the United Nations, the World Bank and the International Monetary Fund, the European Union or the United States Agency for International Development (USAID). Since the 1990s, China, the Dragon Empire, has positioned itself as the "Big Brother" of Africa and as an alternative to the West in perpetuating Africa's dependency syndrome on foreign assistance for the provision of basic amenities and infrastructure.[67] The predominant effect of the dependency syndrome has made the voice of Africa extremely weak on the international scene, due to more pressing messages. According to Andrea Riccardi, the voice of Africa remains "silenced in the great pool of information."[68] Within the Church, the situation is not all that different, as explicitly made clear by René Luneau:

> The churches of Africa are poor . . . How can one experience a relationship of equality when this feeling of "tutelage" from which nothing can really free you seems insuperable? These same churches, perpetually given assistance, will never succeed in making themselves heard by those which are better provided for and that many people, though without daring to say so, think that they have not yet come of age[69].

The attainment of maturity is without doubt much more than numerical strength in terms of both the number of its lay members and the priestly ordinations, with which the Church in Africa seems to have been richly endowed. Catholics in Africa accounted for 17.8 percent of the world's Catholics as at 2017.[70] Regarding priestly vocations, the 2020 Vatican Yearbook, in acknowledging the increase in the number of African priests, stated thus: "Africa, with a positive variation of 15.6%, confirms that it is the geographical area with the greatest potential to cover the needs of pastoral services."[71] Within this context, it is pertinent to reiterate the position of Adrian Hastings. It is not always the number of baptized Christians nor the number of native bishops that was necessarily indicative of the success of a

67. Wanza, "Self-Reliance," 71.
68. Riccardi, "The Social and Political Dynamics," 9.
69. Luneau, "The Expectations," 84.
70. Glatz, "Number of priests declined," line 15.
71. Esteves, "Vatican statistics show decline," lines 34–35.

mission.[72] In the informed viewpoint of Hastings, it was rather the active participation of local churches in the mutual giving and receiving within the universal Church that should become one of the marks of their maturity and autonomy, instead of being perpetual passive recipients of foreign "charity."[73] Cardinal Thiandoum hinted at the same fact at the First African Synod. He acknowledged that the Church in Africa was still a young church in "transition between a mission church and a church on mission, tasting its wings and seeking its way towards maturity, a church of the future with great hopes and optimism."[74] However, the "church is part and parcel of Africa in distress . . . poverty renders cooperation at the continental level very difficult."[75] To achieve financial self-reliance and self-sustainability and to transition from being a receiving church to a giving church remain an uphill task for the Church in Africa, largely due to its historical and geographical location in a poor continent.

Africa is constantly portrayed as a continent whose youthful populations are hampered by limited opportunities. For instance, the 2012 Report on *Africa Economic Outlook*,[76] puts the population of African youth, within the age bracket of 15 and 24 years, to be roughly 200 million. Sadly, the young people within this age bracket account for approximately 60 percent of unemployment in Africa.[77] The gloomy outlook is further compounded by another economic forecast that Africans might not reach parity with the 2015 US citizen's average annual income until the year 2255.[78] Another projection affirms that the population of Africa may hit 2.4 billion people by 2050. If there is no perceptible and substantial increase of the 1.5 percent gross domestic product of the vast majority of African countries, this may mean that more people in the sub-Saharan regions would become impoverished.[79]

Although poverty may remain a dominant feature of the Church in Africa, the Church need not be defined by poverty. The economic weakness of the Church in Africa, as Yusufu Turaki cautioned, "should not translate into

---

72. Hastings, *The World Mission of the Church*, 46.
73. Hastings, *The World Mission of the Church*, 46.
74. Thiandoum, *The Church in Africa*, 7–8.
75. Thiandoum, *The Church in Africa*, 9.
76. The report was prepared for the African Development Bank (ADB), the UN Development Programme (UNDP), and the UN Economic Commission for Africa (ECA).
77. Ighobor, "Africa's Youth," lines 12–15.
78. Brooks, *A Global History of Poverty*, 188.
79. Brooks, *A Global History of Poverty*, 188.

paternalism, dependency and dominance."[80] The local churches in Africa, like other institutions on the continent, will have to shelve their bogus sizes to checkmate their dependence on external aid. Such financial dependency, according to Bishop Patrick Kalilombe, remains "a double-edged sword" because of its potentials to "help the needy out of their predicament only to entrap them in their poverty and powerlessness perpetually."[81] But a self-reliant local church is not realizable through "a naïve unrealistic optimism" or mere words and best intentions without corresponding concrete actions and strategies.[82] It will be realizable through optimism and determination that are well founded on reality. The lack of adequate financial resources need not translate to mental lethargy and paralysis.

A good example is the Irish Church and the mobilization of its lay faithful to participate in the work of modern Irish missionary movements. Placed within the context of the Irish economy, which, until the late 1960s, was in a depressed state, the country itself was one of the poorest countries in Europe at the time.[83] That poverty did not lead to the paralysis of the Irish people and their local church, which in hindsight is not an overstatement to describe as truly heroic their generosity and support to their sons and daughters on mission in many parts of the world. The Catholic Church in Africa, notwithstanding the material poor condition of its teeming population, can equally mobilize them to do likewise, since, ideally, no one is too poor not to give, and no one is too rich not to receive. It can also use its numerical strength as a bargaining advantage, in order to make its voice heard on the international scene without shielding itself with an ultraconservative hard shell. At the end of the 1988 Lambeth Conference of the Anglican Church, a bishop from Africa, in considering the increasing numeric strength of the African bishops, was reputed to have said: "Anyone who wants a resolution passed in 1998, will have to come to terms with the African bishops."[84] The Church in Africa can borrow a leaf from that statement, alongside *la diplomatique de savoir faire* that is highly priced in Vatican politics together with personal connections and characteristics, enhanced by an ecclesiastic's background.[85] The ultimate questions to ask in this regard include: Does the Church in Africa, as the church of the future, possess the mental preparedness

---

80. Turaki, "Evangelical Missiology," 279.

81. Cited in Lucy Wanza, "Self-Reliance," 73.

82. Nwaigbo, "Self-reliance in the 21st," 36; Obiora Ike, "Towards a Self-Sustaining," 8–9.

83. Hogan, *The Irish Missionary Movement*, 127.

84. Cited in Bediako, "Africa and Christianity," 314.

85. Hanson, *The Catholic Church*, 91–92.

and sufficient energy to seize the moment? Will the Church be able to follow through its viable options and proposals? Though materially poor, is the Church willing and able to make itself heard as an equal stakeholder by repositioning itself beyond its present tag as an ultraconservative Church?

AVANT-GARDE FOR HUMAN PROMOTION AND DEVELOPMENT

The Church, as espoused by Karl Barth, is at the service of the state by continually reminding the state of its limits and responsibilities. This is predicated upon the "prophetic mission" of the Church, obliged by its vocation to render an indispensable service to civil society. This prophetic service is envisaged in the realization that the state as a human institution may from time to time derail or renege on its own civic responsibilities towards its citizens. This point of fact renders the prophetic mission of the Church fundamental for the good of society, because the Church's first social mission is to society rather than to politics.[86] As far back as 1986, the "African Report," presented in Mexico at the Second General Assembly of the Ecumenical Association of Third World Theologians, identified human promotion to be a major area of concern for evangelization. The authors of the report termed evangelization as "the announcement of the liberating good news to the poor, the oppressed and the weak."[87] For this very reason, human promotion, understood as evangelization in light of Africa's numerous challenges, ought to be "the priority of priorities."[88]

On the above note, Paul Gifford's insight is appreciated in his identification of two types of contemporary Christianity that are prevalent in Africa as elsewhere around the globe.[89] The two types are manifested in two different ways, together with their specific manners and emphasis. The first manifestation is the "utopian type" that provides moral ideas and illumination for contemporary society to measure itself and its social performance in the welfare of the citizens. In his exposition of the thought of Gifford, Jesse Mugambi notes that this type of Christianity is nurtured by sociology, economics, political science and historical analysis, with the ultimate aim of providing an objective critique of the *status quo*. The second type is the "ideological type," which often serves as a tool in the hands of oppressive

---

86. Couenhoven, "Law and Gospel," 194, 197, 199–200.
87. "African Report," 43.
88. "African Report," 43.
89 As analysed by J.N.K. Mugambi, "African Churches," 209.

regimes to coerce people to accept and conform to the *status quo*.[90] The "ideological type" of Christianity tolerates human suffering and deprivation as the inescapable condition of humanity on earth understood in medieval Catholic theology as "the valley of tears." Sadly, contemporary Christian fundamentalism thrives on this type of Christianity that rejects the social sciences. It seems obdurate in its intent to disregard the geo-economic and geo-political impacts on the concrete realities of society.

Since his research was carried out in the 1990s, Gifford particularly highlighted the figure of the German-American Pentecostal Evangelist, Reinhard Bonnke (1940–2019). He impacted on Africa in the 1990s with his evangelical crusades, with followers across the continent. According to Gifford, preaching a message that seemed to heap the economic woes and backwardness on the devil, Bonnke served as a prime example of the "ideological type" of Christianity. It makes people docile, submissive, fatalistic, and less concerned about their social, political and economic future. As Gifford observes:

> if demons cause every ill, there is no way of dealing with immediate causes of an economic or political nature. If cholera and TB in Mathari Valley are caused by demons, how can one ever proceed to deal with issues like lack of drains, toilets, sewers, doctors and drugs? If evil spirits cause madness and drunkenness, why should one consider the social conditions, the hopelessness, poverty, overcrowding, unemployment and illiteracy? Moreover, if it is Jesus who will change everything miraculously, what need is there for anything except faith? What incentive is there to take control over circumstances and one's future, by planning, strategizing, struggling and mobilizing?[91].

In contrast to the position of Bonnke was the stance of the late great African Statesman, Julius Nyerere of Tanzania, who insisted that the Church ought and must concern itself with the human promotion of Africans and the integral development of Africa. For Nyerere, the local church had no *raison d'être* in the continent, if it failed to get involved in uplifting the downtrodden and deprived Africans as well as speak out and confront institutions of injustice and oppression:

> Unless we participate actively in the rebellion against those social structures and economic organizations which condemn men to poverty, humiliation and degradation, then the Church will become irrelevant to man and the Christian religion will

---

90. Mugambi, "African Churches," 209.
91. Cited in Mugambi, "African Churches," 209.

degenerate into a set of superstitions accepted by the fearful. Unless the Church, its members and its organizations, express God's love for man by involvement in the present conditions of man, then it will become identified with injustice and persecution. If this happens, it will die—and, humanly speaking, deserve to die—because it will then serve no purpose comprehensible to modern man.[92].

It is most likely that sub-Saharan Africa will, in the foreseeable future, be a battleground between Christianity and militant Islam as it formerly was between capitalism and communism. More importantly, it will also witness the contest between mainstream orthodox churches and the prosperity gospel preachers who seem to encourage Africans to engage in day-dreaming and expect a pie from the sky amidst continental stagnation. For the Church in Africa, the shrinking pastoral field of operation on the continent will constitute a major challenge. This will be so, given the louder voices of Bonnke's brand of evangelists that are steadily on the increase in sub-Saharan Africa as well as the brash materialistic lifestyle among a significant number of the Catholic clergy. Since the Church cannot exist outside the life situation of ordinary and poor Africans who make up the bulk of its membership, it faces an uphill task to redefine its message in consideration of the living conditions of the faithful. It is imperative, according to Jean Ndimba, to bridge the wide gap between crowded churches and empty stomachs.[93] In the same vein, it is irreligious and smacks of hypocrisy for any religious organization to promise rewards after death and simultaneously expect material and financial support from the local community. As Mugambi pointedly writes:

> It is deceptive and dangerous to preach a gospel of prosperity in the midst of massive poverty, knowing that socio-structural constraints prevent many African communities from enjoying decent living by any standard[94].

Besides listing the natural resources in Africa, Torild Skard, in her book *Continent of Mothers, Continent of Hope: Understanding and Promoting Development in Africa Today*, directs the attention away from macroeconomic indicators and aggregates to ordinary Africans who bear the brunt of Africa's underdevelopment. She posited questions to highlight the urgency

---

92. Cited in Ogbonnaya, "The Church in Africa," 69–70.

93. "Crowded churches and empties" are taken are from Jean Ndima's thesis, presented at Boston College School of Theology and Ministry in May 2017. The full title of the thesis is: "*Crowded Churches and Empty Stomachs*": *The Paradox of Christianity and Poverty in the Congo-Zaire Opening a Way Towards a Post-Colonial Christianity*,

94. Mugambi, "African Churches," 218.

of accelerating integral development in Africa and to ensure that no person is left behind, especially women in the rural areas. These questions include: "What is Africa really like today for all the ordinary townsmen, villagers, and particularly mothers, breadwinners and children who live there?"[95] Seen through the eyes of the poor, Africa has, since the dawn of independence, intractably been caught in a sinking spiral of poverty, resulting in continuous deterioration in the living conditions of the vast majority of the people.[96] In actuality and without concrete actions, many Africans in the yet undetermined future may continue to "live off the land" and for the female folk in rural communities,

> unless they are lucky enough to live beside a stream, women trek daily for water, for longer and longer distances when the weather is dry. Before cooking over wood in a three-stone fireplace, they spend hours pounding the tubers or grain on which their families largely subsist[97].

Although this varies among communities and nations, it is indisputable that the ultimate tragedy of postcolonial Africa remains the lack of much progress in any form of sustainable development. Contrarily, most of the African countries have rather marched in "step from underdevelopment into maldevelopment, from the margins of potential economic viability in the 1960s into the deep abyss of abundant harvests of poverty" that worsened in the 1990s.[98]

Human welfare indicators point towards the direction that Africa is persistently trapped in a descending and never-ending spiral war of survival characterized by excruciating poverty, unemployment, illiteracy, diseases, corruption, exploitation, civil wars, refugees and economic migrants.[99] In its 1995 World Development Report, the World Bank once depicted Africa as a continent whose human welfare indicators were worsening. The proportion of Africans living below the international standard poverty line has been on the increase ever since. The continent's poverty, in the eyes of the World Bank, was abysmal since "the plight of Africa remains the most serious challenge for the merging world order, with Africa being more of an observant and a victim than a participant."[100] A year after that damning

---

95. Torild Skard, *Continent of Mothers*, 221.
96. Skard, *Continent of Mothers*, 151, 221.
97. Whitaker, *How can Africa Survive?*, 126.
98. Anise, "Descent into Sociopolitical Decay," 340.
99. McGarry, *What Happened at the Synod*, 176.
100. Cited in Ilesanmi, "Leave No Poor Behind," 78.

report, the then Organization of African Unity (OAU) acknowledged the failure of African political leaders and Africa's precarious conditions in its 1996 Yaoundé Declaration:

> We have noted, at the close of the 20th century, that of all the regions of the world, Africa is indeed the most backward in terms of development from whatever angle it is viewed and the most vulnerable as far as peace, security and stability are concerned[101].

This admission was repeated in 2002 by Amara Essy, then Secretary-General of OAU, to indicate that no tangible progress had been made, six years after the 1996 Yaoundé Declaration:

> It is no secret to anyone that Africa, our Continent, has up to now, remained the least developed [o]n the planet. All socio-economic indicators are in the red, thus portraying Africa as the only economic space whose growth has remained constantly negative. This state of affairs . . . verges on catastrophe[102].

Development in the African context is not to be understood in the generic sense, but rather in terms of "bread and butter" for those who lack basic life amenities. Expressed differently, development must be human-centered and become possible when Africans are able to access "the goods they need to develop and realize a conception of a personally and ethically worthwhile life."[103] The five key components of development in the African context, as explained by Adebayo Adedeji, were incisively articulated in September 1995 by an anonymous Somali Elder of Baidoa:

> First, is water. It is the first thing needed to live. Without it, a plant, an animal or a baby dies. Second, is food. Without enough of it, life is miserable and short. Third, once water and food are won, is health—otherwise the human being becomes sick. Fourth, is education, once a human being has water, food and health, he/she needs to learn to open new horizons and unlock new possibilities. And there is a fifth—peace and order. Without these, none of the four basic needs can be sustained[104].

These five cornerstones of development are described in economic terms as quantitative objectives such that failure to pay attention to them results in anti-development or underdevelopment. They collectively constitute the

---

101. OAU, *1986 Yaoundé Declaration*, 16.
102. Cited in Anglin, "The African Peer Review," 238.
103. Ilesanmi, "Leave No Poor Behind," 77.
104. Adedeji, "Democracy and Development," 23.

basis of human security, which implies living in freedom from hunger and abuse. Only the poor can tell the threatening and injurious effects of the worry and fear associated with the uncertainty of not knowing where the next meal may come from. Hunger and starvation deprive people of their human dignity. Food wages war against the destructive hands of hunger that harvest the lives of the poor indiscriminately. It equally enables people to live with dignity. To this end, "human security calls upon states to guarantee all its citizens, without exception, survival, livelihood and dignity."[105] It was in realization of the basic truth that the right to development was created among third-generation rights, including political freedom, economic facilities, social opportunities, and protective security. These rights are understood as indispensable aspects of any sustainable development.[106]

According to Simeon Ilesanmi, human beings are the ultimate beneficiaries of the right to development. This, in turn, remains an essential precondition for the satisfaction of social and economic rights as well as other human rights. It bears stating that, although human rights are important and non-negotiable, they mean nothing,

> when hundreds of millions suffer from malnutrition and vulnerability to disease and starvation. Worse still, it is an insult to them to insist on their 'human right' when there is no realistic prospect of these being upheld[107].

Africa's inability to adequately care for its population in terms of "bread and butter" has made the continent become "the basket case of the planet, the third world of the Third World—and a vast continent in a free fall."[108] This is the picture of Africa, where churches are full on a weekly basis, and even daily in the cities. However, those churches are crowded by people with empty stomachs who incarnate human misery. The poverty of Africa was once measured in relation to the Gulf War fought between 2 August 1990 and 28 February 1991. It was estimated that the cost of one day of the Gulf War amounted to five months of food aid for approximately 20 million people in Africa who were threatened by either drought, famine, war, or all three combined in some places.[109] Placed in the same historical context are the images of death occasioned by the devastating famine in the Horn of Africa between 1984 and 1985 that resulted in roughly two million

---

105. Adedeji, "Democracy and Development," 23.
106. Ilesanmi, "Leave No Poor Behind," 83.
107. Ilesanmi, "Leave No Poor Behind," 83.
108. Anise, "Descent into Sociopolitical Decay," 357.
109. De Gendt, "African Christianity," 104.

deaths.[110] Those macabre images will indelibly remain etched in Africa's collective memory of the twentieth century.

The feminization of poverty majorly colors the continental misery, since women shoulder a disproportionate burden of Africa's material poverty, which sadly "damages women and ends their lives prematurely."[111] The continent is equally a place where personal politics has remained strong without much space for ideological competition among political parties.[112] This is exacerbated by the malaise of the confusion between party and state as well as the blurring lines between public and private enterprise. Despite Africa's complexity, a common preoccupation of politicians across the continent is their focus on the proverbial "national cake," strongly denounced in 1994 by Winnie Byanyima, Head of Uganda's Constituent Assembly Women's Caucus. Although decried within Ugandan political settings, the vivid description of the "national cake" by Madam Byanyima can easily be transposed to other African nations:

> I would like to make some brief remarks about this subject, which delegates have been referring to as the national cake. Most of us born to work in kitchens know that, where cake is, there must be a baker. So, I find the discussion around sharing and eating the cake childish at the very least and irresponsible, selfish, and parasitic at worst. Sections of the press and some politicians have made "eating" acceptable and have placed it right at the centre of political debate. Struggling for the trappings of power is now at the centre stage; it has become acceptable and even fashionable. Values [that] we women care about such as caring, serving, building, reconciling, healing, and sheer decency are becoming absent from our political culture. This eating is crude, self-centred, egoistic, shallow, narrow and ignorant. We should ban eating from our political language... it is a culture [that] we must denounce and do away with if we are to start a new nation[113].

---

110. Riccardi, "The Social and Political Dynamics," 59.
111. O'Sullivan, "Women, Poverty, and Christianity," 103.
112. Engelbert and Dunn, *Inside African Politics*, 207.
113. Cited in Tripp, *Museveni's Uganda*, 39.

CONFRONTING THE "ECCLESIASTICAL CAKE" MENTALITY

Unfortunately, the politicians are not the only ones enmeshed in the crude business of "eating the national cake." Adrian Hastings noticed, in as early as the 1970s, an attitudinal change among some African bishops with regard to flamboyancy and exhibition of materialism. This change of lifestyle began to show itself consequent upon the appointment of African bishops to take the place of missionaries. This was visible in the emergence of palatial episcopal residences, with the resultant effect that local bishops started becoming somewhat aloof from the concrete living realities of their people. Their aloofness led to their isolation as individuals who were uninvolved in the life of their "flock."[114] In this regard, Jean-François Bayart situated the Church within the ambient of the "politics of the belly," comprising of all the strategies and institutions that define contemporary Africa after political independence.[115] Already in 1977, the Cameroonian theologian Fabien Eboussi Boulaga expressed a concern about the "obsession with money" among the emerging African local clergy on the basis of limited financial resources. The concern of Boulaga was reiterated by Jean-Marc Éla in the early 1980s to indicate ecclesiastical materialism that was then becoming one of the continental features of the Catholic Church in Africa. Its contours obviously varied, depending on local and national circumstances. This period saw the construction of Notre Dame de la Paix Basilica in Yamoussoukro (Côte d'Ivoire) between 1985 and 1989 by Félix Houphouët-Boigny, at the cost of over ninety billion CFA francs.[116] At the 1994 African Synod, Bishop Joseph Ajomo of Lokoja (Nigeria) insisted that,

> as leaders of the Church in Africa, we must distance ourselves from unjust rulers, dictators, the corrupt civil authorities, and assume our rightful place as the salt of the earth and light of the world (Matt. 5:13–14)[117].

With regard to the Church, the "politics of the belly" can be regarded as an offshoot of inculturation or assimilation of the Church into postcolonial African society. In the post-missionary phase, as mirrored by postcolonial Africa, ecclesial success on the ecclesiastical strata became akin to social success in civil society. It was symbolized by *homo manducans* (the eating man), whose insignias were concretized by big houses, flashy and expensive

114. Hastings, *A History of African Christianity*, 238.
115. Bayart, "Les Églises chrétiennes," 6, 8.
116. Bayart, "Les Églises chrétiennes," 10.
117. Cited in Ogbonnaya, "The Church in Africa," 76.

cars as well as prominence among the national elites of the postcolonial societies. Between the late 1970s and the early 1980s, Mercedes Benz became the preferred episcopal vehicle *par excellence*, in order to correspond with the new status of local bishops within the social strata of an independent Africa. Similarly, with the entrenchment of the "ecclesiology of chiefdom," the "ecclesiastical cake" became the equivalent of the obnoxious "national cake" sustained by paternalism and clientelism of indigenous monocracies of African leaders. Within the same state of affairs, the nascent local churches in some African countries became afflicted with a similar evil as their political states: factionalism over power and resource control. One resultant effect of the "politics of the belly," at whose centre stand the "national cake" and the "ecclesiastical cake" in postcolonial Africa, is the compromise and reconciliation between the spheres of God and Caesar. Its overall consequence is the dulling of the prophetic impulse among ecclesiastical hierarchies in many local churches. For that reason, muted interventions or outright compromises seemed to have gained the upper hand over prophetic proclamations in favor of social justice and condemnation of corruption and underdevelopment of the continent.[118]

On the eve of the First African Synod, Rose Zoé-Obianga posed an important question to the Church in Africa: "When will you open yourselves up to the enormity of your situation, in the face of which you are adopting an attitude that is both ambivalent and hypocritical?"[119] It was posited against the background of the excruciating pains of the early 1990s, when many parts of Africa were under the strong and destructive grips of poverty, famine, wars, diseases, illiteracy, and endemic underdevelopment. She described those realities as "turbulent, powerful and destructive waves" that swept over Africans, which sadly have remained "the daily lot of our peoples and particularly the women."[120] To a significant extent, the particular churches on the continent embody some of the polarities of postcolonial Africa. Those polarities are characterized by contrasts and extremes. Mrs Odette Kakuze of the Rwanda Association of Christian Workers once highlighted one of those contrasts in an open letter to the bishops at the First African Synod. She underscored the affluent lifestyle of the bishops. In her estimation, such a lifestyle was a major contributing factor that had increased

> the gap between you and us ordinary people. . . You have to teach the Christians about democracy, non-violence and human rights, and help them live these values in their family and places

118. Bayart, "Les Églises chrétiennes," 23.
119. Zoé-Obianga, "When will the Church," 89.
120. Zoé-Obianga, "When will the Church," 88.

of work. Religious leaders clearly ought to be the first ones to live and practice them[121].

That gap is a constitutive element of a binary system of Catholicism in contemporary Africa. It is manifested in the lifestyles of many African clergy, especially as exhibited by a significant minority who indulge in what may be described as "conspicuous consumption." At the same time, the vast majority of Africans are trapped in abject poverty and a daily life of want and penury.[122]

In light of Africa's multiple difficulties, one of the obvious challenges for the Church in Africa, as the church of the future, will be to confront the prevalence of the ethics of munificence and spirit of renter both within and beyond the church's sphere of influence. The pendulum may persistently swing in two directions, in order to maintain an equilibrium. On the one hand, the task will entail a struggle not to turn Christianity into an opium for the materially poor in a continent where religion remains a fulcrum for coping with existential problems. On the other hand, the Herculean challenge will be to avoid a religious ideology for the elite and materially well-off in their quest to justify the oppressive *status quo* that has left the majority of the people behind to wallow in poverty and misery.[123] Jean-Marc Éla once maintained that the Church must not allow itself to be used by African states to "anesthetize the consciousness of the poor and oppressed people of the continent."[124]

It will also mean a simpler lifestyle among Catholic prelates in solidarity with their faithful's living conditions. Cardinal Thiandoum cautioned that bishops must shun the temptation of becoming part of the small cream of affluent elites in a vast sea of human misery on the continent.[125] Beyond a simple lifestyle that is devoid of the trappings of *homo manducans*, it will ultimately demand of the Church and its hierarchies not to be content with the denunciation of social injustice, underdevelopment and corruption, in somewhat vague terms. It will equally mean that the Church must refrain from transforming itself into an additional agency of development when it has not first inquired about and denounced the root causes of poverty and deprivation. In his post-synodal exhortation *Evangelii Nuntiandi*, Pope Paul VI sagely admonished:

121. Cited in Gray, "The Catholic Church," 154.
122. Ronan "The Irish Missionary," 592–593.
123. O'Sullivan, "Women, Poverty, and Christianity," 104.
124. Éla, *My Faith as an African*, 152.
125. Thiandoum, *The Church in Africa*, 12.

> The Church ... has the duty to proclaim the liberation of millions of human beings, many of whom are her own children— the duty of assisting the birth of this liberation, of giving witness to it, of ensuring that it is complete. This is not foreign to evangelization (*Evangelii Nuntiandi* 30).

If the Church in Africa was understood as being somewhat insipid, during the last half of the twentieth century, for its lack of enthusiasm to mobilize the faithful for any meaningful social and political change,[126] a new awakening of its social obligations ought to define its mission in the twenty-first century. Since change is possible when past and present challenges are viewed through the lens of the future, the experiences of poor Africans who constitute the larger number of the faithful as well as their socio-economic and political needs ought to be given prime of place in every consideration by the Church. To re-echo the words of President Canaan Banana of Zimbabwe, their experiences must become "the new burning bush, burning with the intensity of the continual every day struggle for a better life, for meaningful social liberation, for the total liberation of the poor."[127] The 1971 Synod of Bishops, with its overall theme of "Justice in the World," positioned the question of social justice at the very centre of ecclesial ministry and the core of Christian life. Pressing social issues such as poverty, hunger, economic exploitation, discrimination, and lack of access to opportunities, marginalization of the vulnerable, and human rights violations were considered to be within the purview of the Church in its pastoral ministry.[128] Given the enormity of the African situation, where "vampire states"[129] reign supreme, the socio-economic and charitable activities of the Church will no longer be sufficient. This realization is reinforced by the fact that poverty, hunger and other economic issues are never resolved with trickle-down economics. Such activities may be comparable to those provided by non-governmental

---

126. Hastings, *African Catholicism*, 137.
127. Cited in Ranger, "Religion, Development," 53.
128. Turkson, "Roots and Routes of Justice," 6.

129. The term 'vampire states' was used by George Ayittey in his book entitled *Africa in Chaos*. Ayittey describes the functioning of African "vampire states" in this manner: "The African state has been reduced to a mafia-like bazaar, where everyone with an official designation can pillage at will. In effect, it is a "state" that has been hijacked by gangsters, crooks, and scoundrels ... The inviolate ethic of vampire elites is self-aggrandizement and self-perpetuation in power. To achieve those objectives, they subvert every institution of government: the civil service, judiciary, military, media, and banking. As a result, these institutions become paralyzed. ... Regardless of their forms, the effects of clientelism are the same. Politics is viewed as essentially extractive. The state sector becomes fused with the political arena and is seen as a source of wealth, and therefore, personal aggrandizement." Cited in Møller, *Religion and Conflict in Africa*, 16.

organizations (NGOs) whose "charities," to a large extent, help perpetuate a dependency syndrome in Africans.

ECCLESIAL COMMITMENT FOR INCLUSION AND HARMONY

Aware that neither the Church in Africa nor Africa is out of the woods in terms of difficulties and challenges, the pastors of the Church in Africa have an enormous responsibility in the continental project of uplifting the economic and political conditions of Africans. A starting point, according to Cardinal Peter Turkson, citing Pope John Paul II, is to heal "wounded human hearts, the ultimate hiding place for the causes of everything destabilizing the African continent."[130] It is against this background that the 1994 Rwandan genocide marks a very dark spot in the history of African Catholicism towards the twilight of the twentieth century. In his homily, at the opening Mass for the First Africa Synod, John Paul II, while affirming the aspiration of the bishops of Africa, proclaimed:

> With you, gathered in this African Synod, and in communion of spirit with the Bishops of Rwanda who could not be with us today, I feel the duty to *launch an appeal* so that we stop the homicidal hand of violence. With you, I raise my voice and say to all: Stop this violence! Stop these tragedies! Stop these fratricidal massacres![131].

Regrettably, with the disastrous turn of events following the aftermaths of that fratricidal bloodbath, John Paul II sought to distance the official Church from the crime of each member of the Rwandan church. In his letter of 14 March 1996 to Bishop Thaddée Ntihinyurwa of Cyangugu, the then President of the Episcopal Conference of Rwanda, John Paul observed that "Christians have a duty to be truthful witnesses, throughout their existence of this extraordinary gift that God makes, to reach reconciliation and peace."[132] The letter was occasioned by the visit of the papal special emissary to Rwanda in the person of Msgr Paul Josef Cordes, President of the Pontifical Council *Cor Unum*. However, after indicating that justice, equity and truth were indispensable requirements for the reconstruction of Rwanda at the end of the civil war, the Pope would not want the Church to be dragged alongside the misgivings and failures of its members. Pope John Paul II

---

130. Cited in Turkson, "A Special Assembly," 5–6.
131. John Paul II, *Homilies*, §4.
132. John Paul II, *Letter to the President*, §2.

distanced the Church from taking the responsibility for the crimes alleged to have been committed by some members of the Rwandan episcopate:

> The Church as such cannot be held responsible for the faults of those of her members who acted against the Gospel law; they will be called to account for their actions. All members of the Church who sinned during the genocide must have the courage to bear the consequences of what they have done against God and against others[133].

While it might be true that the official Church as a corporate body could not be held accountable for the crimes of its members, it remains nonetheless also true that the Rwandan genocide revealed the many fault lines of Christian evangelization in Rwanda and Africa. The Church in Rwanda was not unique in harboring within itself different competing voices with ethnic undertones. The failings of the Church in Rwanda cannot be adequately treated as the failings of individuals in their private capacity as citizens. Those failings were, without doubt, also institutional failings of the Catholic Church for the implicit roles played by some high-ranking Rwandan ecclesiastics. Whether acceptable or not, the collective failure of the Catholic Church in Rwanda, especially among members of its hierarchy, was before anything else indicative of the superficiality of Christianity in Africa and also proved the inefficacy of the water of baptism in washing away tribal and ethnic blood ties that sometimes can be murderous in its venomous rage if not effectively checkmated.[134] In the opinion of Wolfgang Schonecke, citing the secretary of the pastoral department of AMECEA: "A Church that did not openly address its own ethnic tensions could not speak to society with a united and credible voice."[135] Perhaps, it was for this reason that Pope Benedict XVI insisted, in his post-synodal exhortation *Africae Munus*, that "Reconciliation is a way of life and mission of the Church" (no. 34). Prior to the publication of *Africae Munus*, in his address to the Roman Curia on 21 December 2009, Benedict XVI highlighted the onerous challenges for the Church in Africa and its leaders in building a harmonious and peaceful society for everyone on the continent:

> The task of Bishops was to transform theology into pastoral care, namely into a very concrete pastoral ministry in which the great perspectives found in sacred Scripture and Tradition find application in the activity of Bishops and priests in specific times

---

133. John Paul II, *Letter to the President*, §3.
134. Longman, "Church Politics and the Genocide," 154.
135. Cited in Gray, "The Catholic Church," 154.

and places . . . In fact, the very practical question that Pastors constantly have to face is precisely this: how can we be realistic and practical without claiming a political competence that does not belong to us? . . . The theme of the Synod designated three great words which are basic to theological and social responsibility: reconciliation, justice, peace. Every society needs acts of reconciliation in order to enjoy peace. These acts are a prerequisite of a good political order, but they cannot be achieved by politics alone[136].

As a church of the future, it may be helpful for the Church in Africa to recover some lost ground and rediscover the energy that was visible at work in some local churches around the continent in the immediate post-missionary years. Contrary to some negative assessments of the post-missionary phase of the Church in Africa, the 1990s were marked by social activism in the interventions of some national episcopal conferences in Africa. The Catholic Bishops of Malawi, with their epochal joint pastoral letter of 8 March 1992 entitled "Living our Faith," acted as a catalyst for the spiral of unrest and events that ultimately ended the life-term presidency of Hastings Kamuzu Banda in 1994. The bishops gave voice to their people's long yearning for a new political order and respect for their human dignity, which Banda and the Malawian ruling elite trampled upon without any qualm of conscience.[137] The intervention of the Malawian bishops was by no means an isolated case. In a few other places in the early 1990s, some church leaders emerged on the political stages of their countries as the last vestiges of moral authority and guidance when there was hardly any or no manifestation of public confidence in politicians.

Similar affirmation was true of the Benin Republic, Congo-Brazzaville and Zaire (later the Democratic Republic of Congo), where Catholic bishops played a significant role in the democratization process. The Beninese bishops' pastoral letter of 1989, entitled "Be converted and Benin will live," remains instructive in calling for Benin's political change. Bishop Isidore de Souza of Cotonou became practically the leader of Benin during the transition period from 17 February to 4 April 1991. Bishop Ernest N'Kombo of Owando played a similar role in Congo-Brazzaville, where the bishops insisted, in a pastoral letter, that their churches and places of worship must never be turned into political arenas. Bishop N'Kombo was chosen to oversee the deliberations of the national conference that lasted three months. He was subsequently appointed to head the transitional process. Worthy of

---

136. Benedict XVI, *Address to the Roman Curia and Papal Diplomats*, §6.
137. Mijoga, "The Lenten Pastoral Letter," 57, 60.

note is the open letter of the Zairian bishops to Mobutu SeseSeko, published on 9 March 1990. The bishops asked for genuine political reforms.[138] Shortly afterwards, in 1991, Archbishop Laurent Monsengwo Pasinya of Kisangani was elected to pilot the affairs of the national conference that saved Zaire from further anarchy. Bishop Sanouko Kpodzro of Atakpame presided over the transition process in Togo, as did Bishop Basile Mve Engone of Oyem in Gabon.[139] The role of the aforementioned prelates was made possible by the exceptional concession granted to some bishops to pilot the political affairs of their countries on a *pro tempore* basis. Against that backdrop, Pope John Paul II, in his address to the bishops of the Republic of Congo during their *Ad Limina* visit in 1993, insisted that it was granted in view of the common good of the country involved:

> It can happen that pastors, in an evangelical spirit and with much sincerity and generosity, accept for some time a mission in the political order... for the good of the nation. Such situations remain exceptional. For one entrusted with the care of souls who wishes to be truly a gatherer of the People of God ought to be free in relation to direct political action in the nation[140].

Those intermittent efforts for a better society by some African episcopal conferences, in some remarkable ways already anticipated the social responsibility of the Church as would be consistent with the vision of Pope Francis, especially as articulated in his apostolic exhortation *Evangelium Gaudium* of 24 November 2013. Within the ecclesiology of Pope Francis, the centrality of the social dimension of the Gospel is both an intrinsic aspect as well as a constitutive element of evangelization. It groups under its wings efforts to pursue the just ordering of society, peace and respect of human dignity, particularly of those at the margins of society. It equally means the discarding of a rigid and fundamentalist mindset, which sometimes can prevent the Church from being in touch with the pastoral realities of people's lives.[141] His thoughts in this regard are clearly enunciated in sections 176 to 258 of *Evangelium Gaudium*.

The practical character of Pope Francis' insistence on the social dimension of the Gospel can be a rudder and stimulus for the Church in Africa in responding to the pressing needs of the continent. Worthy of note is the pastoral letter issued by the bishops of Zimbabwe on the precarious situation in their country. Through their pastoral letter, entitled "The March Is Not

---

138. De Gendt, "African Christianity," 109–110; Linden, *Global Catholicism*, 236.
139. Gifford, "Some Recent Developments," 513.
140. Cited in Thiandoum, *The Church in Africa*, 21–22.
141. Gregory, "Pope Francis's Effort," 10, 13, 17.

Ended" of 14 August 2020, the Zimbabwean bishops appeared to have set a new pace for other bishops in terms of pastoral concerns and the prophetic mission of bishops as shepherds of their local churches. The Zimbabwean bishops' pastoral letter chronicled their country's political situation and economic woes, with a repressive government that is equally unresponsive to the plights of their people, especially compounded by official corruption, poverty, and human rights abuses.[142] Their courageous stance, at the moment of great national upheavals and visionless government in Zimbabwe, could act as a springboard and a worthy example for other episcopal conferences on the continent in launching the Church in Africa for the future.

A CONTINENTAL CHURCH CONCERNED ABOUT ECOLOGY

The Church's ecological awakening merged gradually alongside global attention to climate change and other related ecological issues. Of crucial importance, in this instance, is the first United Nations Conference on Human Environment that took place in Stockholm, Sweden, from 5 to 16 June 1972. The Stockholm Conference signaled a significant turning point in global consciousness to environmental matters and the attendant international politics concerning development and ecology.[143] Its main focus, as stated in the preamble, was to consider "the need for a common outlook and for common principles to inspire and guide the peoples of the world in the preservation and enhancement of the human environment."[144] The final declaration of the Conference is divided into two parts: seven "Proclamations" and twenty-six "Principles."

In number two of its "Proclamations" on the protection of the environment, the Conference emphatically stated:

> The protection and improvement of the human environment is a major issue which affects the well-being of peoples and economic development throughout the world; it is the urgent desire of the peoples of the whole world and the duty of all Governments[145].

This Conference statement and its overall position on the need to protect and preserve the natural habitat and ecology drew as their source the

---

142. Zimbabwe Catholic Bishops' Conference, *The March Is Not Ended*, 1–2.
143. *Report of the UN Conference on the Human Environment*, 3.
144. *Report of the UN Conference on the Human Environment*, 3.
145. *Report of the UN Conference on the Human Environment*, 3.

book, *Only One Earth: The Care and Maintenance of a Small Planet*, which was commissioned by the UN Secretary General.[146] It directed the attention of the participants to the causes of environmental degradations such as the persistent pollution of earth, air and water on account of insatiable demands for energy supply, depletion of natural resources, and the destruction of the ecosystem as the ultimate consequences.[147]

Within the universal Church, a heightened ecological awareness took time to evolve. The Church gradually discovered ecological concerns, especially within the Latin American context with its theological and pastoral emphasis on the option for the poor. According to Ian Linden, ecological awareness and environmental articulation by the Catholic Church issued forth from the Church's encounter with the poor as well as the spirituality of indigenous peoples.[148] Environmental questions and ecological concerns were absent in discussions at the Second Vatican Council and in its documents. The Council, particularly in *Gaudium et Spes*, took mainly a positive view about scientific and technological accomplishments of the 1960s. Neither during conciliar sessions nor in its documents was there a critical mention made about the harmful and negative impacts of industrialization on the ecosystem or biosphere. Marvin L. Krier Mich rightly observed that "[t]he council fathers, like many of their contemporaries, were dazzled by the marvels and promise of modern science and technology in 'mastering' nature."[149] It was not until the publication of Pope Paul VI's apostolic letter *Octogesima Adveniens* 14 May 1971 that a perceptible magisterial teaching on environmental issues began to emerge somewhat gradually on the horizon. Although the ecclesial awareness of ecological problems was in its nascent stage, the articulation of Paul VI in 1971 left no trace of doubt that the world might be headed towards the wrong direction, if nothing was done to reverse the dangerous route of the denuding of nature:

> Man is suddenly becoming aware that by an ill-considered exploitation of nature he risks destroying it and becoming in his turn the victim of this degradation. Not only is the material environment becoming a permanent menace—pollution and refuse, new illness and absolute destructive capacity—but the human framework is no longer under man's control, thus

---

146. The final format was edited and published by Barbara Ward and René J. Dubos in 1972, prior to the start of the conference. The book is a collection of the views and studies by many experts from over fifty countries. Although approved by the UN Secretary General, the book acted as a kind of unofficial report for the UN Conference.

147. Ward and Dubos, *Only One Earth: The Care and Maintenance of a Small Planet*.

148. Linden, *Global Catholicism*, 279.

149. Krier Mich, *Catholic Social Teaching*, 386.

creating an environment for tomorrow which may well be intolerable. This is a wide-ranging social problem which concerns the entire human family. The Christian must turn to these new perceptions in order to take on responsibility, together with the rest of men, for a destiny which from now on is shared by all (*Octogesima Adveniens* 21).

Another milestone was reached at the 1971 Synod of Bishops that focused its attention on "The Ministerial Priesthood and Justice in the World." As opined by Thomas Landy, the synodal document, *Justice in the World*, "essentially characterized environmental degradations as a violence carried out by wealthy consumers against the poor."[150] The influence of bishops from the less developed world was remarkably evident in the synodal position on environmental issues:

> Furthermore, such is the demand for resources and energy by the richer nations, whether capitalist or socialist, and such are the effects of dumping by them in the atmosphere and the sea that irreparable damage would be done to the essential elements of life on earth, such as air and water, if their high rates of consumption and pollution, which are constantly on the increase, were extended to the whole of humanity[151].

The Pontifical Commission Iustitia et Pax (Justice and Peace)—a fruit of the 1971 Synod—took up environmental issues. This was reflected in its 1973 publication entitled, *A New Creation? Reflections on the Environmental Issue*. It was largely authored by Lady Barbara Ward, who urged Catholics to rethink their attitude towards nature and creation in general.[152] A clearer picture of the Church's stance on ecological matters came to the fore with the pontificate of John Paul II, albeit also progressively until its apex in 1989 with his message designated for the 1990 World Day of Peace. With his encyclical *Redemptor Hominis* of 4 March 1979, John Paul was concerned that the world economic order was "depleting the earth's resources of raw materials and energy at an ever-increasing rate and putting intolerable pressures on the geophysical environment" (nos. 15 and 16). In the message for the 1990 World Day of Peace, exclusively devoted to ecology and environmental issues, John Paul II described the earth as "the common heritage of all." It is a place where respect for life, for the dignity of the human person ought to be the guiding norms for any sound economic, industrial or scientific

---

150. Cited in Krier Mich, *Catholic Social Teaching*, 386.
151. World Synod of Catholic Bishops, *Justice in the World*, no. 11.
152. Krier Mich, *Catholic Social Teaching*, 387.

progress. On the same earth, peaceful society is not possible without respect for the integrity of the whole of creation denoted as cosmos.[153]

It is important to note the presentation of Bishop Stephen Fumio Hamao of Japan at the 1984 Synod of Bishops in Rome on "Reconciliation." The Japanese prelate stressed the need for reconciliation and harmony between humanity and nature, because

> [w]ork for peace will be effective if all men become aware of their deep connection with nature, especially with all living beings ... man must seek harmony with it and admire in it the beauty, wisdom and love of the Creator[154].

Subsequently, a few national episcopal conferences took up the issues of ecology and the natural environment in their pastoral letters. They included the Episcopal Conferences of Guatemala, the Philippines, the Dominican Republic and the United States of America. Since land distribution was a major source of national crisis that smacked of injustice with respect to the indigenous population, the Guatemalan bishops titled their 1988 pastoral letter, *The Cry for Land*. Their statement reads as follows:

> From the dawn of creation to the Apocalypse, the human person develops in a particular land ... The human person belongs to the earth and the earth also belongs to them since they are charged with the responsibility of tilling and caring for the earth[155].

After listening to tribal people, simple Filipinos, scientists, and environmentalists, the Filipino bishops published their pastoral letter entitled *What is Happening to Our Beautiful Land?* also in 1988. They decried the thoughtless disregard for nature, which sadly leads to "laying waste complex living systems that have taken millions of years to reach their present state of development."[156] They caution that whatever human beings callously dispose of in nature invariably comes back to harm them, even with horrendous consequences at times. The Filipino bishops preceded Pope Francis in calling for an "ecological conversion" to take care of the earth, to watch over it, to protect it and to love it without engaging in any act of despoliation of natural resources.[157] In their 1991 pastoral letter entitled *Renewing*

---

153. John Paul II, *Message for World Day of Peace*, nos. 7–8.
154. Cited in Krier Mich, *Catholic Social Teaching*, 389.
155. See, Christiansen and Grazer, "And God saw that it was good," 282.
156. Catholic Bishops' Conference of the Philippines, *What is Happening*, §15.
157. Catholic Bishops' Conference of the Philippines, *What is Happening?*, §§18, 30; Francis, *Laudato Si*, no. 217: "The external deserts in the world are growing, because the internal deserts have become so vast. For this reason, the ecological crisis is also

the Earth, the bishops of the United States of America called for integral dimensions of ecological responsibility.[158]

Regrettably, the Church in Africa appeared to be unaware of the urgency of the widespread ecological challenges on the continent. The ecological devastations in Africa range from erosion, deforestation, oil spillages, insufficient rainfall to drought and famine that aggravate an already precarious condition for millions of Africans. Against the background of the many ecological problems in Africa, Joseph Ogbonnaya rhetorically once expressed the wish to see a document on ecology issued by SECAM, regional or national episcopal conferences.[159] As a matter of fact, given the poor state of African economies and development, it is reasonable to agree with Jesse Mugambi that Africans have contributed least in the destruction of the global environment, while at the same time they have suffered the most.[160] This again is based on the fact that climate change renders subsistence agriculture unsustainable. It remains the mainstay of livelihood for many Africans, particularly those in the rural areas of the continent.

Geographically, Africa is the only continent in the world that has two vast tropical deserts that run the length and breadth of the continent from the Sahara in the north to the Kalahari in the southern part of the continent. In agricultural terms, this geographical reality poses many challenges to Africans regarding food production, since the continent has more arid and semi-arid lands than arable wetlands. This is compounded by another ecological reality, namely the winds that bring pollutants through the equatorial regions of Africa transverse the continent twice a year during the annual seasonal cycles, since Africa lies evenly within the tropics. The ecological challenges facing Africa and its teeming population seem insurmountable when measured on the scale of declining rainfall that feeds most of the big rivers of Africa, on which many poor African households depend for sustenance, agricultural purposes, and their livestock. The yearly decline in rainfall also has devastating effects on Africa's biodiversity.[161] This realization led Pope Benedict XVI to write in his post-synodal exhortation, *Africae Munus* (no. 80):

> Serious damage is done to nature, to the forests, to flora and fauna, and countless species risk extinction. All of this threatens

a summons to profound interior conversion . . . what they all need is an "ecological conversion . . ."

158. United States Conference of Catholic Bishops, *Renewing the Earth*, §A.
159. Ogbonnaya, "The Church in Africa," 87.
160. Mugambi, "Climate Change and Food Security," 1117.
161. Mugambi, "Climate Change and Food Security," 1118–1122.

the entire ecosystem and consequently the survival of humanity. I call upon the Church in Africa to encourage political leaders to protect such fundamental goods as land and water for the human life of present and future generations and for peace between peoples.

The second 'scramble of Africa' that accelerated since 1998, with China's greater interest in Africa, has aggravated the ecological situation of the continent. Africa can be described as an ecologically conquered continent—from mining to drilling, logging and overfishing. Sanusha Naidu and Martyn Davies maintain that China fuels its industrialization and hunger for energy with Africa's natural resources. For instance, African crude oil is used to smoothen the new Chinese Silk Road, and four African countries, namely Gabon, Congo-Brazzaville, Equatorial Guinea and Cameroon, account for roughly 14 percent of China's wood exports.[162] Ivory Coast stands as a prime example of an African country that was once well-forested. Currently, there are only isolated hardwood trees standing, as most of them have been cut down. In oil-producing countries such as Nigeria, Equatorial Guinea and Angola, the local people endure the harsh realities of the "cursed oil" in their polluted communities, while transnational oil moguls and their African partners enjoy the blessings of oil wealth.[163]

As an ecologically conquered continent, Africa may never sink into oblivion. Perhaps, after crude oil, diamond and other precious mineral deposits have been finally extracted and exploited to the last drop or stone, the next phase of scramble and scavenging would be to exploit Africa's abundant sunshine. The world is going green and global energy supply is increasingly turning to solar and other sources of renewable energy. Africa is pre-eminently rich in sunshine. That will make it a continent of "sun mine" for solar energy. In the not too distant future, solar panels will crisscross the length and breadth of the continent extracting its solar energy for the benefit of the developed world. However, and sad to acknowledge, like other natural resources of the continent, the future exploitation of Africa's solar energy may not benefit the common people of the continent, but further enrich the same African elites who have held the continent captive. Poor Nigeriens have not benefited from the uranium of their country, which is progressively extracted to power the nuclear power plants of France. The inhabitants of the Democratic Republic of Congo perpetually endure the burden of environmental hazards as the by-products of extractive activities of multinational companies in their country. The insatiable greed for

162. Naidu and Davies, "China Fuels its Future," 78.
163. Skard, *Continent of Mothers*, 15, 21.

the Democratic Republic of Congo's myriad of minerals and resources has turned the country into an unenviable world theatre of wars for the ferocious competing combatants who rape and plunder it in equal measure as they please. Zimbabweans bore the brunt of Mugabe's government that literally emptied the mines and platinum of Zimbabwe for the benefits of the Chinese and Zimbabwean elite collaborators.

Ecological issues are a reality, which the Church that is situated in an ecologically conquered continent must confront and address at different levels of episcopal conferences. If for no other reason, the Church in Africa, as the church of the future, ought to be concerned about environmental degradation on behalf of its poor faithful who are vulnerable to food insecurity, since callous depletion of earth's resources threatens their means of livelihood. If concerns for the protection and preservation of the ecosystem and biodiversity can qualify ecology as the "new name for development,"[164] then the Church in Africa cannot bury its head in the sand as if ecological questions did not matter nor rely solely on the Vatican's ecological advocacy to justify its seemingly disinterest. In this regard, what John Paul II wrote about international cooperation as not lessening the individual responsibility of each state to be the vanguard in the protection and preservation of its local environment applies to the Church in Africa.[165] Using the metaphor of the "empty granary," Éla was concerned about the situation of the poor Africans who lament that their fields have been taken away and that "there is no place left to grow millet."[166] He also agonized about the "inattention" of the Church to rural dwellers who suffer hunger and famine as a result of both the government's policy of domination and natural disaster, due to climate change.[167] It will be interesting, for example, to know what the episcopal conferences of oil-rich countries in Africa may say to their various oil-producing communities, whose farming lands have been rendered toxic and their fishing rivers polluted by oil companies.

The Southern African Bishops' Conference seems to have shaken off their own ecological lukewarm attitude. During their Plenary Session held at Mariannhill (South Africa) in August 2019, the bishops approved

164. Iheanacho, "Christian Commitment," 18.

165. John Paul II, *Message for the Celebration of the World Day of Peace*, #9: "The need for joint action on the international level *does not lessen the responsibility of each individual State*. Not only should each State join with others in implementing internationally accepted standards, but it should also make or facilitate necessary socio-economic adjustments within its own borders, giving special attention to the most vulnerable sectors of society."

166. Éla, *My Faith as an African*, 93.

167. Éla, *My Faith as an African*, 175.

the publication of a new pastoral plan for local churches within their jurisdiction. Entitled *Evangelising Community Serving God, Humanity and All Creation*, the pastoral plan highlights the issue of ecology, as the first pages are reserved to the issues of creation and the need for the care of creation, featuring the key components of the vision and mission of the bishops. Strikingly, "care of creation and the environment" conclude the same document. The bishops' interest in ecology is couched as a pledge:

> We, the Church, the family of God in Southern Africa, commit to work together with others for the good of all, by responding to the cry of the poor and the cry of the earth, through Worship, Proclamation of the Word of God, Formation, Advocacy, Human Development and Care of Creation[168].

Elsewhere in the pastoral plan, the bishops explain what "Care of Creation" entails. It means above all

> looking after the soil, our water, our air, the plants, the animals, our dwelling places, our buildings, our resources, our sources of energy—the heritage of our children's children and all the coming generations[169].

In the face of the huge African ecological challenges, no local church can pretend that those issues no longer matter. The future of the church in Africa is needed on the geopolitical, economic and ecological map of Africa, where the issuance of episcopal communiqués may not be sufficient in themselves, but where actual advocacy and activism may be necessary as means of engagement in helping to solve some of the continent's concrete questions.

---

168. Southern African Catholic Bishops' Conference, *Evangelising Community*, 5.
169. Southern African Catholic Bishops' Conference, *Evangelising Community*, 14.

Conclusion

This book set out to trace and articulate the historical contours of the Church in Africa. To be able to do so concisely, it was necessary, albeit briefly, to revisit the earliest Catholic missionary efforts in sub-Saharan Africa before its definitive present state. It recalled the mid-fifteenth century when the popes began to nurse and cherish a long-time dream of a flourishing church in Africa. Their primary attention was on those parts of the continent that were untouched by Islam. It was a dream that successive popes sought to uphold, even when it seemed like a pie in the sky, given the seemingly insurmountable obstacles in its realization. Those obstacles ranged from inaccessible and vast African terrains, shortage of missionaries, subsequent divergent interests between those of the Portuguese monarchy in its hunger for imperialism, and those of the Church. The dwindling fortunes of Portugal in Africa implicitly meant the fading of any reasonable prospect of the Catholic Church in those territories. The Portuguese exploratory adventures had once helped sustain the dream and hope of the popes about the success of papal missionary commitments in sub-Saharan Africa.

In modern times, the modest step to revive that papal dream of a flourishing Church in Africa began with Pope Gregory XVI. This happened with the creation of the Vicariate Apostolic of Upper and Lower Guinea in West Africa that stretched southwards to Angola. He also created the Apostolic Vicariate of Central Africa that ran from Egypt through Algeria to the Red Sea and terminated at the mythical Mountains of the Moon in Eastern Africa. Both vicariates can be considered the mother churches of the Catholic Church in contemporary Africa. From these vicariates came forth most of the local Catholic Churches in Africa, with their peculiar and continental varieties and complexities. An important link in the historical trajectory of the Church in Africa during the nineteenth century re-launching, especially with regard to the Vicariate of Upper Guinea, is the generosity of the Catholic Church in the United States of America. It bankrolled the cost of the first re-launching of the presence of the Catholic Church in that part of the continent. This aspect of the generosity of four American dioceses is not always highlighted in the history of contemporary Catholicism in Africa. That generosity ought to be appreciated against the background that the Catholic Church in America was at the time a poor Church. Similarly, is the recalling of the toils of the missionaries who had to transverse their vast Vicariate of Central Africa. It was once said that life would one day spring forth from their graves!

The discovery and exploration of Equatorial and Central Africa was occasioned by the International Geographic Conference's convocation in Brussels on 12 September 1876, under the patronage of the cunning Belgian King Leopold II. The opening of those parts of Africa coincided with the remaining two years of the pontificate of Pope Pius IX. Through Cardinal Franchi, Prefect of the Propaganda Fide, the pope wanted the Catholic presence to be established in the newly explored areas. For Pius IX and Cardinal Franchi, the new territories were important pathways to further afield in the equatorial and central parts of the continent. However, the launching of the Catholic missionary outreach in those areas became a source of major contention among three missionary institutes, namely the White Fathers, the Combonians, and the Society of African Missions. It was a conflict over territorial boundaries and demarcations.

The further explorations and colonization of Africa equally coincided with the pontificate of Leo XIII, which spanned through the last decades of the nineteenth century. His pontificate was characterized by intensive diplomacy at the international level, within which he inserted Catholic missionary action. The missions were an intrinsic part of the general orientations and policies of Leo XIII. His three missionary encyclicals, with special bearing on Africa, ought to be inserted within his global conception and the role envisaged by him for the Church within the international scheme of affairs. Those encyclicals are *Sancta Dei Civitas* (1880), *In Plurimis* (1888), and *Catholica Ecclesiae* (1890). He built on the legacies of his predecessors with regard to Africa. There were roughly eighty Catholic mission circumscriptions at the time of his death in 1903. Those eighty circumscriptions firmly led the foundation for the next phase of Catholic consolidation in Africa. They began to take proper shape after the publication of *Maximum Illud* in 1919 by Pope Benedict XV. He placed emphasis on the formation and ordination of the local clergy in mission territories as well as their elevation to the episcopate.

Catholic missions in Africa benefited from Benedict XV's practical oriented reform and reorganization of the Church's missions. The continuation of his missionary vision by Pope Pius XI gave Africa its first indigenous Bishop in the person of Bishop David O'Leary of South Africa on 8 September

1925. This great milestone in contemporary African Catholicism's history is regrettably often passed over without notice. The reason may be due to his White race. By contrast, the episcopal ordinations of Bishops Joseph Kiwanuka (Uganda) and Ignatius Ramarosandratana (Madagascar) by Pope Pius XII in Rome on 19 October 1939 received more attention. If the record must be straightened, Bishop O'Leary deserves a prominent place in the Church's contemporary history in Africa. His ordination was the first effort towards the indigenization of the Church on the continent. Another distinctive mark is the establishment of an Apostolic Delegation in 1922, which took place in South Africa. The Apostolic Delegation in Pretoria can be described as providing the pattern followed by the Holy See in the establishment of other delegations in sub-Saharan Africa. As institutions in the hands of the Holy See, the apostolic delegations became important tools for the implementation of the Vatican's missionary policy of indigenization in Africa.

Adhering strictly to the mandates given to them by the Holy See through the Propaganda Fide, the apostolic delegations helped the Holy See shortcut resistances that would have naturally come from missionary institutes and their powerful superiors general. This is against the realization that not everyone enthusiastically signed the policy of transferring ecclesiastical authority to emerging young African clergy. The wave of independence that blew across the African continent, from the late 1950s to the late 1970s, offered the Vatican ample opportunities and the freehand to widen its diplomatic tentacles. It created new apostolic delegations in many countries following their declarations of independence. In some instances, the Holy See ignored France's protestation. For instance, it attached some West-Central African colonies to the Apostolic Delegation in Lagos, Nigeria, that had recently attained its independence from Britain in 1960. Similar overriding of the French concerns by the Vatican also occurred over the nationality of papal delegates. The Vatican preferred Italians to French prelates in the soon would-become ex-French Africa.[1] Those differences signaled the freedom of the Vatican to manoeuvre in its diplomatic negotiations with the newly independent African countries and the pursuance of its policy of Africanization of the African episcopate. It became a centerpiece of attention for Popes Pius XII, John XXIII, and Paul VI, as it was considered through the prism of *plantatio ecclesiae* that began with Popes Benedict XV and Pius XI in the first decades of the twentieth century.

To a large degree, the Church in Africa came of age during the pontificate of Paul VI, who became the first pope to visit Africa in 1969. During the Second Vatican Council, the Church in Africa was grouped together

---

1. Gori, "Santa Sede e Francia," 198.

with the Church in Asia as "Young Churches." The old mission system of *ius commissionis* was replaced with the *mandatum* system that placed the duty of growth and development of the local churches on the shoulders of their local hierarchies. They were charged with the responsibilities of participating in the general missionary work of the Universal Church; contributing to the disciplinary and institutional organization of the Church, and making doctrinal contributions as they make their way towards spiritual growth and ecclesiastical maturity.[2] In the course of his thirteen-year pontificate, Paul VI often returned to those obligations, which the Holy See under him insisted, must not be executed over and above Rome. For example, the emergence of the local churches with their nascent local hierarchies did not mean isolation from the centre. Certainly, also, the end of the missionary phase did not imply an end in missionary cooperation between the young churches and the older churches. This was against the background of the declaration of the All Africa Conference of Churches (AACC) in Lusaka, with its call for a "moratorium" on foreign missionaries and money to Africa. At the 1974 Synod of Bishops in Rome, the African bishops distanced themselves from that position. They underscored their preference for continued collaboration in mutual respect between their local churches in Africa and their counterparts in Europe and North America. The Church in Africa is generally believed to have attained some maturity in 1974 after its missionary tutelage.

Notwithstanding that attainment of maturity, the same Church, through the 1970s and 1980s, collectively struggled to find ways to articulate its self-identity. It inquired about what it meant to be a local church with other sister churches under the bigger umbrella of the Catholic Church. It predicated most of its energy and attention on "inculturation." Although helpful to some extent, that preoccupation sapped it of energy that otherwise would have been expended in the development of other areas. The *terminus ad quem* of that long process was the First Synod of African Bishops. That Synod was not incredibly unique in itself, since it ought to be placed within the context of the 1990s that can be described as the decades of "synods." Similar other continental synods took place in Rome.

As for the African Synod, Rome, of its own accord, decided for the African bishops on account of their failure to agree whether they wanted a council or a synod. This was occasioned by the disunity among the bishops, especially as bishops from English-speaking churches tended to view with suspicions the bold demands of their French-speaking colleagues, particularly those from Cameroon and Zaire (the Democratic Republic of Congo).[3]

---

2. Tshinbango, "The Mission and Responsibility," 128.
3. Luneau, "The Expectations of the Catholic Church," 85.

The Church in Africa is broadly considered as the Church of the future on account of its growing population. One of the basic tenets of this book is that it must close its ranks, seize its moment, and reposition itself as a formidable equal stakeholder in global Catholicism. Although materially poor, due to its location in an impoverished continent, it has a numerical strength it can leverage to discard its status as a marginal local church at the fringe of the Universal Church.

Most appropriately, what Joseph Ki-Zerbo, the Burkinabé historian, said of Africa in Stockholm on 31 December 1997 can fittingly be applied to the Catholic Church in Africa. The Universal Catholic Church needs a local church in Africa that is "able to stand up, to walk on its feet rather than on crutches or on its head, in a vacuous mimicry or escapism."[4] This applies to the local church's faltering steps towards financial maturity and self-reliance. It goes beyond the massaging of its ego as the "spiritual lung" of the world. In a poor continent with bleak economic prospects for its young population and the feminization of poverty, as the Church of the future, it has to stand up on its feet to confront the sources of political and economic despondencies that have continued to hold its faithful under bondage. As an avant-garde for human development in a continent of mothers, it is preeminently positioned to be the voice of its children. It bears reiterating that the convocation of two African synods in Rome hardly matters for poor Africans who, most of the time, fill their local churches with empty stomachs. Put differently, those synods may remain hollow if they have no bearing on the actual reality of the common people.

As many of its people may likely "live off the land" in the foreseeable future, it becomes imperative and incumbent upon the Catholic Church in Africa to also concern itself with ecological matters on the continent. The poor who constitute the vast majority of the church members equally make up the bulk of vulnerable victims of ecological disasters in a continent that is becoming ecologically conquered. The future shape of the Church in Africa may be determined by how it engages itself with the concrete realities that affect its faithful, in particular, and the continent, at large. If "inculturation" and the quest for self-definition characterized the history of African Catholicism in the post-missionary period, social and economic issues, ethnic cohesion even within the Church, poverty, migration, and ecology may define its future on the continent. These issues may provide the roadmap as the church of the future travels along those routes in order to reach a destination that is not presently known.

4. K-Zerbo, "Acceptance Speech," lines 96–98: "The Africa which the world needs is a continent able to stand up, to walk on its own feet rather than on crutches or on its head, in vacuous mimicry or escapism."

Bibliography

Adedeji, Adebayo. "Democracy and Development: A Complex Relationship." In *Challenges of Conflict, Democracy and Development in Africa*, edited by Khabele Matlosa et al, 19–32. Johannesburg: EISA, 2007.
"African Report." In *Third World Theologies: Commonalities and Divergences*, edited by K. C. Abraham, 28–56. Oregon: Wipf and Stock, 1990.
Albanese, Giulio. "Africa, Quo Vadis? (Africa, Where Are You Going?)." In *Paul VI and the Church in Africa*, 148–154. Brescia: Istituto Paolo VI, 2015.
Allen, John. "To bongos and bass guitar, pope calls Africa an 'immense spiritual lung.'" https://www.ncronline.org/blogs/ncr-today/bongos-and-bass-guitar-pope-calls-africa-immense-spiritual-lung?_ga=2.208578578.1880434726.1595841250-12390 45515.1595841249.
Anglin, Douglas G. "The African Peer Review of Political Governance: Precedents, Problematics and Prospects." In *Democratic Reform in Africa: Its Impact on Governance and Poverty Alleviation*, edited by Muna Ndulo, 236–275. Oxford: James Currey, 2006.
Anise, Ladun. "Descent into Sociopolitical Decay: Legacies of Maldevelopment in Africa." In *Africa in the Contemporary International Disorder: Crises and Possibilities*, edited by Mulugeta Agonafer, 337–362. New York: University Press of America, 1996.
Annals of the Propagation of the Faith (June 1919). Conserved in Archives of Propaganda Fide, *Nuova Serie*, Vol. 620 (1919).
Arinze, Francis. "Paul VI and the African Episcopate." In *Paul VI and the Church in Africa*, 30–37. Brescia: Istituto Paolo VI, 2015.
Augustin Planque—Yesterday and Today. Rome: Sisters of Our Lady of the Apostles, 1984.
"Avant-propos." In *Des Prêtres noirs s'interrogent*, 15–18. Paris: Les Éditions du Cerf, 1956.
Bacchio, Gian Luca. *Leone XIII: Il rinnovamento della Chiesa nelle sue encicliche*. Canterano: Gioacchino Onorati, 2019.
Ballard, Martin. *White Men's God: The Extraordinary Story of Missionaries in Africa*. Oxford, Westport: Greenwood World, 2008.
Bane, Martin J. *The Popes and Western Africa: An Outline of Mission History 1460s-1960s*. New York: Alba House, 1968.
Bartoccetti, Vittorio. "L'elemento giuridico nel problema del clero indigeno." *Il Pensiero Missionario* 8 (1936) 289–307.
Bate, Stuart C. *Missiology Notes*. Cedara: Unpublished, 1995.

Bate, Stuart C. "The Church under Apartheid." In *The Catholic Church in Contemporary Southern Africa*, edited by Joy Brain and Philippe Denis, 151-186. Pietermaritzburg: Cluster Publications, 1999.

Baur, John. *2000 Years of Christianity in Africa*. Nairobi: Paulines Publications Africa, 1994.

Bayart, Jean-François."Les Églises chrétiennes et la Politique du Ventre: le Partage du Gâteau ecclesial." http://politique-africaine.com/numeros/pdf/035003.pdf.

Bediako, Kwame. "Africa and Christianity on the Threshold of the Third Millennium: The Religious Dimension." *African Affairs* 99:395 (2000) 303-323.

Benedict VI. *Homily at the Opening Mass of the Second Special Assembly for Africa of the Synod of Bishops*. http://www.vatican.va/content/benedict-xvi/en/homilies/2009/documents/hf_ben-xvi_hom_20091004_sinodo-africa.html.

Benedict XVI. Post-synodal Apostolic Exhortation *Africae Munus*. http://www.vatican.va/content/benedict-xvi/en/apost_exhortations/documents/hf_ben-xvi_exh_20111119_africae-munus.html.

Benedict XVI. *Address to the Members of Roman Curia and Papal Representatives*. http://www.vatican.va/content/benedictxvi/en/speeches/2009/december/documents/hf_ben-xvi_spe_20091221_curia-auguri.html.

Bevens, Stephen B. and Schroeder, Roger P. *Constants in Context: A Theology of Mission for Today*. New York: Orbis, 2004.

Birmingham, David. "Merchants and Missionaries in Angola." *Lusotopie* 5 (1998) 345-355.

Boyle, Patrick M. "Beyond self-protection to prophecy: The Catholic Church and political change in Zaire." *Africa Today* 39:3 (1992) 49-66.

Brasseur, Paule. "L'Eglise Catholique et la Décolonisation en Afrique noire." In *Les chemins de la décolonisation de l'empire français, 1936-1956: Colloque organisé par l'IHTP le 4 et 5 octobre 1984*, edited by Charles-Robert Ageron, 723-745. Paris: CNRS Éditions, 1986.

Britannica, T. Editors of Encyclopaedia. "Diogo Cão." *Encyclopedia Britannica*, 2016. https://www.britannica.com/biography/Diogo-Cao.

Brockman, Norbert and Pescantini, Umberto. *A History of the Church*. Nairobi: Paulines Publications Africa, 2004.

Brooks, Andrew. *A Global History of Poverty and Prosperity*. London: Zed, 2017.

Brou, Alexandre. "L'Œuvre du Cardinal van Rossum." *Études* 213 (1932) 345-356.

Brown, Stephen J. "France the Missionary." *An Irish Quarterly Review* 17:68 (1928) 649-463.

Bruls, J. "From Missions to 'Young Churches'." In *The Christian Century: The Church in a Secularised Society*, edited by Roger Aubert, 385-437. London: Darton, Longman and Todd, 1978.

Bühlmann, Walbert. "The African Church: The Council of Jerusalem to Vatican II." *Concilium* 13:35-54. New York: Paulist, 1966.

Bühlmann, Walbert. "Passato e futuro della evangelizzazione." In *Sacrae Congregatione de Propaganda Fide Memoria Rerum (1622-1972)*, Vol. III/2:1815-1972, edited by Josef Metzler, 578-6. Roma: Herder, 1976.

Bühlmann, Walbert. *The Coming of the Third Church*. Slough: St Paul Publications, 1977.

Bühlmann, Walbert. *Mission on Trial - Addis Ababa, 1980: A Moral for the Future from the Archives of Today*. Slough: St Paul Publications, 1978.

Bühlmann, Walbert. "Mission in the 1980s: Two Views." *Occasional Bulletin of Missionary Research* 4:3 (1980) 98–99.

Bujo, Bénézet. "Vincent Mulago—An Enthusiast of African Theology." In *African Theology: The Contribution of the Pioneers*, Vol. 1, edited by Bénézet Bujo and Juvénal I. Muya, 13–38. Nairobi: Paulines Publications Africa, 2003.

Camps, Arnulf. *Studies in Asian Mission History 1956–1988*. Leiden: Brill, 2000.

Carreño, J. "A Truly African Church." In *What Happened at the African Synod?*, edited by Cecil McGarry, 51–66. Nairobi: Paulines Publications Africa, 1995.

Castle, Tony and McGrath, Peter. *On This Rock, The Popes and Their Times: St Peter to John Paul II*. London: St Paul's, 2002.

Catholic Bishops' Conference of the Philippines. *What is Happening to Our Beautiful Land*, 1988. https://www.silene.org/en/documentation-centre/declarations/what-is-happening-on-our-beautiful-land-pastoral-letter-on-ecology/#What-is-Happening-to-our-Beautiful-Land.pdf

Chioccheta, Pietro. "Le Vicende del Secolo XIX nella Prospettiva Missionaria." In *Sacrae Congregationis de Propaganda Fide, Memoria Rerum (1622–1972)*, Vol. III/1, 1815–1972, edited by Josef Metzler, 3–38. Roma: Herder, 1976.

Clarke, Richard F. Ed. *Cardinal Lavigerie and the African Slave Trade*. Cambridge: Cambridge University Press, 2009.

Colzani, Gianni. "La teologia della missione dopo il Vaticano II." In *La Missioni senza confini: Ambiti della missione ad agentes. Miscellanea in onore del R. P. Willi Henkel, OMI*, edited by Marek Rostkowski, 45–62. Roma: Missionari Oblati di Maria Immacolata, 2000.

Comby, Jean. *Duemila anni di Evangelizzazione: Storia dell'espansione Cristiana*. Torino: Società Editrice Internazionale, 1994.

Comby, Jean. *How to Understand the History of Christian Mission*. London: SCM, 1996.

Connolly, Timothy. "Pope Pius XII and Foreign Missions." *The Furrow* 8:3 (1957) 150–155.

Costantini, Celso. *Va e annunzia il regno di Dio*, Vol. II. Brescia: Morcelliana, 1943.

Costantini, Celso. *Ricerche d'Archivio sull'Istruzione "De Clero Indigena."* Roma: Edizioni di Storia e Letteratura, 1947.

Couenhoven, Jesse. "Law and Gospel, Or the Law of the Gospel?: Karl Barth's Political Theology Compared with Luther and Calvin." *Journal of Religious Ethics* 30:2 (2002) 181–205.

Dederen, Raoul. "Karl Rahner's The Shape of the Church to Come: A Review Article." https://digitalcommons.andrews.edu/cgi/viewcontent.cgi?referer=https://www.google.com/&httpsredir=1&article=1355&context=auss.

De Gendt, Rik, "African Christianity in European Public Opinion." In *Towards the African Synod*, edited by Giuseppe Alberigo and Alphonse N. Mushete, 104–111. London: SCM, 1992.

Delavignette, Robert C. *Christianity and Colonialism*. New York: Hawthorn, 1964.

Delisle, Philippe. "La campagne antiesclavagiste de Lavigerie et Léon XIII devant 'l'opinion missionnaire' française." In *The New Papacy and the New World Order. Vatican Diplomacy, Catholic Opinion and International Politics at the time of Leo XIII / La Papauté et le nouvel ordre mondial. Diplomatie vaticane, opinion catholique et politique internationale au temps de Leo XIII*, edited by Vincent Viaene, 395–411. Leuven: Leuven University Press, 2005.

Denis, Philippe. "Clergy Training." In *The Catholic Church in Contemporary Southern Africa*, edited by Joy Brain and Philippe Denis, 124–150. Pietermaritzburg: Cluster Publications, 1999.

Dichiarazione finale dei Vescovi Africani. "Evangelizzazione e corresponsabilità." In *Le nuove vie del Vangelo: I Vescovi Africani parlano a tutta la Chiesa*, edited by Giuseppe Butturini, 287–291. Bologna: EMI, 1975.

Drehmanns, Joseph M. *Kardinal van Rossum: KorteLevensschets*. Romen: Roermond-Masseik, 1935.

Dries, Angelyn. *Missionary Movement in American Catholic History*. New York: Orbis Books, 1998.

Duquesne Studies, Spiritan Series 1: A History of the Congregation of the Holy Ghost 222–225. https://dsc.duq.edu/spiritan-dsss.

Éla, Jean-Marc. *African Cry*. Oregon: Wipf & Stock, 2005.

Éla, Jean-Marc. *My Faith as an African*. Oregon: Wipf and Stock, 2019.

Englebert, Pierre and Dunn, Kevin C. *Inside African Politics*. Cape Town: UCT Press, 2014.

Esteves, Junno A. "Vatican statistics show decline in number of consecrated men, women." https://www.globalsistersreport.org/news/religious-life/vatican-statistics-show-decline-number-consecrated-men-women.

Filesi, Teobaldo. "L'Evangelizzazione del Regno del Congo: il contributo religioso e storico della 'missio antiqua' dei Capuccini (1645–1835)." In *Evangelizzazione e culture II: Atti del Congresso Internazionale Scientifico di Missiologia*, Roma, 5–12 Ottobre 1975, 297–344. Roma: Pontificia Università Urbaniana, 1976.

Fisher, Henry P. "The Catholic Church in Liberia." *Records of the Catholic Historical Society of Philadelphia* 40:3 (1929) 249–310.

Foster, Elizabeth A. "A Mission in Transition: Race, Politics, and the Decolonization of the Catholic Church in Senegal." In *In God's Empire: French Missionaries and the Modern World*, edited by Owen White and J. P. Daughton, 257–273. Oxford: Oxford University Press, 2012.

Foster, Elizabeth A. *African Catholic: Decolonization and the Transformation of the Church*. Massachusetts: Harvard University Press, 2019.

Francis. Encyclical Letter *Laudato Sì*. http://www.vatican.va/content/francesco/en/encyclicals/documents/papa-francesco_20150524_enciclica-laudato-si.html.

Francis. Apostolic Exhortation *Evangelii Gaudium*. https://www.vatican.va/content/francesco/en/apost_exhortations/documents/papa-francesco_esortazione-ap_20131124_evangelii-gaudium.html.

Gahamanyi, Jean-Baptiste. "I sacerdoti e i catechisti sono poveri." In *Le nuove vie del Vangelo: I Vescovi Africani parlano a tutta la Chiesa*, edited by Giuseppe Butturini, 172–173. Bologna: EMI, 1975.

Gampiot, Aurélin M. *Kimbanguism: An African Understanding of the Bible*. University Park: Penn State University Press, 2017.

Gargan, Edward T. "Introduction." In *Leo XIII and the Modern World*, edited by Edward T. Gargan, 3–12. New York: Sheed and Ward, 1961.

Gifford, Paul. "Some Recent Developments in African Christianity." *African Affairs* 93:373 (1994) 513–534.

Glatz, Carol. "Number of priests declined for first time in decade, Vatican says." https://www.ncronline.org/news/world/number-priests-declined-first-time-decade-vatican-says.

Gori, Luca. "Santa Sede e Francia: La decolonizzazione dell'Africa nera francese (1953–1960)." *Studi Storici* 43:1 (2002) 193–213.

Gray, Richard. "The Catholic Church and National States in Western Europe during the Nineteenth and Twentieth Centuries: From a Perspective of Africa." *Kirchliche Zeitgeschichte* 14:1 (2001) 148–155.

Greenwell, Andrew M. "Leo XIII's In Pulrimis: Natural Law and Slavery." Part 1. http://lexchristianorum.blogspot.com/2011/01/leo-xiiis-in-plurimis-natural-law-and.html.

Gregory XVI. Brief *In Supremo*. https://www.vatican.va/content/gregorius-xvi/it/documents/breve-in-supremo-3-dicembre-1839.html.

Gregory, William P. "Pope Francis' Effort to Revitalize Catholic Mission." *International Bulletin of Mission Research* 43:1 (2019) 7–19.

Groves, C. P. *The Planting of Christianity in Africa*, 1878–1914, Vol. 3. London: Lutterworth, 1955.

Groves, C. P. *The Planting of Christianity in Africa* 1914–1954, Vol. 4. London: Lutterworth, 1958.

Guatemalan Bishops' Conference. *The Cry for Land*, 1988. http://www.inee.mu.edu/documents/20CryforLand_000.pdf.

Guerriero, Elio. "Prefazione." In Massimo Marcocchi, *Colonialismo, Cristianesimo e Culture Extraeuropee: L'Istruzione di Propaganda Fide ai Vicari apostolici dell'Asia Orientale 1659*, 4–10. Milano: Jaca, 1981.

Hanson, Eric O. *The Catholic Church in World Politics*. New Jersey: Princeton University Press, 1987.

Hastings, Adrian. *The World Mission of the Church*. London: Darton, Longman & Todd, 1964.

Hastings, Adrian. "In the Field." In *The Church is Mission*, edited by Edna McDonagh, 80–98. London: Geoffrey Chapman, 1969.

Hastings, Adrian. "The Ministry of the Catholic Church in Africa, 1960–1975." In *Christianity in Independent Africa*, edited by Edward Fashoé-Luke et al, 26–43. London: Rex Collings, 1978.

Hastings, Adrian. *A History of African Christianity 1950–1975*. Cambridge: Cambridge University Press, 1982.

Hastings, Adrian. *African Catholicism*. London: SCM, 1989.

Hastings, Adrian. *The Church in Africa 1450–1950*. Oxford: Clarendon, 1996.

Healey, Joseph G. "Historical Development of Small Christian Communities/Basic Ecclesial Communities in Africa." https://smallchristiancommunities.org/historical-development-of-the-small-christian-communitiesbasic-ecclesial-communities-in-africa/.

Hebga, Meinrad. "Christianisme et Négritude." In *Des Prêtres noirs s'interrogent*, 189–204. Paris: Les Éditions du Cerf, 1956.

Hebga, Meinrad. "Englebert Mveng – A Pioneer of African Theology." In *African Theology: The Contribution of the Pioneers* Vol. 1, edited by Bénézet Bujo and Juvénal I. Muya, 39–46. Nairobi: Paulines Publications Africa, 2003.

Hebga, Meinrad. "Cinquante ans après, où en sommes-nous?." In *Des Prêtres noirs s'interrogent. Cinquante ans après. . .*, 295–299. Paris: Karthala et Présence Africaine, 2016.

Henriot, Peter. "The Second African Synod: Challenge and Help for Our Future Church." *Hekima Review* 41 (2009) 8–18.

Hepzi, Joy R. J. History and Development of Education of Women in Kerala." PhD diss., University of Kerala, 1993. https://shodhganga.inflibnet.ac.in/bitstream/10603/173433/8/08_chapter%203.pdf.

Hickey, Raymond, ed. *Papal Missionary Documents and Africa*. Dublin: Dominican Publications, 1982.

Hildebrandt, Jonathan. *History of the Church in Africa: A Survey*. Achimota: Africa Christian, 1981.

Hofmeyr, J. W. and Pillay, Gerald J, eds. *A History of Christianity in South Africa*, Vol. 1. Pretoria: Haum Tertiary, 1994.

Hogan, Edmund M. *The Irish Missionary Movement: A Historical Survey*, 1830–1980. Dublin: Gill and MacMillan, 1992.

Holmes, Derek. *The Triumph of the Holy See*. London: Burns & Oates, 1978.

Howard, David M. "Editorial: A Moratorium on Missions?." https://missionexus.org/editorial-a-moratorium-on-missions/.

Iacobelli, Pedro. "The Vatican's Shift of its Missionary Policy in the Twentieth Century: The Mission of the Augustinian Fathers of Assumption in Manchuria." *Asian Cultural Studies* 36 (2010) 91–104.

Ighobor, Kingsley. "Africa's Youth: A "Ticking Time Bomb" or an Opportunity?." https://www.un.org/africarenewal/magazine/may-2013/africa%E2%80%99s-youth-%E2%80%9Cticking-time-bomb%E2%80%9D-or-opportunity.

Iheanacho, Valentine U. *Maximum Illud and Benedict XV's Missionary Thinking: Prospects of a Local Church in Mission Territories*. Starbrücken: Scholar's, 2015.

Iheanacho, Valentine U. "Maximum Illud and its Relevance in Contemporary Mission." *Tripod* 39:194 (2019) 82–93.

Iheanacho, Valentine U. "Christian Commitment in the Contemporary World in the Light of Papal Teachings." *The Catholic Voyage* 15 (2019) 3–22.

Iheanacho, Valentine U. "Plantatio Ecclesiae in Africa: From Tutelage to Maturity." *Studia Historiae Ecclesiasticae* 46:1 (2020) 1–17.

Iheanacho, Valentine U. "Maximum Illud and the African Church: Yesterday and Tomorrow." *Abuja Journal of Philosophy and Theology* 10 (2020) 25–40.

Ike, Obiora. "Towards a Self-Sustaining and Self-Reliant Church: Theological Perspectives from the Social Teaching of the Church and Local Experiences in Development." https://www.obioraike.com/docs/towards-a-self-sustaining-and-self-reliant-church-theological-perspectives-from-the-social-teaching-of-the-church-and-local-experiences-in-development.pdf.

Ilesanmi, Simeon O. "Leave No Poor Behind: Globalization and the Imperative of Socio-Economic and Development Rights from an African Perspective." *The Journal of Religious Ethics* 32:1 (2004) 71–92.

Isichei, Elizabeth. *A History of Christianity in Africa: From Antiquity to the Present*. London: SPCK, 1995.

Joly, Léon. *Le Christianisme et l'Extrême Orient: Missions Catholiques de l'Inde, de l'Indo-Chine, de la Corée*, Vol.1. Paris: Lethielleux, 1907.

Joly, Léon. *Le Christianisme et l'Extrême Orient: Missions Catholiques du Japon*, Vol. 2. Paris: Lethielleux, 1907.

John Paul II. Encyclical Letter *Redemptor Hominis*. http://www.vatican.va/content/john-paul-ii/en/encyclicals/documents/hf_jp-ii_enc_04031979_redemptor-hominis.html.

BIBLIOGRAPHY 175

John Paul II. *Homily at the Opening Mass of the Special Assembly for Africa of the Synod of Bishops.* http://www.vatican.va/content/john-paul-ii/en/homilies/1994/documents/hf_jp-ii_hom_19940410_sinodo-africano.html.

John Paul II. *Message for the Celebration of the World Day of Peace.* http://www.vatican.va/content/john-paul-ii/en/messages/peace/documents/hf_jp-ii_mes_19891208_xxiii-world-day-for-peace.html.

John Paul II. *Letter to the President of the Rwandan Bishops' Conference.* http://www.vatican.va/content/john-paul-ii/it/letters/1996/documents/hf_jp-ii_let_19960314_episc-conf-rwanda.html.

Kachama-Nkoy, Stephen. "Reflections on the Church in the Congo." *An Irish Quarterly Review* 50:199 (1961) 298–311.

Kaggwa, Robert. "The New Catholicity: Rethinking Mission in an Age of Globalisation with Special Reference to the African Situation." *New Blackfriars* 86:1002 (2005) 185–203.

Kalilombe, P. A. "The African local churches and the world-wide Roman Catholic communion: Modification of Relationships as Exemplified by Lilongwe Diocese." In *Christianity in Independent Africa,* edited by Edward Fashoé-Luke et al, 79–95. London: Rex Collings, 1978.

"Kalliombe, Patrick." https://dacb.org/stories/malawi/kalilombe-patrick/.

Kazingufu, Gilbert. "Synods in the Life of the Church and in Particular the African Synod." In *What Happened at the African Synod?,* edited by Cecil McGarry, 12–32. Nairobi: Paulines Publications Africa, 1995.

Kendall, Elliot. *The End of an Era: Africa and the Missionary.* London: SPCK, 1978.

Kenny, Joseph. *The Catholic Church in Tropical Africa 1445–1850.* Ibadan: Ibadan University Press, 1983.

Kilby, Karen. "Karl Rahner's Ecclesiology." *New Blackfriars* 90:1026 (2009) 188–200.

Ki-Zerbo, Joseph. "Acceptance Speech." https://www.rightlivelihoodaward.org/speech/acceptance-speech-joseph-ki-zerbo/.

Korieh, Chima J. and Njoku, Raphael C. "Introduction." In *Missions, States, and European Expansion in Africa,* edited by Chima J. Korieh and Raphael C. Njoku, 1–10. London: Routledge, 2007.

Koschorke, Klaus et al, eds. *A History of Christianity in Asia, Africa, and Latin America, 1450–1990: A Documentary Sourcebook.* Michigan: William B. Eerdmans, 2007.

Krier Mich, Marvin L. *Catholic Social Teaching and Movements.* Bayard: Twenty-Third Publications, 2003.

Kroeger, James. "Papal Mission Wisdom: Five Mission Encyclicals 1919–1959." In *A Century of Catholic Mission,* edited by Stephen B. Bevans, 93–100. Oxford: Regnum International, 2013.

La Bella, Gianni. "Leo XIII and the Anti-Slavery Campaign." In *The New Papacy and the New World Order. Vatican Diplomacy, Catholic Opinion and International Politics at the time of Leo XIII / La Papauté et le nouvel ordre mondial. Diplomatie vaticane, opinion catholique et politique internationale au temps de Leo XIII,* edited by Vincent Viaene, 381–394. Leuven: Leuven University Press, 2005.

Latourette, Kenneth S. *A History of the Expansion of Christianity: The Great Century in Northern Africa and Asia, A.D. 180 -A.D. I914,* Vol. VI. London: Eyre & Spottiswoode Ltd, 1944.

Latourette, Kenneth S. *A History of the Expansion of Christianity: Advance Through Storm AD. 1914 and After,* Vol. VII. London: Eyre & Spottiswoode, 1947.

Latourette, Kenneth S. *Christianity in a Revolutionary Age: A History of Christianity in the Nineteenth and Twentieth Centuries: The Roman Catholic, Protestant and Eastern Churches*, Vol. IV. New York: Harper & Brothers, 1961.

Lavergne, Bernard."Préface." In François Méjan, *Le Vatican contre la France d'Outre-Mer*, 3. Paris: Librairie Fischbacher, 1957.

Lavigerie, Charles. "Le memoir secret sur l'Association Internationale Africaine de Bruxelles et l'Évangélisation de l'Afrique Équatoriale addressé à Son Éminence le Cardinal Préfet de la S. C. de la Propagande par Mgr l'Archevêque de Alger." In *Rapports du Père Planque, de Mgr Lavigerie et de Mgr Comboni sur l'Association Internationale Africaine*, edited by Marcel Storme, 75-136. Brussels: J. Duculot, 1957.

Leo XIII. Encyclical Letter *Catholicae Ecclesiae*. http://w2.vatican.va/content/leo-xiii/en/encyclicals/documents/hf_l-xiii_enc_20111890_catholicae-ecclesiae.html.

Leo XIII. Encyclical Letter *Sancta Dei Civitas*. http://w2.vatican.va/content/leo-iii/en/encyclicals/documents/hf_l-xiii_enc_03121880_sancta-dei-civitas.html.

Longman, Timothy. "Church Politics and the Genocide in Rwanda." *Journal of Religion in Africa* 31:2 (2001) 163-186.

Lopez-Gay, J. "The Clergy and the Native Hierarchy in Japan." In *Native Clergy in the Young Churches and the Pontifical Work of St. Peter the Apostle*, 69-71. Rome: Pontifical Missionary Union, 1976.

Luneau, René. "The Expectations of the Catholic Church." In *Towards the African Synod*, edited by Giuseppe Alberigo and Alphonse N. Mushete, 83-87. London: SCM, 1992.

"Mabathoana, Emmanuel Gregory." https://dacb.org/stories/lesotho/mabathoana-emmanuel/.

Majawa, Clement. "African Christianity in the post-Vatican II Era." In *The Routledge Companion to Christianity in Africa*, edited by Elias K. Bongmba, 214-231. London: Routledge, 2016.

Malula, Joseph. "Per cristianizzare l'Africa, Africanizzare il cristianesimo." In *Le nuove vie del Vangelo: I Vescovi Africani parlano a tutta la Chiesa*, edited by Giuseppe Butturini, 127-130. Bologna: EMI, 1975.

Marcocchi, Massimo. *Colonialismo, Cristianesimo e Culture Extraeuropee: L'Istruzione di Propaganda Fide ai Vicari apostolici dell'Asia Orientale 1659*. Milano: Jaca, 1981.

Martina, Giacomo. *Pio IX 1846-1850*. Roma: Editrice Università Gregoriana, 1974.

Mathew, David. "Catholicism in Africa." *Blackfriars* 33:382 (1952) 3-5.

Maurice, Cheza. "Le Symposium des Conférences épiscopales d'Afrique et de Madagascar: Le SCEAM". *Revue Théologique de Louvain* 21:4 (1990) 472-476.

Mba, Paul A., "L'affranchissement du clergé indigène et des chrétiens autochtones." http://theses.univ-lyon2.fr/documents/getpart.php?id=lyon2.2006.essono-mezui_h&part=112260.

Mbiti, John S. "Foreword." In *Anthology of African Christianity*, edited by Isabel A. Phiri et al, xvii-xxi. Oxford: Regnum International, 2016.

Méjan, François. *Le Vatican contre la France d'Outre-Mer*. Paris: Librairie Fischbacher, 1957.

Metzler, Josef. "La Santa Sede e le Missioni." In *Storia della Chiesa: dalle Missioni alle Chiese Locali (1846-1965)*, Vol. XXIV, edited by Josef Metzler, 129-159. Milano: Edizione Paoline, 1990.

Metzler, Josef. "The Legacy of Pius XI." *International Bulletin of Missionary Research* 17:2 (1993) 62–65.
Mijoga, Hilary B. P. "The Lenten Pastoral Letter: A First Public Declaration of the Hidden Transcript." *J. Humanit* 10:11 (1996–7) 55–67.
Miotk, Andrzej. "The Historical Significance and Prophetic Resonance of the Apostolic Letter Maximum Illud on the Centenary of its Publication." *Verbum SVD* 60:1–2 (2019) 11–38.
Miranda, Salvador. "The Cardinals of the Holy Roman Church." http://cardinals.fiu.edu/bios1965.htm.
Møller, Bjørn. *Religion and Conflict in Africa with a Special Focus on East Africa DIIS Report 2006:6*. Copenhagen: Danish Institute for International Studies, 2006.
Moody, Paul F. "The Growth of the Catholic Missions in Western, Central and Eastern Africa." In *Sacrae Congregationis de Propaganda Fide, Memoria Rerum (1622–1972)*, Vol. III/1, 1815–1972, edited by Josef Metzler, 203–225. Roma: Herder, 1976.
Mugambi, J. N. K. "African Churches in Social Transformation." *Journal of International Affairs* 50:1 (1996) 194–220.
Mugambi, J. N. K. "Theological Method in African Christianity." In *Theology and the Transformation of Africa - Tangaza Occasional Papers* 10, 69–100. Nairobi: Paulines Publications Africa, 2000.
Mugambi, J.N.K. "Climate Change and Food Security: A Challenge for African Christianity." In *Anthology of African Christianity*, edited by Isabel A. Phiri et al, 1117–1132. Oxford: Regnum International, 2016.
Mukuka, George. "The Establishment of the Indigenous Catholic Clergy in South Africa." *Studia Historiae Ecclesiaticae* 34:1 (2008) 1–30.
Müller, Karl. "The Main Principles of Centralized Government for the Missions." *Concilium* 13, 11–33. New York: Paulist, 1966.
Murphy, Francis X. *The Papacy Today*. London: Weidenfeld and Nicolson, 1981.
Mutig, John. "Archbishop Lefebvre Defies Pope Paul: The Conflict Intensifies." https://www.scd.org/sites/default/files/201706/Vol_2_No_81_Archbishop_Lefebvre_Defies_Pope_Paul.pdf.
Mveng, Engelbert. "The Historical Background of the African Synod." In *African Synod: Documents, Reflections, Perspectives*, edited by Maura Browne, 20–31. New York: Orbis, 1996.
Naidu, Sanusha and Davies, Martyn. "China Fuels its Future with Africa's Riches." *South African Journal of International Affairs* 13:2 (2006) 69–83.
Nasimiya-Wasike, Anne. "Christology and an African Woman's Experience." In *Liberation Theology - An Introductory Reader*, edited by Curt Cadorette et al, 92–103. Oregon: Wipf and Stock, 1992.
Ndimba, Jean-Christian N. *"Crowded Churches and Empty Stomachs": The Paradox of Christianity and Poverty in the Congo-Zaire Opening a Way Towards a Post-Colonial Christianity*. https://dlib.bc.edu/islandora/object/bc-ir:107475/datastream/. . ./citation.pdf.
Negash, Tekeste. *Italian Colonialism in Eritrea, 1882–1941: Policies, Praxis and Impact*. Stockholm: Almquist & Wiksell International, 1987.
Neill, Stephen. *A History of Christian Missions*. London: Penguin, 1986.

Ngulu, Joseph M. "The Church in Africa during the Twentieth Century and the Meaning of the Pontificate of Paul VI: General Historical Lines." In *Paul VI and the Church in Africa*, 12–29. Brescia: Istitutio Paolo VI, 2015.

Njoroge, Lawrence M. *A Century of Catholic Endeavour: Holy Ghost and Consolata Missions in Kenya*. Nairobi: Paulines Publications Africa, 2000.

Nwaigbo, Ferdinand. "Self-reliance in the 21st Century Church in Africa." *African Ecclesiastical Review* (2002) 35–61.

Oborji, Francis A. *Trends in African Theology since Vatican II: A Missiological Orientation*. Rome: Leberit SRL, 2005.

Oborji, Francis A. "Catholic Mission in Africa 1910–2010." In *A Century of Catholic Mission: Roman Catholic Missiology 1910 to the Present*, edited by Stephen B. Bevans, 11–23. Oxford: Regnum International, 2013.

Oborji, Francis A. "The Mission ad gentes of the African Churches." https://sedosmission.org/old/eng/oborji_2.htm.

O'Connell, James. "The Church in Africa: Will its 'Success' Continue?." In *The Church in Africa*, edited by William J. Wilson, 1–23. New York: Maryknoll Publications, 1967.

Oduyoye, Mercy A. "A Letter to My Ancestors." http://www.wcc-coe.org/wcc/assembly/or-mo-e.html.

Ogbonnaya, Joseph. "The Church in Africa: Salt of the Earth?." In *The Church as Salt and Light: Path to an Ecclesiology of Abundant Life*, edited by Stan Chu Ilo et al, 65–87. Oregon: Wipf and Stock, 2011.

Okigbo, Pius. "The Future Haunted by the Past." In *Africa Within the World: Beyond Dispossession and Dependence*, edited by Adebayo Adedeji, 28–38. London: Zed, 1993.

Oliver, Roland. *The Missionary Factor*. London: Longmans, 1969.

O'Malley, John W. *What Happened at Vatican II?* Massachusetts: Harvard University Press, 2008.

Onaiyekan, John O. "Paul VI and the Church in Africa." In *Paul VI and the Church in Africa*, 97–115. Brescia: Istituto Paolo VI, 2015.

O'Sullivan, Michael. "Women, Poverty, and Christianity in Relation to Africa." *Milltown Studies* (1999) 103–129.

Pass, Steven. *The Faith Moves South: A History of the Church in Africa*. Michigan: Kachere Series, 2006.

Patterson, Collin. "What has eschatology to do with the gospel? An analysis of papal documents on mission *ad gentes*." *Missiology: An International Review* 47:3 (2019) 285–299.

Paul VI. Apostolic Letter *Africae Terranum*. http://www.va/content/paul-vi/it/apost_letters/documents/hf_p-vi_apl_19671029_africae-terranum.html.

Paul VI. *Homily at the Conclusion of The Symposium Organized by the Bishops of Africa*. http://www.vatican.va/content/paul-vi/en/homilies/1969/documents/hf_p-vi_hom_19690731.html (accessed: 16 April 2020).

Paul VI. Apostolic Exhortation *Evangelii Nuntiandi*. http://www.vatican.va/content/paul-vi/en/apost_exhortations/documents/hf_p-vi_exh_19751208_evangelii-nuntiandi.html.

Paul VI. *Speech to Participants at the Symposium of Episcopal Conferences of Africa and Madagascar*. http://www.vatican.va/content/paul-vi/fr/speeches/1975/documents/hf_p-vi_spe_19750926_simposio-africa.html.

Paul VI. Apostolic Exhortation *Octogesima Adveniens*. http://www.vatican.va/content/paul-vi/en/apost_letters/documents/hf_p-vi_apl_19710514_octogesima-adveniens.html.

Pengo, Polycarp. "Missionaries to Yourselves: The Legacy of Vatican II and the Identity of the Church in Africa." In *Paul VI and the Church in Africa*, 1–11. Brescia: Istituto Paolo VI, 2015.

Pierli, Francesco. "Daniel Comboni: An Unquenchable Passion for Africa." In *Gateway to the Heart of Africa: Missionary Pioneers in Sudan*, edited by Francesco Pierli et al, 26–58. Nairobi: Paulines Publications Africa, 1999.

Pius XII. *Speech to Pontifical Mission Societies*. https://w2.vatican.va/content/pius-xii/it/speeches/1944/documents/hf_p-xii_spe_19440624_opere-missionarie.html.

Pius XII. Apostolic Exhortation *In Auspicando Super*. http://w2.vatican.va/content/pius-xii/it/apost_exhortations/documents/hf_p-xii_exh_19480628_in-auspicando-super.html.

Pius XII. Encyclical Letter *Evangelii Praecones*. http://w2.vatican.va/content/pius-xii/en/encyclicals/documents/hf_p-xii_enc_02061951_evangelii-praecones.html.

Pius XII. Apostolic Letter *Cupimus Imprimis*. http://w2.vatican.va/content/pius-xii/it/apost_letters/documents/hf_p-xii_apl_19520118_cupimus-imprimis.html.

Pius XII. Encyclical Letter *Ad Sinarum Gentem*. http://w2.vatican.va/content/pius-xii/en/encyclicals/documents/hf_p-xii_enc_07101954_ad-sinarum-gentem.html.

Pius XII. *Radio Message to the Episcopate and Faithful of South Africa*. http://w2.vatican.va/content/pius-xii/en/speeches/1951/documents/hf_p-xii_spe_19510429_fedeli-sud-africa.html.

Pius XII. Encyclical Letter *Fidei Donum*. http://w2.vatican.va/content/pius-xii/en/encyclicals/documents/hf_p-xii_enc_21041957_fidei-donum.html.

Pouconta, Paulin. "Meinrad Pierre Hegba: Theologian and Healer." In *African Theology in the 21st Century: The Contribution of the Pioneers*, Vol. 2, edited by Bénézet Bujo and Juvénal I. Muya, 70–92. Nairobi: Paulines Publications Africa, 2006.

Présence Africaine. "Modern culture and our destiny." *Présence Africaine* 8–9–10 (1956). Special edition dedicated to the 1st International Conference of Negro Writers and Artists (Paris, Sorbonne, 19–22 September 1956).

Prudhomme, Claude. "Stratégie missionnaire et grandes politiques sous Léon XIII le heurt des logiques." In *The New Papacy and the New World Order. Vatican Diplomacy, Catholic Opinion and International Politics at the time of Leo XIII / La Papauté et le nouvel ordre mondial. Diplomatie vaticane, opinion catholique et politique internationale au temps de Leo XIII*, edited by Vincent Viaene, 351–379. Leuven: Leuven University Press, 2005.

Prudhomme, Claude. *Missioni Cristiane e Colonialismo*. Milano: Jaca, 2006.

Prudhomme, Claude. "Le Cardinal van Rossum et la politique missionnaire du Saint-Siège sous Benôit et Pie XI (1918–1923)." In *Life with a Mission: Cardinal Willem Marinus van Rossum C.Ss.R 1854–1932*, edited by Vefie Poels et al, 123–141. Nijmegen: Trajecta, 2011.

Racque, Élise. "The Evolution of Catholicism in Africa." https://international.la-croix.com/news/the-evolution-of-catholicism-in-africa/5210.

Radclife, Timothy. "The Shape of the Church to Come." https://www.americamagazine.org/issue/693/article/shape-church-come.

Rahner, Karl. *The Shape of the Church to Come*. London: S.P.C.K., 1974.

Rahner, Karl. "Towards A Fundamental Theological Interpretation of Vatican II." http://cdn.theologicalstudies.net/40/40.4/40.4.4.pdf.

Ranger, Terence. "Religion, Development and African Christian Identity." In *Religion, Development and African Christian Identity*, edited by Kirsten H. Petersen, 29-58. Uppsala: Scandinavian Institute of African Studies, 1987.

Renault, Gilbert. *The Caravels of Christ*. New York: G.P. Putnam's Sons, 1959.

Riccardi, Andrea. "The Social and Political Dynamics of Africa after the End of the Political Presence of the Soviet Union." In *Towards the African Synod*, edited by Giuseppe Alberigo and Alphonse N. Mushete, 59-67. London: SCM, 1992.

Riccardi, Andrea. *Il Potere del Papa da Pio XII a Giovanni Paolo II*. Roma: Editori Laterza, 1993.

Robert, Rweyemamu D. "The Development of the Local Clergy in Africa." In *Native Clergy in the Young Churches and the Pontifical Work of St Peter the Apostle*, 84-90. Rome: Pontifical Missionary Union, 1796.

Ronan, Nessan J. "The Irish Missionary in Africa: An Endangered Species." *The Furrow* 45:10 (1994) 592-593.

Russell, H. *Africa's Twelve Apostles*. Boston: Daughters of St Paul, 1981.

Salamone, Frank A. and Mbabuike, Michael. "The Plight of the Indigenous Catholic Priest in Africa: An Igbo Example." *Rivista trimestrale di studi e documentazione dell'Istituto italiano per l'Africa e l'Oriente* 49:2 (1994) 210-224.

Sangu, James D. *Report on the Experiences of the Church in the Work of Evangelisation in Africa* (Presented in Rome on behalf of the Episcopal Conferences of Africa at the 1974 Synod on "The Evangelisation of the Modern World").

Schelkens, Karim et al. *Aggiornamento?: Catholicism from Gregory XVI to Benedict XVI*. Leiden: Brill, 2013.

Serapião, Luis B. "The Preaching of Portuguese Colonialism and the Protest of the White Fathers." *A Journal of Opinion* 2:1 (1972) 34-41.

Seumois, André. "La Mission 'Implantation de l'Église' dans les documents ecclésiastiques." *Sonderdruckaus Missionswissenchaftliche Studien* (1951) 39-53.

Seumois, André. "Local Clergy and Inculturation of the Church." In *Native Clergy in the Young Churches and the Pontifical Work of St Peter the Apostle*, 20-25. Rome: Pontifical Missionary Union, 1976.

Shorter, Aylward. *Christianity and the African Imagination: After the African Synod - Resources for Inculturation*. Nairobi: Paulines Publications Africa, 1996.

Shorter, Aylward. *Cross and Flag in Africa: "The White Fathers" during the Colonial Scramble 1892-1914*. New York: Orbis, 2006.

Skard, Torild. *Continent of Mothers, Continent of Hope: Understanding and Promoting Development in Africa Today*. London: Zed, 2003.

Southern African Catholic Bishops' Conference. *Evangelising Community Serving God, Humanity and All Creation*. Pretoria: SACBC, 2019.

Stanley, Brian. *The Bible and the Flag: Protestant Missions and British Imperialism in the Nineteenth and Twentieth Centuries*. Leicester: Apollos, 1990.

Stoetzer, Carlos O. "Preface." In Martin J. Bane, *The Popes and Western Africa: An Outline of Mission History 1460s-1960s*, iii-vi. New York: Alba House, 1968.

Sundkler, Bengt and Steed, Christopher. *A History of the Church in Africa*. Cambridge: Cambridge University Press, 2004.

Tasie, Godwin and Gray, Richard. "Introduction." In *Christianity in Independent Africa*, edited by Edward Fashoé-Luke et al, 3-15. London: Rex Collings, 1978.

BIBLIOGRAPHY 181

Thiandoum, Hyacinthe. *The Church in Africa and her Evangelising Mission towards the Year 2000. "You shall be my witnesses" (Acts 1:80)*. Vatican City: Editrice Vaticana, 1994.

Tinchese, Stefano. *Roncalli e le Missioni: L'Opera della Propagazione della Fede tra Francia e Vaticano negli anni '20*. Brescia: Società Editrice Internazionale, 1989.

Tomko, Jozef. "Un Grande Africano." In *Il Cardinale Bernardin Gantin: Missionario Africano a Roma, Missionario Romano in Africa*, edited by Giulio Cerchetti et al, 139–140. Città del Vaticano: Libreria Editrice Vaticana, 2010.

Toniolo, Elia. "The First Centenary of the Roman Catholic Mission to Central Africa, 1846–1946." *Sudan Notes and Records* 27 (1946) 99–126.

Tragella, Giovanni Battista. "Le vicende d'un opuscolo sul clero inideno e sul autore." In *Der einheimishce Klerus in Geschichte und Gegnwart, Festschrift* for L. Kilger, edited by Johannes Beckmann, 189–202. Shöneck-Beckenried 1950.

Tripp, Aili M. *Museveni's Uganda: Paradoxes in a Hybrid Regime*. Boulder: Lynne Rienner, 2010.

Tshinbango, T. "The Mission and Responsibility of New Formed Churches." *Concilium* 13, 128–141. New York: Paulist, 1966.

Turaki, Yusufu. "Evangelical Missiology from Africa: Strengths and Weaknesses." In *Global Missiology for the 21st Century*, edited by William D. Taylor, 271–283. Michigan: Baker Academic, 2000.

Turkson, Peter K. A. "Roots and Routes of Justice Ministry in Africa." https://afjn.org/download/newsletters/Turkson%20Talk%20-%20%203.2.2013%20AFJN%20Web%20Edition.pdf.

Turkson, Peter. "A Special Assembly of the Synod of Bishops for Africa II: Le Profezie, Risorse, Ricadute." http://www.iustitiaetpax.va/content/dam/giustiziaepace/presidenteinterventi/2010/2010_FIRENZE_PKAT_ENG.pdf.

United Nations. *Report of the United Nations Conference on the Human Environment, Stockholm, 5–16 June 1972*. New York: United Nations, 1973. https://www.un.org/ga/search/view_doc.asp?symbol=A/CONF.48/14/REV.1.

United Nations. *UN Conference on the Human Environment (Stockholm Conference)*. https://sustainabledevelopment.un.org/milestones/humanenvironment.

United States Conference of Catholic Bishops. *Renewing the Earth*, 1991. https://www.usccb.org/issues-and-action/human-life-and-dignity/environment/renewing-the-earth.

Uzukwu, Elochukwu E. "The Birth and Development of a Local Church: Difficulties and Signs of Hope." In *African Synod: Documents, Reflections, Perspectives*, edited by Maura Browne, 3–8. New York: Orbis, 1996.

Viaene, Vincent. "Introduction. Reality and Image of the Pontificate of Leo XIII." In *The New Papacy and the New World Order. Vatican Diplomacy, Catholic Opinion and International Politics at the time of Leo XIII / La Papauté et le nouvel ordre mondial. Diplomatie vaticane, opinion catholique et politique internationale au temps de Leo XIII*, edited by Vincent Viaene, 9–29. Leuven: Leuven University Press, 2005.

Wanza, Lucy. "Self-Reliance: A Management Strategy for Socio-Economic Sustainability of the Church in Africa." *African Ecclesiastical Review* 57:1–2 (2015) 60–84.

Ward Barbara and Dubos, René J. *Only One Earth: The Care and Maintenance of a Small Planet*. London: Penguin, 1972.

Wheeler, Andrew. "Gateway to the Heart of Africa: Sudan's Missionary Story." In *Gateway to the Heart of Africa: Missionary Pioneers in Sudan,* edited by Francesco Pierli et al, 10–25. Nairobi: Paulines Publications Africa, 1998.

Wiest, Jean-Paul. "Learning from the Missionary Past." In *The Catholic Church in Modern China: Perspectives,* edited by Edmond Tang and Jean-Paul Wiest, 181–198. New York: Orbis, 1993.

Winters, Bartholomew. *Priest as Leader: The Process of the Inculturation of a Spiritual-Theological Theme in a United States Context.* Roma: Editrice Pontificia Universitá Gregoriana, 1997.

Whitaker, Jennifer S. *How can Africa Survive?.* New York: Harper & Row, 1988.

World Synod of Catholic Bishops, 1971. *Justice in the World.* https://www.cctwincities.org/wp-content/uploads/2015/10/Justicia-in-Mundo.pdf.

Yago, Bernard. "La responsabilità delle chiese locali." In *Le nuove vie del Vangelo: I Vescovi Africani parlano a tutta la Chiesa,* edited by Giuseppe Butturini, 177–178. Bologna: EMI, 1975.

Yaoundé Declaration, 1996. https://archives.au.int/bitstream/handle/123456789/587/AHG%20Decl%203%20%28XXXII%29%20_E.pdf?sequence=1&isAllowed=y.

Young, Ernest P. *Ecclesiastical Colony: China's Catholic Church and the French Religious Protectorate.* Oxford: Oxford University Press, 2013.

Zimbabwe Catholic Bishops' Conference, *The March is not Ended,* 2020. https://spotlight.africa/wp-content/uploads/2020/08/ZCBC-The-March-is-not-ended.pdf.

Zoé-Obianga, Rose. "When will the Church in Africa become African?." In *Towards the African Synod,* edited by Giuseppe Alberigo and Alphonse N. Mushete, 88–91. London: SCM, 1992.

Index

Abessole, Paul Mba, 103
Achebe, Chinua, 129
Adedeji, Adebayo, 144
Adolf, Hitler, 116
Aelvoet, Walter, 132
Afonso I, King of Congo, 2, 4
Agbedi, Majola (Vincent David), 88–89
Albanese, Giulio, xviii
Alvaro, King of Congo, 6
Ajomo, Joseph, 147
Arinze, Francis, xxi
Aggrey, James Kwegyir, 9
Anthony Claret, Saint, 49
Augustine of Canterbury, Saint, 59, 62

Bacchio, Gian Luca, 35
Banana, Canaan, 150
Banda, Hastings Kamuzu, 153
Bane, Martin, 37
Barbier, 24
Barghash ibn Said, Sultan of Zanzibar, 33
Barnabo, Alessandro, 24
Barron, Edward, xix, 17–22, 25–26, 49, 97
Barret, David, 135
Barros, 13
Barth, Karl, 140
Bartoccetti, Vittorio, 76
Baur, John, 10
Bayart, Jean-François, 126, 147
Benedict XV, Pope, ix–x, xix, 68–74, 76, 90, 99, 164–65
Benedict XVI, Pope, 129, 152, 159

Bessieux, Jean Remi, 49
Benezet, Anthony, 16
Beya, Bernadette Mbuye, 132
Bigirumwmi, Aloys, 100, 107–8
Bissainthe, Gérard, 113
Boilat, David, 97
Bolano, Alphonsus, 4
Bonaparte, Napoleon, Emperor, 11, 23, 50
Boniface, Saint, 59
Bonnke, Reinhard, 141–42
Bonomelli, Geremia, 34
Boulaga, Fabien Ebuoussi, 119, 147
Boyle, Patrick M., 98, 118
Brasseur, Paul, 90
Brockman, Norbertand, 22
Broderick, Thomas, 98
Brou, Alexandre, 74
Bühlmann, Walbert, 9, 118–19, 121
Bujo, Bénézet, 114
Buthelezi, Peter, 108
Byanyima, Winnie, 146

Cameron, Lovett V, 39
Căo, Diogo, 3
Capet, Joseph, 63–64
Caufee, Paul, 16
Ciurcia, Aloysius, 50
Clark, Francis Xavier, 65
Clement of Alexandria, Saint, 58
Clement VII, Pope, 5
Clement VIII, Pope, 5
Clement XI, Pope, 7–8
Clement XIII, Pope, 23

INDEX

Colt, Samuel, 27
Comboni, Daniel, 24–25, 28–31, 41–43, 50, 52–53, 55
Cordes, Paul Josef, 151
Costantini, Celso, xix–xx, 61
Curci, Carlo Maria, 34
Czacki, Wladimir, 34

Da Silva, Rodrigo A, 39
Davies, Martyn, 160
De Clapiers, Luc, 117
De Castro, Matthew, 90
Ddungu, Adrian, 108
De La Condamine, Charles Marie, 9
De Galicourt, 23
Delisle, Philippe, 41, 46
Della Piane, 92
D'Ormesson, Wladimir, 116
Dlamini, Bonaventura, 108
Dodds, Prosper, 100
Duval, Léon-Étienne, 88

Ekandem, Dominic, xxi
Éla, Jean-Marc, 126, 147, 149, 161
Emechete, Paul, 98
Emonet, Ambroise, 54–56
England, John, 20
Engone, Basile Mve, 154
Essy, Amara, 144
Eugene IV, Pope, 4

Fardy, J, 120
Feliciani, Antonio, 64
Ferry, Jules, 11
Finley, Robert, 16
Foster, Elizabeth, 86
Franchi, Alessandro, 29–30, 42, 44, 164
Francis Pope, 154, 158
Franco, Francisco, 110
Fridoil, Arsène, 97
Fumio, Stephen, 158

Gahamanyi, Jean-Baptiste, 119
Gantin, Bernard, xxi
Gargan, Edward T, 34
Gatu, John G, 120
Gifford, Paul, 140–41
Gijlswijk, Bernard Jordan, 91

Gouvei, Teodosio Clemente de, 110, 112
Gregory the Great, Pope, 62
Gregory XVI, Pope, ix–x, xvii, 14, 20–21, 30, 36, 41, 50, 61, 163
Groves, Charles, 56

Ham, 45
Hastings, Adrian, 1, 28, 60, 75, 103, 106, 110, 117, 122–23, 137–38, 147
Hegba, Meinrad Pierre, 114, 120–21
Henrique, Dom, 4, 58
Henry, Portuguese prince, 110
Herskovits, Melville Jean, 131
Hickey, Raymond, 131
Hinsley, Arthur, 91
Hopkins, Samuel, 16
Houpouët-Boigny, Félix, 147

Ilesanmi, Simeon, 145
Ingoli, Francesco, 67
Innocent X, Pope, xviii, 6, 59
Isabel, Princess, 39

Javouhey, Anne-Marie, 23, 96–97
Javouhey, Rosalie, 96
Jefferson, Thomas, 16
John, Apostle, Saint, 58
John XXIII, Pope, 2, 69, 85, 100, 165
John Paul II, Pope, 123–26, 151, 154, 157, 161
Joly, Léon, 89
Joseph, Faye, 100

Kagame, Alexis, 114
Kakuze, Odette, 148
Kalilombe, Patrick, x, 120–21, 139
Keith, George, 16
Kelly, John, 19, 21
Kenny, Joseph, 2, 4
Kibanga, Muhilh, 133
Kilby, Karen, 128
Kiwanuka, Joseph, 100, 102, 107–8, 165
Ki-Zerbo, Joseph, 167
Korieh, Chima, 8
Kpodzro, Sanouko, 154

Krich-Mich, Marvin L., 156

La Bella, Gianni, 41, 43
Lagos, Polono de, xviii, 4
Landy, Thomas, 157
Lavergne, Bernard, 117
Lavigerie, Charles, 21–22, 29–32, 34, 41, 43–56
Ledóchoneko, Maria Teresa, 47
Ledochwski, Mieczyslaw H, 55
Lefebvre, Marcel, 81, 92–94, 105
Leo Africanus, 6
Leo X, Pope, 4–5, 58, 61, 74
Leo XIII, Pope, ix–x, xxi, 12, 21, 29, 32–37
Leopold II, King of Belgium, 29, 40, 43–47, 50, 51, 52, 56, 91, 116, 164
Libermann, Francis, 21–23, 25
Linden, Ian, 156
Livingstone, David, 40
Livinhac, Léon, 54
Lopez, Duarte, 6
Lopez, Gregory, 90
Lucas, Martin, 91
Luneau, René, 137

Mabathoana, Emmanuel G, 98
Machel, Samora, 111
Malula, Joseph, x, xxi, 117–18, 122, 130
Manna, Paolo, 90
Manuel, John, 4
Marion-Brésillac, Melchior de, 29
Marocchi, Massimo, 59
Martin of Tours, Saint, 59
Martin V, Pope, 1–2
Masson, Joseph, 131
Matembele, Kalenga, 121–22
Matthew, David, 85
Mathew David, Apostolic Delegate, 94
Mazrui, Ali, xxii
McCann, Owen, 88
Méjan, François, 115–16
Menelik II, Emperor, 10
Mikado of Japan, 33
Milingo, Emmanuel, 112
Miotk, Andrzeji, 70

Mohasi, Raphael, 98
Monroe, James, 16
Moody, Paul, 23, 56
Morse, Samuel, 27
Moussa, Jean-Pierre, 97
Muaca, Eduardo, 111
Mugabe, Robert, 161
Mugambi, Jesse N K, 134, 140, 142, 159
Muganda, Eduard, 97
Mukuka, George, 98
Mulago, Vincent, 114
Mveng, Engelbert, 113

Naidu, Sanusha, 160
Napoleon III (Louis), 11
N'Dayen, Joachim, 122
Ndimba, Jean, 142
Nell, Stephen, vii, 119
Njoku, Raphael, 8
N'Kombo, Ernest, 153
Ntihinyurwa, Thaddée, 151
Nunes, Francisco, 112
Nwaigbo, Ferdinand, 136
Nyerere, Julius, 141

Oborji, Francis A, xx–xxi, 101, 134
Ogbonnaya, Joseph, 135, 159
Okigbo, Pius, xviii
O'Leary, David, 164–65
Oliver, Roland, 9
Oliveira, Salazar António de, 110
O'Malley, John, 86
Otunga, Maurice, xxi, 108

Pasinya, Laurent M, 154
Patrick, Saint, 59
Paul V, Pope, 61–62, 69
Paul VI, Pope, x, xx–xxi, 2, 23, 87–88, 102, 112–13, 124–25, 149, 156, 165–66
Pedro II, Emperor, 39
Pereira, Custodio Alvim, 112–13
Pescantini, Umberto, 22
Peter Claver Saint, 47
Pigafetta, Filippo, 6
Pierli, Francesco, 28
Pinder, Denis, 19, 21

Pinheiro, Didacus, 4
Pius II, Pope, xviii, 4, 41
Pius VII, Pope, 23
Pius IX, Pope, x, xvii, 21, 28–30, 32, 36, 50, 52, 164
Pius X, Pope, 19
Pius XI, Pope, xix–xx, 69, 73–77, 79, 90, 99, 165
Pius XII, Pope, xix, 2, 26, 69, 77–83, 87, 100, 110, 165
Planque, Augustin, 12, 29–32
Pouconta, Paulin, 133
Poullard des Places, Claude F, 21
Prouvost, Henri, 75, 92
Prudhomme, Claude, 32–33

Raffaello Sanzio, 74
Rahner, Karl, 84–85, 123, 128–29
Ramarosandratana, Ignatius, 100, 165
Rampolla, Mariano, 47
Raponda-Walker, André, 97
Resende, Sebastiao Soares de, 112
Rhodes, Alexandre de, 59
Ribeiro, Felix Niza, 112–13
Riccardi, Andrea, 137
Romano, Anthony, 6
Roseberry, Lord, 11
Rosmini, Antonio, 33
Ross, Ronald, 9
Rossum, Willem van, 71–74
Roy, Alexandre le, 54
Rugambwa, Laurian, 85, 88, 102
Russell, H, 46
Rütti, Ludwig, 130

Sangu, James D, 88, 131
Sankara, Thomas, 127
Sanon, Anselm T, 127–28
Sara, Robert, xxi
Sarpong, Peter, 122
Sastre, Robert, 114
Schmandt, Raymond H, 35

Segura, P B, 131
Serapiăo, Luis, 113
SeseSeko, Mobutu, 154
Seumois, André, 71
Scott, Kenneth, 28
Simeoni, Giovanni, 55
Sixtus V, Pope, 6
Skard, Torild, 142
Skhakhane, Jerome, 109
Souza, Isidore de, 153
Steed, Christopher, 51
Stoetzer, Carlos, 2
Storme, Marcel, 30
Strebler, Joseph-Paul, 94–95, 107
Sundkler, Bengt, 51, 101
Sutter, Fedele, 55

Tardy, Michel-François, 105
Tasie, Godwin, 103
Terrasse, 96
Thiandoum, Hyacinthe, xxi, 124, 130, 138, 149
Thomas Aquinas, Saint, 33
Truffet, Benedict, 49
Turaki, Yusufu, 138
Turkson, Peter, xxi, 151

Urban VIII, Pope, 76
Uzukwu, Elochukwu, 117

Viaene, Vincent, 32
Vilhegas, Diego Ortiz de, 5

Ward, Barbara, 157

Yago, Bernard, 93

Zedong, Mao, 80
Zoa, Jean, 130–31
Zoé-Obianga, Rose, 148
Zoungrana, Paul, xxi, 88, 122, 132

CPSIA information can be obtained
at www.ICGtesting.com
Printed in the USA
LVHW021329151121
703324LV00003B/9

9 781666 731309